GCSE for AQA

Business & Communication Systems

Second Edition

Jonathan Sutherland &
Diane Canwell

GW00992963

© 2009 Folens Limited, on behalf of the authors

United Kingdom: Folens Publishers, Waterslade House,
Thame Road, Haddenham, Buckinghamshire HP17 8NT
Email: folens@folens.com

Ireland: Folens Publishers, Greenhills Road, Tallaght, Dublin 24
Email: info@folens.ie

Folens publications are protected by international copyright laws.
All rights are reserved. The copyright of all materials in this publication,
except where otherwise stated, remains the property of the publisher
and the author. No part of this publication may be reproduced, stored
in a retrieval system, or transmitted, in any form or by any means, for
whatever purpose, without the written permission of Folens Limited.

The authors hereby assert their moral right to be identified as the
authors of this work in accordance with the Copyright, Designs and
Patents Act 1988.

**Consulting Editor: Ann Bennett, Subject Leader Business
Studies, Icknield High School, Luton**

**Subject and Exam question reviewer: Siân Parry**

Project development: Rick Jackman (Jackman Publishing Solutions Ltd)
    and Adrian Moss (Instructional Design Ltd)
Editor: Louise Wilson
Design and  layout: Patricia Briggs
Index: Indexing Specialists (UK) Ltd
Cover design: EMC Design
Cover image: Fotolia/AlienCat

First published 2007 by Folens Limited
This edition first published 2009

British Library Cataloguing in Publication Data. A catalogue record
for this publication is available from the British Library.

ISBN 978-1-85008-457-0
Product code FD4570

# Contents

# Introduction: Studying and the exam

### What is the unit about?

Unit 8 provides an idea of how business and communication systems assist organisations in achieving their objectives. You will also see how ICT (Information and Communications Technology) systems have an influence on the way people work, and how they can be used to improve internal and external communication. The unit looks not only at the benefits of ICT, but also at some of the risks, such as health and safety and data security. It is split into three parts, each looking at different aspects of ICT systems in business. The first part explores administration, the working environment, health and safety and data systems. The second looks at aspects of human resources and the importance of people in helping businesses achieve their objectives. The final part deals with communication, its purpose, systems and how ICT is used.

The unit headings, and the amplification (additional information and required coverage) exactly match the specification. Business terminology is kept to a minimum throughout.

### Why is it important?

It is rare for a business not to use ICT systems. This unit explains how and why businesses use these systems, and how they can help businesses achieve their aims and objectives. ICT systems make businesses far more efficient, helping them to organise their work, deal with information, communicate and sell products or services, and provide support to their customers or clients.

Unit 8 provides a sound base of information on how ICT systems are used routinely by a variety of businesses and organisations. The unit looks at the importance of ICT, and the rest of the GCSE focuses on how businesses use ICT in a more practical way. ICT has changed the way in which some people work. The unit covers how ICT has radically changed the way in which businesses communicate with one another and with their customers. You will also find out how ICT has led to businesses being able to offer customers products and services 24 hours a day, 365 days a year, through the use of the Internet.

### What is the assessment like?

The assessment for Unit 8 is a 1-hour written examination paper, worth 40% of the entire GCSE mark. There will be 60 marks available on the paper, equivalent to one mark per minute. All the questions in this book are based on that formula; in other words, if a question is worth 4 marks you should spend no more than 4 minutes on it, otherwise you will find that you will not have enough time to answer other questions that may be worth more marks. Timing is only one consideration, however. The quality of the answer is also very important.

| ASSESSMENT OBJECTIVE | WHAT IT SAYS | HOW IMPORTANT IS IT? |
|---|---|---|
| A01 | Recall, select and communicate knowledge and understanding of concepts, issues and terminology. | 12% of the marks for this unit and 30% of the overall GCSE. |
| A02 | Apply skills, knowledge and understanding in a variety of contexts and in planning and carrying out investigations and tasks. | 14% of the marks for this unit and 35% of the overall GCSE. |
| A03 | Analyse and evaluate evidence, make reasoned judgements and make appropriate conclusions. | 14% of the marks for this unit and 35% of the overall GCSE. |

## How do I get a good grade?

Examiners use a uniform marking system, which means that you will need 36 marks out of 60 (60%) to achieve a grade C, or 54 marks (90%) to achieve an A*. However, it is important to remember that whatever your mark for this paper, your final GCSE mark is gained across the three units.

Examiners are particularly interested in the *quality* of your answer. They have set three assessment objectives, as shown in the table above.

So we can see that Unit 8 is worth 40% of the GCSE. The examiners will also be interested in ensuring that you produce good-quality written English:

- Writing needs to be legible.
- Words must be spelt correctly.
- Punctuation and grammar should be accurate.

- Your meaning should be clear.
- You should use a style of writing that is appropriate.
- You should organise your information clearly, and use specialist words when needed.

Wherever you see this logo: you will find a section of text specifically designed to help you extend your understanding of a particular aspect of the specification. These sections will help you analyse and evaluate information in a manner required by the examiner for the assessment objective AO3.

Each of the double-page spreads has a set of questions on the right-hand side, all of which follow the mark-a-minute system. You should pay attention to the marks offered for each question. For example, if a question asks you for 'three advantages' but

offers six marks, you know that it is not looking for a three-word answer, but requires a little more depth. Similarly, it is important to provide explanations when required, or to show your working out when doing a calculation.

At the end of each section there is a revision guide with a set of integrated questions. The sections build up to this final spread, which takes questions from a broad area of the specification – not simply what you have just read. The deeper you get into the unit, the more likely you are to come across questions that require you to apply knowledge gained from other parts of the unit, just as you would in the exam. This is excellent practice for the exam, and it is a very good idea to get into the habit of answering all the questions you come across in the book.

# The purpose of setting objectives

YOU WILL FIND OUT:
- why businesses set objectives
- how businesses choose their objectives

## Why do businesses set objectives?

There are good reasons why a business should set objectives, rather than simply plodding along and hoping for the best:

- It helps with decision-making – the decisions have to be properly thought out.
- Targets can be set, which helps motivate employees and managers.
- The business can measure its own progress.
- The business can make sure that all of its different parts work together to achieve the objectives.

This is why some of the most successful organisations produce very clear general **mission statements**.

It is no good for a business to have aims and objectives if it does not really know how to achieve them. A business needs to set out its strategies and tactics in a **business plan**.

A strategy is a major plan used by a business to set out its long-term objectives. A good example would be: 'We want to be the best-known retailer in the high street in five years' time, by offering first-class customer service'.

Tactics are the individual parts of a strategy. They are short-term and flexible. An example would be: 'In order to become the best-known retailer in the high street, we need to open at least ten new stores each year'.

In order to meet objectives, the strategy states what the business needs to do and the tactics describe how to achieve the strategies. Setting aims and objectives will help the business to understand its purpose and give it a clearer view of its future.

The two most common objectives of business organisations are survival and making a profit. These objectives do not apply to organisations that do not need to generate money in order to keep running, such as a government department, which is funded by the taxpayer. No business can survive for very long if it does not cover its costs. It must at least do this, otherwise its money will run out and no one will lend it any more. Making a profit simply means selling products and services for more than they cost the business to buy, make or provide to customers.

## How do businesses choose their objectives?

In order for a business to achieve its long-term objectives, it needs to make short-term plans. The table opposite shows examples of how short-term plans can help a business in achieving its long-term objectives.

Some businesses will design a mission statement that tries to express the purpose of the business and what broad products and services it offers. The mission statement is designed to give the management, employees, customers and potential investors a quick guide to the aims and objectives of the business. It also allows the business to be described in no more than three or four sentences.

When we look at business plans later in this unit (see pages 24–9), we will see that mission statements are also a good starting point in helping to explain the direction in which the business wants to be moving and the way in which its future is mapped out.

### For example Tesco's mission statement

Tesco PLC's mission statement is: 'To create value for customers to earn their lifetime loyalty'. Tesco recognises, as do many successful businesses, that customers are of vital importance. If they are treated in the right way, they will come back and shop with the business again.

| LONG-TERM OBJECTIVE | SHORT-TERM PLAN |
|---|---|
| Expand into Europe | • Investigate different countries and their markets<br>• Find suitable premises<br>• Recruit staff for overseas work |
| Develop new products | • Investigate the market<br>• Research possible competition<br>• Plan to buy new machinery<br>• Recruit new staff |
| Become the best | • Improve products and services<br>• Investigate the competition<br>• Retrain the sales team<br>• Plan a major advertising campaign |
| Reduce waste | • Find out how much waste is produced now<br>• Find out where the waste is produced<br>• Find out how similar businesses deal with waste<br>• Bring in a waste management consultant |

A mission statement should say what the business is, what it does, what it stands for and why. Out of this mission statement, the business can then identify its objectives and aims, as well as the strategies and tactics that will help it to achieve these.

A mission statement can therefore state:

- the purpose of the business
- who the business serves
- the type of customers
- the needs that the business fulfils
- how those needs are fulfilled
- the values of the business.

By using a mission statement as the building block of the aims and objectives, the business can produce measurable results.

> Strategies are the broad ways in which the business can accomplish its mission. Goals and actions flow out of each strategy.

A mission statement is broadly a shortened version of more complex objectives. It needs to mean something – otherwise it has no value to the business. It needs to state a purpose and how that purpose will be achieved. If it clearly states the aims and objectives of the business, then the strategies and tactics to achieve them can be created. If the mission statement is vague, it may be impossible to come up with a way of achieving those aims and objectives.

### KEY TERMS

**Mission statement** ▶ a paragraph, a set of points or even just a sentence that summarises what the organisation stands for, as well as its principles.

**Business plan** ▶ a detailed report of a business's future proposals. It also examines the present market and provides financial details. The business will use its business plan to help in meeting its aims and objectives.

## QUESTION TIME
*10 minutes*

The Lewis Hamilton Foundation (LHF) is a registered charity that provides funding for a wide range of different charities and good causes. Its main focus is to improve the lives and opportunities of children and young people who are living in poverty around the world.

Lewis Hamilton had the help of his family, friends and others to realise his ambition to become a Formula 1 racing driver. The LHF aims to provide the tools and skills to help others to fulfil their dreams and meet their objectives. The LHF also helps existing charities, particularly those involved with seriously ill children, with children and young people with disabilities, and with children trapped by poverty.

Source: adapted from the Lewis Hamilton Foundation

**1** What might LHF's mission statement be? *(4 marks)*

**2** Lewis Hamilton is considered to be an ideal role model. How might his involvement in the charity help it to fulfil its aims and objectives? *(6 marks)*

3

# What are business aims and objectives?

## What are business aims and objectives?

Every business will establish short-term goals or aims. The short-term aims form the business's long-term objectives, setting out what the business wants to achieve in the future.

The objectives of different businesses are obviously going to vary. They can depend on things like how old the business is, how big it is, and the state of the market or markets in which it operates. Above all, they need to be realistic and achievable.

Objectives can also be affected by difficult economic conditions, when there might be high unemployment and the company's regular customers simply do not have enough money to spend.

A business can settle on many objectives, but really there are two main ones:

- to survive, which means making enough money to cover its costs – survival in itself is not enough in the long term
- to make a profit, so that the business owner can take out a wage, or employees can have a share in the profits, or shareholders can receive a reward for their investment (see also pages XX–XX).

## Breaking even

The first thing a business has to do is to make at least as much money (income) as it spends (expenditure). Once it does this, the business has broken even. Any more income it receives will be profit. However, simply making a profit might not be enough. The business has to excel in one area or more in order to satisfy its **stakeholders**.

## Making a profit

The first way to judge the success of a business is by the size of its profit. The more profit a business makes, the better it is seen to be performing. However, profit is only one measure of success.

An extremely large business, with expensive assets (such as large buildings or expensive machinery), is likely to make a large profit. But is this profit really so large compared to what it cost the business to produce it?

### For example

A business may have assets, such as factories and equipment, worth £100 million and may make a net profit of £10 million.

By dividing the net profit by the capital employed, we can calculate the return on capital employed as a percentage. In this case, it would be 10%.

$$\frac{\text{Net profit}}{\text{capital employed}} \times 100$$

So in our example:

$$\frac{\text{£10 million}}{\text{£100 million}} \times 100 = 10\%$$

Another way of judging the success of a business is to look at its sales compared to the total sales in the market. This market share percentage can be calculated as follows:

$$\frac{\text{sales of the business}}{\text{total sales in the market}} \times 100$$

### For example

If the total sales in the market were £150 million and the business achieved sales of £15 million, then it has a 10% market share.

If sales do increase, it is worth checking to see if the total sales in the market have also increased. If they have, then the business may not in fact have increased its market share.

## Creating jobs and wealth

Another measure of business success, certainly one measured by government or potential employees, is job creation. It brings new wealth to an area and is also good for the government, as less money needs to be paid out in benefits.

A business can also create wealth in other ways. This can be measured in terms of what it owns, such as the land, factories or offices. Theoretically, the more a business owns, the more money it should be able to make. Wealth can also be measured by what the business is providing for its employees in terms of increasing their skills and making them more productive. Other businesses associated with the company are also affected by its wealth – suppliers receive more orders from a wealthier business. And the local area benefits from the wealth, because employees spend money on shopping, housing and taxes.

## KEY TERMS

**Stakeholder** ▶ an individual or group with a direct interest in the business, such as an employee, owner or shareholder.

**Dividend** ▶ a share of the profits, paid out on each share held by the shareholder.

Shareholders of a business will be looking to see how much of the profit made by the business is passed on to them through **dividends**. Businesses do not always pass on all of their profits via dividends. They may keep – or retain – some of the profits to give them a cash reserve. This is known as 'retained profit'. They will retain this profit to invest in a specific project or buy a particular asset, or to help cash flow in the future.

Shareholders will also be looking at sales growth. This shows that the business is being very active and seeking out new customers, or encouraging existing customers to consume more.

Another type of stakeholder will be affected by increased sales – employees. They will be busier and there will be a need to employ more people.

## Why are business aims and objectives important?

Aims and objectives are often written with clear benefits in mind, such as:

- To increase …
- To reduce …
- To improve …

They are often described as SMART targets:

**S** PECIFIC *they have a clear focus*

**M** EASURABLE *it is easy to determine when they have been achieved*

**A** TTAINABLE *they are realistic and not impossible.*

**R** ESULTS-ORIENTATED *they focus on the results rather than the methods*

**T** IME-SPECIFIC *they have a clear end date*

Defining the aims and objectives is important. They give the business greater direction and focus; they allow all employees and managers to have a greater understanding of the purpose of the business and they help external groups to understand the business. Clear aims and objectives can often help businesses solve problems.

Aims and objectives can be applied across the whole business, as can be seen in the diagram.

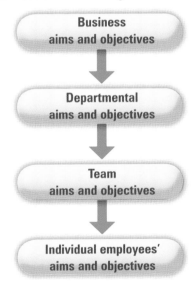

The business aims and objectives might be very general, but the aims and objectives of individual parts of the business are clearer steps. If individuals achieve their aims and objectives, then the team reaches its aims, and so on.

## QUESTION TIME
*8 minutes*

A business operates in a market with total sales of £120 million. It has sales of £6 million. The market increases in value to £150 million total sales and the business manages to increase its sales to £8 million.

**1** Calculate the business's original market share. *(4 marks)*

**2** Calculate the new market share of the business. *(4 marks)*

5

# Types of business aims

**YOU WILL FIND OUT:**

- about survival, profit and growth
- about market share and customer satisfaction
- about ethical and sustainable businesses

## Survival, profit and growth

### Survival

For a small business, survival in the first few months, or even years, can be a challenging aim in itself. As we saw in Section 1.1.5, start-up businesses are far more likely to fail in the first year or two than a more established business.

New businesses often find it difficult to set aims and objectives. For a new business, before anything has been sold to a customer, everything is an expense, so they need to be extremely careful about their spending. They may therefore see survival as the only thing they can aim for in the beginning. Even this is hard to achieve, as it is very difficult for new businesses to break even.

### Profit

In the longer term, the new business must, like any other business, try to make a profit. This is also difficult.

As all business activity costs money. Businesses need to pay for items such as **stock**, wages and salaries, and other running costs. To cover their costs, businesses must sell the goods and services they produce. However, if the income that a business receives from selling its products is less than its costs, the business will make a loss. If the income of a business is the same as its costs, the business will break even. Only if its income is greater than its costs, will the business make a profit.

A business cannot afford to continue to make a loss. It needs to make a profit to pay for what it has bought and to put the money back into the business to develop it, pay off loans and pay tax.

Making a profit is a common aim, as it gives the owners of the business a reward for investing in the business. It also allows them to reinvest in the business, to make it even more successful in the future.

But not all businesses aim to make a profit. If businesses such as social enterprises or charities make more money than they spend, they put all of it back into the business or organisation.

### Growth

Growth is another aim of most businesses. They might want to open more stores or move to larger premises. They might want to increase their range of products and services, to buy more efficient equipment, or to advertise to a wider group of customers.

Growth can be measured in many different ways, but the two key ways are:

- **Increased turnover** – this means that the value of the sales being made is greater than before. For example, instead of selling £15,000 of products a month, the business now sells £20,000 of products a month.
- **Greater profit** – the business is actually making more money on each sale it makes. Instead of making £5 every time it sells a £20 item, it is now making £6 per item. It will be able to do this if it can make or buy the item cheaper than before.

In order to increase its market share, a business may decide to reduce the price of its products in order to attract customers from other suppliers. However, in the short term, reducing the price may lead to lower profits. The business must decide whether to sacrifice short-term profit in the hope that achieving its aim of increased market share will lead to higher profits in the future. This can mean that objectives can sometimes conflict with each other.

## Market share and customer satisfaction

The market for a product consists of all the buyers and sellers of that product. All businesses operate in the markets for their products. The more buyers – or customers – that a business has for its product, the higher the volume of sales it will achieve. Higher sales can mean more income and therefore more profit.

The market share of a business is the value of its sales as a percentage of the total sales by all businesses operating in that market (see also the equation on page 14). Another aim of most businesses is therefore to increase their market share in order to make more profit. However, in achieving that extra market share, the business may have to drop prices for a while to attract more customers. This might force a competitor out of the market, because they cannot compete by selling at that price. Once that happens, the business that dropped the price can charge more again and make back the lost profits.

Most customers will be looking for a business that can offer them the best quality at the lowest price. To attract and keep customers, a business must always aim to provide a high-quality product. However, there is no point in providing the best product if no one can afford to buy it, so a business also needs to balance the costs involved in improving the quality with the price it will need to charge for it. Customers will expect value for money.

Customer satisfaction is another important aim. This means that the customer is pleased – or even delighted – with the products that the business sells them and, as importantly, is satisfied with the service provided by the business. So the business needs to consider staff training (giving the customer advice and support), its systems (making it easy for the customer to buy from and communicate with the business) and good service after the product has been sold (ongoing help and advice). If a customer is satisfied, they will come back to the business and buy again, and will tell their friends and colleagues about their positive experience. Poor customer service can mean that customers will not return and will tell their friends about their bad experience.

── **K E Y   T E R M** ──

**Stock** ▶ materials that will be used to make products, work in progress (part-made products) or finished products waiting to be sold.

## Ethical and sustainable businesses

Growth and expansion are often seen in a negative light. By using profits to stimulate greater growth and to increase profits, businesses are often accused of being greedy and having little regard for social, ethical and environmental concerns.

Low wages, for example, are not ethically acceptable. Nor is the use of underpaid overseas employees. These both bring the business into conflict with the law and attract bad publicity on television or in the newspapers. Businesses need to balance growth and profit by showing that they care about these issues. Most businesses have to show a degree of social and ethical responsibility, regardless of whether these beliefs are genuine.

Being ethical means doing things and making decisions that are morally correct. This does not just mean not doing something illegal. It means thinking about buying things from other ethical businesses, not exploiting suppliers or employees, not damaging the environment, not treating animals badly, checking where materials and stock come from and making sure that it too has been ethically produced.

Sustainability is another aspect of a business taking on social and environmental responsibilities. It means running a business that does not affect the environment, cause pollution or use up scarce resources that cannot easily be replaced.

# QUESTION TIME
*14 minutes*

**T**wo friends decide to set up a DVD home delivery service. They borrow £8,000 to buy their stock and £6,000 to buy two mopeds to deliver the DVDs to their customers. They also rent a small unit on an industrial estate, which costs them a total of £4,000 each year.

As an introductory offer, customers can borrow as many DVDs a month as they wish for £120 per year.

**1** How many customers would they need to cover all their costs so far? *(4 marks)*

**2** If the two friends wanted to earn £12,000 per year each, how many more customers would they need? *(4 marks)*

**3** Suggest what new services the business might offer to attract more customers. *(6 marks)*

# The criteria for judging the success of a business

## Why is it important to be successful?

It is easy for business start-ups to fail. The first few months or even years, when the business is small, are the most difficult. The company may lack finances, resources, and the skills and talents needed to survive.

There are many reasons why things can go wrong:

- **Lack of systems** – no systems or procedures are in place to sort out problems. Problems are dealt with as they arise, because the business could not predict them.
- **Lack of direction** – the company owners do not know where the business is heading; they have no clear goals. Survival is their main goal.
- **No financial planning** – no one looks at how much money is being made and spent until it is too late.
- **Relying on one or two people** – small businesses are often built around the skills of one or two people. If they leave or are ill, the company falls apart.

- **Not knowing who the customer is** – the business has not identified its key customers and does not know how to tell them about its products and services.
- **Not knowing about the market or the competition** – the business may not realise that tastes are changing or that a major competitor is taking all the customers.
- **Lack of communication** – the business owners do not explain what is needed to their employees or suppliers, or they are useless at communicating with customers.
- **Lack of quality standards** – the company has no way of ensuring that quality levels are maintained.
- **Lack of money** – the business is simply spending too much and earning too little.
- **Concentrating on the job, not the business** – the owners are so busy doing the job that they forget all their other business activities and responsibilities.

Success is vital for businesses and social enterprises for many different reasons. For example:

- The organisation may have borrowed money to set itself up. This needs to be repaid. If the business fails, it may still end up having to pay the money back.
- Investors are relying on the business to be careful with their money.
- Businesses and social enterprises provide employment.
- They contribute to the local economy by paying Council Tax and spending money with other local businesses.

The bigger a business becomes, the more important it is for it not to fail, because so many people and other organisations are relying on its continued success. These different groups, some closely related to the company and others less so, are known as 'stakeholders' (see also Section 1.2.5). They have an interest in the business and are concerned that it does well and survives.

8

## Who cares about success?

Everyone in the business and everyone related in some way to the business should care whether or not it is successful. Some may rely on the business to pay wages; some may be owed money by it; others may have paid the business money and are expecting it to provide them with products or services. All of these groups are examples of stakeholders: for one reason or another they need the company to be a success and would suffer if it failed.

In difficult economic times, business failures are all too common. Nearly 2,000 businesses failed in 2008. In 2009, this figure is expected to rise to over 32,000. In recent times the worst year for business failures was back in 1992, when 34,000 businesses failed.

Every time a business fails, people lose their jobs. The business owners find themselves in debt. Investors lose the money they put into the company. Suppliers who have provided the business with products and services do not get paid. Customers who have paid for products and services to be supplied, lose out. Property owners who rented the building to the business lose money, and many other groups and individuals are affected.

No matter how big or small the company, failure affects far more people than just those directly involved in it.

> All businesses rely on other businesses. They are all part of a network that supplies products and services to one another, as well as to their customers. One business failing and owing other businesses money can have a knock-on effect. If a really large company fails, owing lots of money to several smaller businesses, then the effect can be disastrous.

## QUESTION TIME
### 10 minutes

In 2003, the village shop in the small village of Woodton in East Anglia closed down. Villagers had to go to other villages and towns to do their shopping. In 2005 the shop was reopened, and now sells everything from newspapers to local farm produce. The village, with 650 homes, now has its own place to buy groceries.

**1** In what ways might a shop such as this be important to the local community? *(6 marks)*

**2** What other local businesses might benefit from the re-opening of the shop? *(4 marks)*

9

# Stakeholders and their objectives

YOU WILL FIND OUT:

- what stakeholders are
- why stakeholders are important
- what stakeholders want

## What are stakeholders?

A stakeholder is an individual or group affected in some way by a business, or with an interest in its activities. Many groups will have a stake in the success of a business and will benefit if the business does well or suffer if it fails.

Each type of stakeholder will have a slightly different view of the business. Some may actually work within the business (internal stakeholders), while others are external to it (external stakeholders).

Employees
Managers
Directors/owners
Shareholders
Trade unions
Customers

BUSINESS

INTERNAL    EXTERNAL

Local community
Suppliers
Banks and lenders of finance
HM Revenue & Customs
Government
Pressure groups

### Internal stakeholders

- **Employees** have a stake in the business because their livelihoods rely on its success. If the business does well, they may receive more money and benefits. If it fails, they may have to take a pay cut or even lose their jobs. Increasingly, organisations encourage employees to become shareholders, to reinforce the link.
- **Managers** at different levels of an organisation are ultimately responsible for the decisions that affect its success or failure. Managers are often rewarded with high salaries and **bonuses**, or with additional benefits, such as private healthcare or company cars.
- **Directors, owners and share-holders** are often interchangeable, with some kind of financial stake in the business. They might own shares or be outright owners of the business. The directors and owners will make day-to-day decisions that affect the future of the business.

   Shareholders look to these people to make the right decisions, so that they receive a share of the profits. Shareholders literally own a

share of the business. Shares might go up or down in value, depending on the success or failure of the business. Shareholders receive a dividend as their part of the profits.

- **Trade unions** are employee organisations that support employees at work. They ensure that employees are treated fairly and receive reasonable pay and benefits. They are stakeholders because they represent employees, who are key internal stakeholders.

### External stakeholders

Most businesses have a complex network of external stakeholders. Some have a relatively close relationship with the business; others influence the business without becoming involved on a daily basis.

- **Customers** want low prices and the best quality available. They weigh up what they can gain from a choice of businesses. Customers are always looking for new products and services and want businesses to offer what they need.
- Businesses buy goods and services from **suppliers**. A builders' merchant will buy from businesses supplying timber, bricks, concrete, and a host of other products. The business and the suppliers rely on

one another. The business needs the supplier to have in stock the products it needs; the supplier needs to be paid by the business.

- **The Government** will often directly influence a business because it passes laws that the business must take note of and apply, such as health and safety regulations or laws about payment. The government is involved in collecting taxes from businesses via Her Majesty's Revenue & Customs. Businesses are also influenced by regulations from the **European Union**.
- Wherever a business is located, it will have an impact on **the local community**. Some impacts will be positive (such as buying products and services from local suppliers); others negative (such as increased traffic, or a threat to other local businesses due to competition).
- **Banks and finance providers** lend to businesses so that they can fund special projects or expand. Banks and other finance providers will not want a company to make decisions that could affect its ability to pay back the loans. Before agreeing to lend it any money, they will look closely at its profitability.

10

**Bonuses** ▶ additional pay made to directors, managers and other employees, as a reward for their efforts towards the success of the business.

**European Union** ▶ an agreement between many European countries to make trade between them easier, to allow people to move around freely and to gradually have more similar laws.

⏩ All the stakeholders in a company have their own expectations, so the business itself must balance the wishes of the various stakeholders. Higher wages would please employees, management and trade unions, but would not please owners and shareholders. The increase would cause business costs to rise and the profitability of the business would probably fall.

If the business focused solely on providing profits for its owners, then it would find itself in difficulties with its employees and the trade unions. These groups would consider themselves to be exploited and undervalued. This could in turn affect their performance and the overall profitability of the business.

Pleasing all groups at all times may be impossible. However, an organisation must try to take into account the needs of each stakeholder group. This becomes even more complicated when the external stakeholders are brought into the equation.

## Why are stakeholders important?

A business or a social enterprise needs to take account of the needs of all its stakeholders. Some stakeholders will be employed by the business and will rely on the owners making the right decisions so that they get paid and keep their jobs. Others, like the local community, may be affected by the activities of the business, having to put up with extra traffic, more noise and pollution but also benefiting from more jobs and money for local people and other local businesses.

More pay for employees (which would please them) means higher costs. This probably means less profit, so less money for investors and shareholders. It is possible to balance things; the business might offer extra pay for employees if sales targets are met. This means that the business has made better profits than before, so everyone can share in the success – employees and shareholders alike.

It may not always be possible for a business to satisfy all of its stakeholders.

## What do stakeholders want?

Each stakeholder group is looking for something slightly different from a business:

- The government wants the business to stick to the laws and regulations.
- Investors want the business not to take too many risks. They want a return on their investment.
- Customers want quality products and services at a fair price.
- Local communities want to limit any negative impact on the local area.
- Suppliers want the business to be fair in its dealings with them.

A business normally tries to rank the importance of its stakeholders, working out how powerful they are and what influence they have on the business. But each business, regardless of its size, has an obligation to all its stakeholders.

## QUESTION TIME
*12 minutes*

The Millennium Dome (now the O₂ Arena) was built after a massive campaign to find out the opinions of local stakeholders. Letters were sent out to 7,000 local residents and 120,000 leaflets were distributed, asking for views. The concern was that the massive venue would disrupt the lives of the local community, but the developers claimed that it would also bring benefits.

11

1 **Suggest THREE ways in which the building of the venue might disrupt the local community.** *(6 marks)*

2 **Suggest THREE ways in which the venue has brought benefits to the local community.** *(6 marks)*

# The influence of stakeholders

YOU WILL FIND OUT:

● about stakeholders and owners

● about management and employees

● about customers and community

● about suppliers and competitors

● about the government

## Stakeholders and owners

As a business grows, there will be changes in the relationships it has with its various stakeholders. Stakeholders are individuals or groups affected in some way by the activities of the business. Typically, the key stakeholders are the owners, the employees themselves, the customers, and the local community, as well as the business's suppliers and competitors.

There will always be tensions between stakeholders; some will want something that will affect another stakeholder in a negative way. If shareholders want higher returns on their investments, there could be less left to reinvest in the business. There may also be a pressure to keep wages and salaries low, and prices could rise, meaning that suppliers will be offered less for their products and services. In this case, some stakeholders may accept slight changes because they appreciate the position that the business is in, but others will find the situation unacceptable.

Balancing the needs and demands of stakeholders is always a difficult job for any business. More often than not it will have to meet the needs of its most powerful stakeholders first and then try to sort out any problems that may arise from the others.

The bigger and more complicated the business, the more difficult it is for its owners to keep control of what is happening from day to day. Many of the largest businesses are owned by thousands of shareholders. Hardly any of these shareholders have anything to do with the running of the business. They simply have to trust the skills and expertise of the managers to protect their investment.

## Management and employees

The owners of a small business may have complete responsibility for its management. However, as a business gets larger, more people will take on responsibility for making decisions. They will set the strategy of the business and decide on its aims and objectives. They will have managers and supervisors to carry out the work for them. This means that in many organisations there is a big difference between owning the business and running or controlling it.

## Customers and community

Customers want reliable, high-quality products and services at a reasonable price. Businesses want to offer these products and services to match the needs of the customer, but at the lowest cost to the business. This often causes problems, when the levels of quality that the business thinks are acceptable are not acceptable for the customers. Businesses need to be flexible and responsive to customer needs. They need to offer good service but make sure that their costs remain as low as possible to ensure that they make a profit.

The local community can be affected by changes in the size of a business. To begin with there may be new employment in the area. There is also a knock-on effect, as local suppliers will receive more business from the growing organisation, generating even more jobs. The net result, on the positive side, is that there will be more money in the local economy.

On the negative side, however, the local community may have to suffer additional transport movement in the area, disruption, construction work and busy roads, as the employees of the business come into and out of work each day.

The relationship between a major stakeholder and the business needs careful management. For businesses the owners are major stakeholders who want the business to generate profit. However, another major stakeholder is the business's customers. They do not want to pay high prices and want high-quality products and reliable service. It is not always easy to balance the needs of these two key groups. Compromises have to be made: sometimes profits have to be cut to provide for customer needs and sometimes customers have to pay slightly more than they would wish to in order to ensure that the business makes a profit.

## Suppliers and competitors

Suppliers are other businesses with products and services to sell. Just like the businesses they supply, suppliers have their own aims and objectives. They will, for example, want to be making a profit so they will not be prepared to offer their products and services more cheaply than makes sense to them. Suppliers and their customers will always try to negotiate over prices and delivery dates, trying to get the best deal for themselves.

Competitors can also have an influence on a business. Every organisation faces competition. Sometimes competitors will do things that will have a negative impact on the business, such as lowering prices or opening a store nearby. The business needs to react and, better still, try to predict what their competitors might do before they do it. If the competitor gets the upper hand then the business risks losing some of its market share.

## Government

Businesses are influenced by central, local and even European governments. At each level there are rules and regulations that control the way in which businesses operate. However, all governments want businesses to be successful; they want them to create jobs and to generate income. Any profits that the business makes will mean that it pays more money to the government in taxes.

If businesses are seen to be behaving in an unacceptable way then they run the risk of the government using the law to stop them.

## QUESTION TIME
### 22 minutes

**1** Define the term 'stakeholder'. *(2 marks)*

**2** Identify and explain the expectations of three stakeholders of a business. *(6 marks)*

**3** Identify and explain which stakeholders are affected by a business that is making a loss. *(6 marks)*

**4** Why might a business find it difficult to satisfy the expectations of a manager, customer and owner all at the same time? *(8 marks)*

13

# Business administration

## What is business administration?

All businesses have administrative systems to coordinate their activities and allow decision-makers to plan for the future. All organisations will work in different ways and have different systems and procedures. The procedures are sets of rules, or the business's preferred steps. Administration procedures are important because a business's activities need to be coordinated and planned. The business needs to be effective and efficient and it needs to be able to access relevant information when needed.

Some administrative procedures are still paper-based, but increasingly they have become electronic systems. Everything is available through a networked computer system. Administrative procedures or systems are in fact a series of smaller steps or tasks that determine exactly how information is handled, how it is routed around the organisation, where it is stored and how long it is kept.

Information will need to be passed around different parts of the organisation. Ultimately it will then be stored away, but it may still need to be retrieved from storage at any time in the future.

## The flows of key business information

Perhaps the easiest way of understanding how business information is handled is to consider it as a series of inputs and outputs. Information will come into the business, such as:

- Information received via the telephone
- An order from a customer
- Details of a new law
- Information about new products or services
- Communication from a supplier or a customer
- Money from customers
- Bills from suppliers

The business has to have an administrative procedure in place to handle each type of information. Certain information will automatically be sent to a particular individual or part of the business, such as a cheque being sent to the accounts department. In smaller organisations, people will carry out administrative duties as part of their normal work, and will have other responsibilities as well. In larger organisations there may be a separate administration department.

Once information is received by the organisation, it needs to be processed. This may mean simply ensuring that the right person is given the information, or it may mean distributing it to a number of people.

The administration system will provide a support system to handle all the resources and information that is used. It will:

- Keep records relating to the activities of the business
- Monitor the performance of business activities
- Know where information is stored and how it can be retrieved

The business may have to act on the information that it receives, and in order to do this the information has to be sent to the right part of the organisation or the correct individual. It will be their responsibility to deal with the information on behalf of the business.

### For example Handling complaints

A business receives a complaint from a customer. They have been overcharged for a service that they have received. The information needs to be sent to someone who can make a decision about authorising the overpayment to be cancelled, or a refund to be arranged. This individual may be in customer services or may be in accounts. The procedure may be that Customer Services handles it by agreeing that action needs to be taken, and then authorises accounts to make the refund to the customer.

14

## The purpose of business information

A vast amount of information can come into a business. The administrative procedures are there to organise that information, and make sure the right person has sight of it and then that it is stored in the correct location so that it can be found later.

The administrative procedures ensure:

- Consistency – every piece of information has been dealt with in the same way.
- Effective use of time – although administrative procedures can be time-consuming, they do save time in the long run.

The overall purpose of providing this support is to:

- Ensure that managers and decision-makers have access to the information they need to make decisions.
- Support departments so that when they need particular information they can access it in order to carry out their work.

## Types of administrative support

As we will see, business and administration support covers a wide range of different areas of the business. All managers and departments will need this support so that they have the latest information. The following list gives some examples of typical types of support:

- Meetings – organising them, supporting the meeting while it is going on and providing records of the meeting for future use.
- Documents – preparing basic blank documents, such as forms or letterheads so that the same types of forms, with the necessary information, are used by all parts of the business and that copies can be made and sent to the correct part of the business.
- Arranging events, travel and accommodation for key managers.
- Handling data – dealing with documents and other information and distributed to the relevant people, and stored in an accessible and secure manner.

## QUESTION TIME
*12 minutes*

**1** Define the term business administration. *(2 marks)*

**2** Suggest TWO types of information that a business might receive and how each might be handled. *(4 marks)*

**3** What might be the consequences to a business if it does not set up effective administrative procedures? *(6 marks)*

15

> Although ICT can make the function of business administration more efficient, a vast amount of information still comes into a business by other routes. There are telephone messages, documents, brochures, catalogues, letters and a host of other paper-based documents, such as invoices, statements of account and delivery notes. Without an effective administrative process it is impossible for the business to know what has arrived, who is meant to deal with it and whether it has been dealt with at all.

# The role of administration

**YOU WILL FIND OUT:**
- about storage of information
- about electronic filing
- about processing of information
- about retrieving and disseminating information

## Storage of information

The words 'storage' and 'retrieval' can be confusing if you haven't worked in an office. In fact, they mean 'filing'. This word can also cause a reaction – often one of groans and moans! Filing is often thought of as boring and routine, and, in essence, it is. Nowadays, however, storage and retrieval also includes the computerised systems of storing and retrieving information.

The safe and secure storage of information and the easy access or retrieval of that information is imperative if an organisation is to function successfully and efficiently. Obviously this involves a logical and effective way of recording documents and storing them in an efficient system which will allow the easy retrieval of that information when required.

Filing is the basis of record-keeping and entails the processing, arranging and storing of documents so that they can be found when required. The documents are placed in consecutive order and preserved in that system until they are required for reference.

## Electronic filing

Obviously, all information stored on computer must also be protected. Electronic filing is now widely used by businesses, and companies using it must ensure that:

- back-up copies of documents are made and safely stored
- passwords are used by the staff using the computer, and these should be changed regularly
- user codes are used in addition to passwords, if necessary. These are known only to those who are authorised to access the information, and relate to specific files or documents stored.

## Processing of information

All businesses are awash with information. On a daily basis, data, including facts and figures, come into the business or are generated by the business. One of the most important tasks of employees and managers is to be able to understand the relevance of what arrives on their desks. It would be impossible for everyone to read every relevant piece of information. It is therefore vitally important that someone has responsibility for analysing the data and the figures and identifying what may be relevant and what is not.

Also, many facts and figures are presented in ways which are not immediately useful, either to the business or to particular departments. Again someone has to take the responsibility of looking through the data, deciding what is relevant and then presenting it in a useable format.

## Retrieving and disseminating information

Obviously, the main purpose of filing paperwork away is being able to find it again when it is needed, either by yourself or by someone else. Being able to find the right information in a filing system is known as retrieving information and would be necessary in order to:

- add more information to the contents of the file
- obtain some information from the contents of the file.

But giving information away can prove complicated. If someone takes individual documents from a file they may go missing forever. You should never allow just one or two pages to be taken from a file unless:

- most of the information contained in the file is confidential and the person needing the one or two documents cannot see the rest of the confidential information
- the information contained in the file is much too large to take away.

Not all facts and figures coming into a business or being generated by it have obvious relevance to the work going on in any of its departments. This does not necessarily mean that the information can be ignored or discarded, as there may be something hidden within it that is of relevance, though it is not immediately obvious.

16

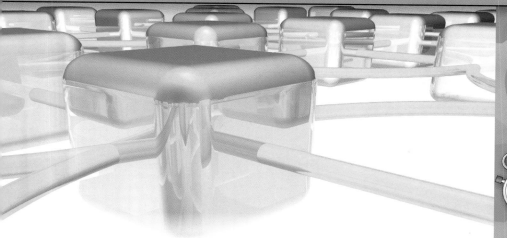

As you have probably realised, different parts of a business often need the same information, but in more or less detail. Some will need very detailed facts and figures in order to make decisions. Others will only need to know the highlights of facts and figures in order to help them make decisions. Whenever a business is required to analyse, extract or adapt information, it needs to think about what is, and what is not, relevant to the person or group of individuals they are preparing the information for. The more relevant the information, and the shorter the summary of that information, the more likely the reader is to be able to understand the relevance of what they are being shown.

## For example Sharing data

In many businesses, the same data will have to be adapted for various purposes. Here is an example of how one set of figures can be relevant in several different ways:

- A sales department would be interested in all aspects of sales figures because they would tell it exactly what had been sold, when and where.
- Purchasing would be interested in sales figures because they would wish to make sure that products that have been sold were re-ordered.
- Finance and Accounts would be interested in sales figures because they are concerned with the total amount of money received by the business. They will also analyse individual product sales figures so that they can see which of the products are providing the business with the most profit.

- The owners of the business will be interested in the sales figures because they will show them how well the business is performing and how much profit it is making.
- Human resources departments are interested in sales figures because, if sales are increasing, they may need to employ more sales staff. Alternatively, if sales are falling, they may have to consider reducing the number of sales staff.

## QUESTION TIME
*12 minutes*

1 What do you understand by the term 'indexing'? *(2 marks)*

2 How might electronic filing of information be more efficient than paper-based filing? *(4 marks)*

3 Explain why every piece of information generated or received by a business needs to be analysed and distributed? *(6 marks)*

17

# How administration supports business functions

**YOU WILL FIND OUT:**

● how administration supports the functions of a business

● about the key functions of a business

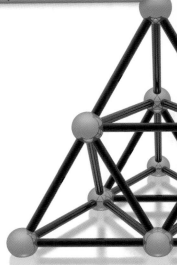

## How administration supports the functions of a business

A functionally-based organisational structure is usually designed around the different parts of the organisation that produce, market and sell the product or service. The different departments or functions will all be controlled by a board of directors, that elects or appoints a managing director. The managing director is supported by a range of senior managers, each of whom has responsibility for one particular function of the organisation.

These functions are, in fact, the different areas or departments of the business. The business needs to be organised in the best possible way in order to meet the objectives that have been set for it. This helps to define what individuals do and precisely what departments are responsible for.

Using this type of organisational structure, a company can group certain functions that it carries out logically under a particular manager. There are usually four ways of grouping employees, or grouping what the business does:

- by what they produce (the product)
- by their function, or what they do for the organisation
- by process (how they do it), for example by having various regional offices
- by the type of customer they deal with, for example if they deal with other businesses, or with retail outlets (shops).

## The key functions of a business

The functional areas, or departments, of an organisation all have their own specific jobs to do. The particular roles of each department within an organisation are explained below.

### Finance/Accounting

The finance or accounts department of an organisation supervises all matters involving money. Its main role is to use the data it collects to find out whether or not the business is making a profit. It checks that the business's revenue (the money coming into the business) is greater than its costs (the money being spent). The information the finance department generates is handed on to the directors, shareholders and senior managers of the business in the form of written documents, including balance sheets and profit-and-loss accounts.

### Human Resources

Human Resources recruits suitable new employees and organises them so that they provide the type of work the organisation needs to meet its objectives. The department is also sometimes known as the 'personnel department'. It closely monitors the selection of new employees. It aims to ensure that employees are trained and developed adequately, and, if particular employees are suitable, that they are given higher and often better-paid jobs (promotion) within the business.

### Sales

The sales department's main responsibility is to create orders for the business's products or services. The greater a business's emphasis on selling to individual customers, the larger the sales force. Those businesses that rely on large amounts of advertising to gain interest in its product or service can have quite a small sales force. Much of the information that the sales department provides is analysed by the marketing department. Often the sales department will also develop what is known as 'point of sale' materials. These include posters, leaflets, brochures, pamphlets and catalogues.

### Marketing

The main function of the marketing department is to try to meet customers' needs and to predict what they may need in the future. Working closely with the sales department, the marketing department carries out a great deal of research to try to discover what customers want, where they want to buy it and how much they are prepared to pay for it. Marketing also researches and designs the best way of informing customers what the business is offering for sale.

18

We already know that the functional, or departmental, way of organising a company means that the different departments all have their own areas of work. They are all striving to make sure that the business meets its main aims or objectives. In a way, each of the departments is specialising in one particular aspect of the business. The employees who work in that department could be regarded as specialists in that particular function of business activity.

## Research and development (R&D)

The main function of the research and development department is not just to come up with new products or services. It also has to come up with the most efficient and effective way of producing them. It will, after carrying out lots of tests, pass on its designs and proposed ways of producing the product to the production department. The production department will then take over the responsibility of putting the new product into production.

## Customer Service

The customer service department is the main point of contact that customers have with a business. It could be that the customer has a complaint to make, or that they require more detailed information from the department.

## IT services

The information technology (IT) or computer services department will have the responsibility for the hardware and the software that a business uses.

## Production

The production department is involved in all functions which revolve around actually producing the products or services for the customer. This department will monitor levels of wastage to ensure the most efficient use of resources. It will also check the cost of raw materials and parts purchased to make sure that profit margins are maintained.

## Purchasing

The purchasing department is responsible for assisting the other departments of the business in ordering and buying the goods and services required. It keeps a stock of catalogues and price lists from suppliers. When the purchasing department's employees receive a purchase requisition (a request to purchase) from one of the other departments, or individuals, within the organisation, it researches the various suppliers until it finds the right product, at the right price, with the right delivery time.

## Distribution

The effective and efficient distribution of a business's products is the responsibility of the distribution department. In situations when an organisation provides a delivery service to the customer, it is essential that the most efficient and cost-effective routes are used. This is often carried out using computer software.

## QUESTION TIME
*16 minutes*

**1** Who are departmental or functional managers usually responsible to in an organisation? *(2 marks)*

**2** How might the work of the IT functional area streamline the work of other functional areas of the business? *(6 marks)*

**3** If a business receives a complaint from a customer who has been overcharged for products and services and has had received damaged goods, which functional areas of the organisation might be involved and why? *(8 marks)*

19

# The importance of accuracy

## How administration provides support

Obviously, all organisations work in different ways and have different systems and procedures that they expect their staff to carry out in the course of their day-to-day duties. This section of the book briefly outlines the different types of administrative procedures. Throughout the unit, the particular skills, duties and tasks required to carry them out are discussed in more detail.

The operation of administrative procedures is important since the activities of the organisation must be coordinated and planned. If inadequate administrative procedures are in operation, then the organisation may suffer from a lack of efficiency since it does not have access to all relevant information. Administration inevitably involves some form of filing, whether it be a paper-based filing system or a computer-based system.

The systems an organisation has in place should aim to establish a means of assessing the operations it carries out. Most administrative systems are a series of sub-systems that can be split into additional sub-systems. It is therefore important that the organisation monitors all parts of the system. The systems should be designed in such a way that they can be changed to meet the requirements of the organisation.

An organisation's administrative procedures are the means by which it is able to operate as a cohesive entity. Any organisation can have good ideas and well-motivated employees, but, without procedures to ensure that functions are carried out, these may not be carried through. Information received by the organisation has to be processed in some way before it can either be stored (in which case it could later be retrieved) or disseminated (sent to different people) in the various departments. Alternatively, the information may need to be sent out from the organisation in a different format.

Most businesses create systems by talking to those who carry out the duties relating to them. These individuals are most aware of what is involved in each particular type of task. By asking the experts how they would ideally do a particular job, the business can begin to create a handbook which outlines the procedures. These manuals can then be used as a reference for those carrying out these tasks in the future. The manuals can be updated as procedures change or are amended for various reasons.

Businesses do not usually circulate copies of a manual and expect people to read it from cover to cover and understand what is now required. Instead, new procedures are often supported by training events or by encouraging individuals who were involved in the writing of the manual to provide support for others. This is known as mentoring, and the mentor can be considered to be an expert.

In order to assess whether the new procedures are being used properly, and to track their effectiveness, a business may create a series of new documents or forms. These forms will need to be completed by those using the new procedures, to confirm that particular steps have been followed and to highlight any difficulties.

In larger organisations where new procedures are being put in place, it may not be possible for those using the new procedures to contact those who have designed them. These larger organisations need to provide support to their staff. This is often achieved by encouraging individuals encountering difficulties to send memos or emails to named people responsible for dealing with the particular problems.

20

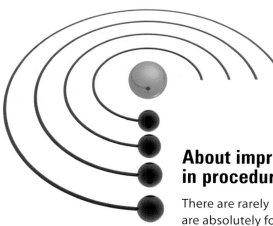

## About procedural difficulties

Despite the fact that the business may have spent considerable amounts of time and money on designing new procedures, printing manuals, organising training and mentoring, the procedures may still cause difficulties. They may be unclear and there may be people, such as new members of staff, who have missed the training events. Equally, some people may not have realised that the procedures applied to them, but in later weeks or months the procedures now do apply and they may need support.

There may also be aspects of the procedures which the business had not considered when they were written. A vital stage in the procedure may have been left out. The business may also have forgotten to include useful and vital tracking documents, which again could cause problems.

## About improvements in procedures

There are rarely procedures which are absolutely foolproof or ideal for every situation. There will always be a need to interpret procedures in certain cases, as the organisation may not have thought about particular circumstances. The procedures may have been designed to apply to the most usual circumstances, but there are always unusual cases that don't seem to fit the procedures. This means that there is always room for improvement and is the reason that tracking documents are useful.

Also, it is vital that users are encouraged to contact those responsible for designing procedures if they have any serious suggestions for practical improvements.

Procedures should be seen as being able to gradually develop rather than being set in stone. Businesses want their procedures to work in all circumstances and for employees to be sure of their actions in every event.

## QUESTION TIME
*14 minutes*

**1** Explain why clear administrative procedures are so important to businesses. *(6 marks)*

**2** Why is it important for a business to constantly review the way in which it handles information? *(8 marks)*

21

It is vital that all business information is stored, even if it does not seem to be important at the time. Businesses need to log, circulate, store and retrieve a vast amount of information in order to ensure that crucial pieces of information are not lost or ignored. Such losses can be disastrous for a business as it may be required by law to react to the information, or may lose a valued customer or a business opportunity if the information is overlooked. In an increasingly information-overloaded world it is often difficult to pick out what is really valuable, and this has become an increasing problem for businesses.

# Job roles

YOU WILL FIND OUT:

- job roles
- organisational structures and trees
- layers of management
- hierarchies and spans of control

## Job roles

There are a number of different job roles in any organisation, and their titles may not make it immediately clear what they are. The important thing to remember is that different job roles give authority and responsibility to the individual.

- **Managers** undertake tasks and duties delegated to them by directors, and take day-to-day responsibility for making decisions and implementing policies. They have a good working knowledge of the business.
- **Supervisors** tend to be on the next level down from, and report to, managers. They are team leaders or organisers of specific projects or functions of the organisation and tend to deal with day-to-day tasks. They do not always have wider managerial responsibilities.
- **Operatives** – this term can be applied to a variety of different job roles. Operatives often carry out manual labour or operate machinery or equipment. However some non-manual activities can be carried out by operatives, such as in the fast food outlet McDonald's, whose counter staff are called operatives.
- **Support staff** – this job title implies a junior role in an organisation where the support staff would assist a more senior member of staff. Examples include shop assistant, catering assistant, and administrative assistant. These job roles can be vital to an organisation because the support staff help the manager to carry out his or her own job.

## Organisation charts

The traditional way of visualising the organisational structure of a business is to create an organisation chart, which illustrates:

- each of the departments and how they are broken down
- the levels of responsibility of managers, by showing different managers who have the same level of responsibility at the same level in the chart. This can also show how departments and their managers work with one another
- the lines of communication within the business, showing how information passes up and down the organisation (from senior management down and then back up to the senior management via the layers of management).

## Organisation trees

The West Yorkshire Fire and Rescue Service organisation chart below is a simplified organisation tree. It shows five individuals answering directly to the Chief Executive, all with the same level of responsibility for one or more management

areas of the organisation, such as Human Resources or Training and Development. Underneath this senior management group, there will be managers responsible for each geographical area and each fire station, and beneath them will be the firefighters and other support staff.

As you can see from the illustration opposite, organisation trees often look like pyramids. There are only a handful of individuals at the top, but there are more and more managers, supervisors and employees as you move down the tree. Those employees at the bottom report, through successive layers of management, to the senior managers. This is known as a **hierarchy**.

By organising the business in a strict order, it is possible to identify and place individual managers and employees in areas of specialism.

The ways in which businesses are organised are determined by the nature of the work involved. Some departments are functional (actively involved in doing the business's work), while the rest are in support roles, such as administration.

**EXAMPLE OF AN ORGANISATION CHART**

SOURCE: WWW.WESTYORKSFIRE.GOV.UK

**EXAMPLE OF AN ORGANISATION TREE**

SOURCE: WWW.EMERALDINSIGHT.COM

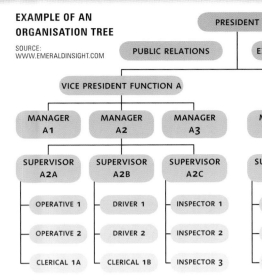

## Layers of management

Not all organisations look like tall, thin pyramids. Some are very flat. These have few layers of management between the key decision-makers and the employees. These types of organisation are called flat structures. They usually use teams of employees to carry out tasks and solve problems.

Many smaller organisations use flatter structures. These make it easier for everyone to understand the objectives of the business and learn how to work closely together. It is easy to tell just how many layers of management there are in a business by counting the number of managers or supervisors between the key decision-makers at the top of the organisation and the employees at the bottom of the structure. Obviously the more layers there are, the more complicated it can become to get messages and instructions up and down the structure.

The arrangement of layers is often called the chain of command. It traces the exact lines of responsibility and communication from, for example, the managing directors to retail assistants.

Messages can easily get lost or changed in complicated structures with several layers of management. Smaller businesses find it easier to pass on information directly and ensure that it is correct. The problem arises, however, when the business gets larger and needs more employees.

## Hierarchies

Another major consideration regarding complicated pyramid structures with multiple layers of management is that they are very hierarchical. This means that each layer of management hangs onto its authority and responsibility, making sure that it is always part of any decision-making process. Information must pass through each level, both up and down the organisation.

## Spans of control

A supervisor or manager's span of control is made up of a number of individuals who directly report to him or her. Even the most talented and efficient manager can only handle a limited span of control. Once the span gets beyond about eight individuals, it becomes difficult for the manager or supervisor to devote enough time to each subordinate.

### — K E Y   T E R M S —

**Hierarchy** ▶ the arrangement of the levels of authority in a business, with successively more authority and responsibility as you go up the organisation tree.

## QUESTION TIME
*16 minutes*

**1** What are the main differences between a manager and a supervisor? *(6 marks)*

**2** What is meant by de-layering? *(2 marks)*

**3** What is meant by the term hierarchy? *(2 marks)*

**4** What is meant by a chain of command and a span of control? Why are they different? *(6 marks)*

23

# Routine and non-routine tasks

## Routine tasks

The activities of an organisation may be classified as routine or non-routine. Routine activities are those carried out on a regular basis – for example, administration functions include:

- opening the mail each morning
- filing business documents in a filing cabinet.

Other activities are non-routine and require individuals to be more adaptable, as the demands of each day will differ and cannot be predicted with any great accuracy. On a single day, an individual may have a series of meetings or tasks to perform without prior notice or instruction.

Routine functions can be easily organised if the correct procedures are in place. An organised office will base its procedures on previous experience and will be able to predict the demands that will be placed upon it. In situations where an individual or department must carry out a non-routine function, they must be able to rely upon a separate series of procedures to support them.

Organisations will have their own sets of procedures, but generally they will all have a way of keeping track of the following:

- the cost of purchases made
- the names of those the business has made purchases from
- sales levels
- customers who have bought the business's products or service
- any customer enquiries received
- payments made by customers
- payments outstanding from customers
- payments made to suppliers

- payments outstanding to suppliers
- information about the employees (human resources) of the business (employee records)
- details of training undertaken or required by employees
- information about stock levels
- records of internal meetings held.

Procedures allow a business to carry out all its activities in an organised way. Decisions will be made about the organisation's objectives and then the procedures will help the business's managers and employees to achieve them.

If a business's employees carry out their activities or tasks in an organised way, then the impression they give their customers and the general public will be good. This good image is important for businesses and they will try to achieve it through their procedures in the following ways:

- All paperwork leaving the business gives a good impression because it is neat, accurate and well-presented.
- All information requested is sent out quickly to the right person, at the right time.

- All messages received are dealt with promptly and efficiently.
- All customers, or people likely to become customers, receive the same high level of service from the employees.
- Employees are aware of the need to keep confidential or sensitive information safe.
- The business's buildings and employees are kept healthy and safe.
- The business is following government laws in the way in which it carries out its activities.

Organised businesses will also have the following benefits:

- The business's customers are more likely to return and buy again (repeat business).
- The business's customers are more likely to recommend the business to others, which could bring them new customers.

## Non-routine tasks

The ability to use information sources, deal with a combination of routine and non-routine tasks to identify and solve routine and non-routine problems are important skills for any

---

**For example** Security officer

A security officer in a college might be expected to:
- plan to perform routine tasks and duties, allowing for flexibility to attend unscheduled incidents reported by others. This will result in reorganising and reprioritising the routine tasks.
- liaise with members of the college community to fulfil the routine and non-routine tasks and duties, so that mutual schedules and agendas are adhered to.
- in the absence of the Team Supervisor, prepare team briefings and deploy staff according to operational requirements and with respect to the various duties.

24

In developing a new product, the manufacturing process needs to be considered alongside the development itself. This will involve:

- testing proposed designs to see if they can be manufactured cost-effectively
- designing new products with an eye to minimising the number of components
- reducing assembly complexity
- using standard parts wherever possible, – inexpensive and easy to source
- using parts that are already used in existing products
- ensuring standardisation if production volumes will be low
- buying-in components that can be sourced at competitive prices.

## QUESTION TIME
*12 minutes*

**1** Choose a new product or service that you would like to see on sale. Work through the stages of new product development and suggest how the process might work for your product. *(12 marks)*

employee or manager in a business. Employers look for a willingness and an ability to perform routine and non-routine tasks effectively, in ways that may be needed to respond to changing circumstances.

Businesses cannot predict what may be needed of their employees and many aspects of their work could be described as being non-routine. These are either unexpected situations or problems, or they may be tasks that are out-of-the-ordinary compared to the everyday work of the employee. Examples of non-routine work may include new product development, research, or planning and handling complaints.

Non-routine work needs:

- knowledge
- skills
- appropriate attitude.

As an example of non-routine work, the table below looks at how new product development takes place, and how unpredictable the stages can be so that they require employees to be very flexible in their approach.

| STAGE | PROCESS | EXPLANATION |
|---|---|---|
| 1 | Idea generation | New product development ideas can come from a variety of different sources such as the employees themselves, competitors, customers, distributors and suppliers, so the business needs to constantly look for ideas and leads. |
| 2 | Screening | This process involves looking through the ideas generated above and selecting ones that are feasible and workable to develop. Pursuing non-feasible ideas can be very costly to the business, so this needs a flexible approach. |
| 3 | Concept development and testing | Once the business has decided that the idea is a good one, it needs to be tested on the potential customers. This involves finding out what they think of the idea. Is it practical and feasible? Would they buy it? Will it offer them the benefits that the business thinks it will? Has the business overlooked something about the idea? Can this problem be put right? Again, at this stage the business needs to figure out the best way to present the idea to the target group and to collect and analyse its reactions. |
| 4 | Marketing strategy and development | Now the business needs to decide how it will launch the product or service to the market. It will have to figure out a marketing strategy that would work. It needs to be able to target the right type of potential customer and be able to persuade them to try the product or service. |
| 5 | Business analysis | So far so good. But now the business has to make a major investment in the idea. Is it financially worthwhile? Will it generate sales and profits? How much will it cost the business to produce the product, provide the service and market it to the customers? How much market share would be considered to be a success? |
| 6 | Product development | This is the final stage before the launch of the product or service. Now the last-minute developments and changes take place. Final testing takes place, and last changes are made. This is a crucial time as there will be no second chances. |
| 7 | Test marketing | The product or service is launched into a specific region or market. The reaction of the customers to the marketing and the product or service itself will tell the business whether it has got things right. |
| 8 | Commercialisation | Now the product or service can be nationally launched. Timing is important, and constant checks on progress are essential. |

# Routine and non-routine decision-making

## Decision-making

Managers make problem-solving decisions with varying amounts of certainty, risk and uncertainty. When there is certainty and a little risk, decisions tend to be easier as they are more routine and predictable. When decisions have uncertainty and risk, they tend to be non-routine – the manager may not have had to make this type of decision before. We will return to these three aspects of **decision-making** later, but what is decision-making?

Decision-making involves identifying and choosing alternatives based on the values and preferences of the decision-maker. Decision-making is the process of sufficiently reducing uncertainty and doubt about alternatives to allow a reasonable choice to be made.

### ——— K E Y   T E R M S ———

**Decision-making** ▶ looking at alternative choices, then choosing the one that has the highest probability of success and that best fits with the goals of the business.

**Contingency plan** ▶ a plan or series of actions designed to help a business get through a crisis situation.

**Brainstorming** ▶ meeting to collect ideas and suggestions about how to solve a problem. The group discusses each of them and comes up with the best solution.

**For example  Stock control**

Instead of taking regular decisions to re-order stock, many businesses use computer programmes to make these decisions for them. They set up the system so that stock will automatically be re-ordered when it falls below a predetermined level.

## Routine decision-making

For routine decisions, the manager will usually have access to all the information necessary to make the right choice. This type of decision is likely to have been made before in similar situations. This type of decision-making is therefore relatively simple.

Some situations arise on a regular basis, in which case the manager can use tried and tested responses or make automatic decisions.

Some decisions can also be approached in this kind of systematic way. They are straightforward problems and the information needed to solve them is clear. There is a range of problems that can be anticipated in this way, for example Human Resources decisions relating to pay rises, promotions, holiday requests or dealing with absences.

## About non-routine decision-making

New and unfamiliar problems also arise for which there is no automatic answer. In these cases, the manager will need to have access to all the information to make the right choices. The manager needs to understand the situation and be aware of the alternatives, and it is likely in these cases that the decision will be based on the manager's judgement. The business will be relying on the manager's judgement to make the right decision at the right time, but there is no guarantee that the chosen solution will work. This type of situation is fairly common for managers, even though it is non-routine, and responsibility is greater the more senior the manager.

A crisis is another type of non-routine problem that could lead to a disaster if not handled in the

## For example Managing in a crisis

A manager receives a telephone call early in the morning telling her that the offices have just been opened by the cleaning staff and the ground-floor rooms are flooded. The manager will have to decide how to react, whether to tell the staff not to come into work, reschedule meetings, arrange a clean-up and decide whether or not to go to the office immediately.

correct way. It is likely to need a quick solution and means that the manager will have only a short time to consider the alternatives and come up with the ideal solution.

Many businesses set up **contingency plans** which are designed to predict and then deal with crisis situations. The contingency plan can immediately swing into action and everyone will know what they have to do and when it has to done. This is also known as crisis management.

Sometimes managers will face situations they have not faced before, where the level of information is very poor. This makes it difficult to come up with a list of alternatives. These situations require a manager who is good at creative problem-solving. Sometimes, the business will bring together a group of people to **brainstorm** the situation and come up with alternatives. In reality, none of them are working on anything more than guesses or opinions, so good judgement is vital.

By coming up with contingency plans, many non-routine decisions can be handled in a more routine way. It is not possible to design a contingency plan that works for every crisis or non-routine situation, but where it is possible, it does help to create a way of thinking through a problem before it happens and setting up a series of actions to assist in dealing with it.

 There are several basic kinds of decision:

- **Decisions whether** – these are yes/no, either/or decisions that must be made before selecting an alternative.
- **Decisions which** – these involve a choice of one or more alternatives from a set of possibilities. The choice is based on how well each alternative measures up to a set of criteria.
- **Contingent decisions** – these are decisions that have been made, but put on hold, until some condition is met.

## QUESTION TIME
*12 minutes*

**1** A shop manager has to make a decision. A regular customer wants her money back, as the goods she bought as a present are not wanted. The shop has a strict policy of no refunds after 14 days; the purchase was made three weeks ago. What kind of decision has to be made by the manager and why? *(4 marks)*

**2** A business investor needs to make a decision. If she invests £10,000 in company A and it is successful she will make £50,000. If it fails she will lose her £10,000. If she invests in company B with the same amount and it is successful, she will make £15,000, but if it fails she will get back £7,000 of her investment. What kind of decision is being made and why? *(8 marks)*

27

# Prioritising and planning

## Prioritising

Generally speaking, planning will help you to work efficiently and effectively. This means that you will need to deal carefully with all the aspects of your job and the tasks which have been given to you. Getting a task completed begins with planning, so it is appropriate to begin there.

## Planning

The classic way to approach target setting is to remember the word SMART. SMART is an acronym (a word made up of initials) and stands for:

**S** PECIFIC
**M** EASURABLE
**A** TTAINABLE
**R** ESULTS-ORIENTATED
**T** IME-SPECIFIC

All the major goals or targets set for a team should be broken down into manageable pieces. In other words, teams and individuals can achieve short-term goals (which are more under their own control) on the road to achieving the major goals. These steps along the way need to be put in order of priority (the most important first). Teams should also put their goals down in writing, so that there is no doubt about what they are. It is also useful to write down the ways in which you achieved those goals on the way. This means that as the goals are achieved they can be ticked off and the next one can be looked at.

Planning is a crucial element of every job, but few people ever get

| PLANNING AND PRIORITISING STAGE | DESCRIPTION |
|---|---|
| Get the facts about the task | What do you need to do, when does it need to be done, how does it have to be done, who do you need to contact (or refer to) and who can help you to do it? |
| Clarify what has to be done | Ask questions before you get on with the task. If you need help or assistance in deciding what has to be done, ask at the outset. |
| Is the task part of your normal job? | It may not be clear to you whether the task fits what you are normally supposed to do. If you are not trained to do the task, you could say this, but you do need to be flexible at times. |
| Identify the resources you will need | Resources can fall into three categories:<br>• Equipment<br>• Materials<br>• Information<br>Identify what you need and whether it is available. |
| Prioritise | Routine tasks may have to be set aside if the task is important or urgent. |
| Be flexible | Priorities can change. What is important or urgent to some is not to others. You may also experience changes in the deadlines. Be prepared to re-plan to scrap what you have already started! |

any training about how to plan effectively. Most people can get by with their own personal planning to handle their own responsibilities, but planning as a part of a team can be quite difficult.

A good plan needs to be 'alive' and flexible. A good plan can also take a lot of pressure off the team and the team leader. It offers them a 'map' to achieve objectives and targets.

Planning can involve the following:

• deciding on the objectives of the team
• deciding which of the team's goals need to be achieved to reach the objectives
• deciding on the strategies needed to achieve the objectives (how to do it)

• deciding who will do what in the team to achieve the objectives.

Team planning usually takes place at meetings set aside to decide what the team has to do and how it will achieve these goals. In the meeting the following would be looked at:

• evaluation of progress (where they are at the moment)
• deadlines for achieving particular goals
• prioritisation of goals or deadlines
• agreement on all of the above so that everyone has had a chance to be involved
• allocation of individual responsibilities to team members
• allocation of resources to team members to help them achieve and deal with the responsibilities that they have been given.

28

# Consequences of poor planning

There is a saying: 'Failing to plan is planning to fail'. The most important responsibilities of someone organising work are planning, integrating and executing. As we have seen, planning in general is the function of selecting objectives and establishing the policies, procedures and programmes necessary for achieving them. The key reasons to make sure that a plan is in place are:

- to eliminate or reduce uncertainty
- to improve efficiency of the operation
- to obtain a better understanding of the objectives
- to provide a basis for monitoring and controlling work.

However, many managers and business owners do not plan because:

- it takes time
- they have to think
- it involves paperwork
- they have to follow procedures
- they are committed to getting the job done within a time period.

The consequences of failing to plan are:

- starting something without knowing why or how to judge when it is completed
- enthusiasm at the beginning, but this quickly disappears
- chaos, as no one has a defined role.

Financially it may be problematic for the business, as people will have been spending time for no good reason or outcome. Routine work may not have been completed and it will reflect badly on the business if customers, suppliers or distributors are involved.

## QUESTION TIME
*12 minutes*

**1** **Using the Namibia example, what should have been planned and prioritised by the Ministry of Education before the ordering of the computer equipment? Suggest how it should have been planned and prioritised and what should be done now.**
*(12 marks)*

29

### For example

Here is an example of how poor planning can affect thousands of people. In Namibia in southern Africa a N$9 million batch of computer equipment was bought by the country's Ministry of Education in early 2007 for distribution to 40 schools. It has not yet reached its intended destinations. These computers have been kept in storage at the Ministry's National Education Technology Service and Support Centre because of lack of proper infrastructure at most of the schools that had been identified. Many of these schools do not have the necessary power points. There is also a concern about the lack of security at some of the schools. Another major problem is that Namibia does not have enough computer teachers.

# Workplace organisation

## Workplace organisation

Organisations differ a great deal, but they all have some common features, including:

- They all use resources, such as people, money and materials.
- They all provide something; either a product or a service.
- They usually compete with other business organisations.

Each business undertakes a variety of tasks or functions in order to operate effectively within its area of work. Some of these tasks are:

- Managing employees – usually through a human resources department.
- Selling products or services – by providing customers with required products or services.
- Distributing products or services – by choosing an appropriate way in which products or services can be delivered to customers.
- Purchasing products or services – by ordering them from other business organisations.

- Marketing products or services – by carrying out research to find out what customers need and publicising what they have to sell so that customers know it is available.
- Keeping financial records – monitoring the money that comes into and out of the business.

Organisations have to make sure that when they are making a choice it is the right one. Part of this is to ensure that they are organised in the right way. We have already seen that businesses have different organisational structures. But what about the physical working environment? This is the actual working area used by the managers and the employees to carry out their day-to-day work. It is impossible to make sweeping generalisations about how a workplace is organised because every business organisation is different.

The following section will focus on some of the common ways in which the workplace is organised and how it has changed and continues to change.

### ——— K E Y  T E R M S ———

**Community charge** ▶ a tax payable to the local government by every household, based on the value of the property.

**Grant** ▶ funding provided by central government or by the European Union to support local services.

## Different types of business organisation

It is important to note that not all business organisations are either the same size or have the same complexity of tasks to carry out. Also they do not necessarily have the same aims and objectives. Many businesses are privately owned, which means that they have owners or shareholders. Their primary interest is to serve their customers in the most profitable way they can. There are also non-profit making organisations, which are either referred to as social enterprises or charities. The main aim of these is not to make a profit, but to provide service or support to their customers or clients while ensuring that they have sufficient funds to continue operating.

Government departments – or the Civil Service – are another type of business organisation. These are responsible for running central government activities. At a more local level there are county, metropolitan, borough and district councils. All of these provide services to the community and are funded by the **community charge** and **grants** from central government. They all need to be as organised and structured as a privately owned business that focuses on profit. They have similar tasks to perform and consist of different departments with a wide range of responsibilities. They need to be efficient and they also need to have an administrative system that supports their work.

30

# Functions of organisations

Workplaces will tend to be organised according to the different functions that need to be carried out. Although not all organisations break down these functions in the same way, there are common sets of functions that could form the basis of how the workplace is split up:

- *Finance and accounts* – the part of the organisation that supervises all matters involving money. It will record and monitor sales, costs, wages, salaries and budgets
- *Human Resources* – responsible for recruiting new employees and organising them. It also deals with training and development and is responsible for maintaining employee records and dealing with issues such as retirement.
- *Production* – if the business actually makes something (a manufacturer) then this department will be the one that does the manufacturing, so it will be the direct user of raw materials or components, which it will and transform into new products.
- *Research and Development (R&D)* – looks to create new products and services to match customer demand.
- *Sales and Marketing* – the sales force deals directly with customers and consumers and will be involved in trying to persuade them to buy products and services. The marketing area will carry out research, but it will be primarily involved in promoting the business's products and services to potential customers.

- *Distribution* – responsible for storing and transporting products into and out of the business.
- *Purchasing* – this may be part of the accounts area, but some businesses keep it separate. The purchasing department is responsible for ordering or buying products and services needed by the business.
- *Customer services* – this may be either part of Sales and Marketing or a separate department. It is the main point of contact for customers with complaints, queries and issues that might arise after some of the business's product has been purchased.
- *IT* – responsible for maintaining the business's computer and telecommunication systems, including the hardware and software.
- *Administration* – as we already know, this area controls the paperwork and supports the other departments.

> Some businesses have centralised services, so that the areas are separate but support one another. All administrative work will be carried out by one department and all accounts and finance by another. A decentralised system means that each department or function would be responsible for its own administration and financial matters.

## QUESTION TIME
*21 minutes*

1  Name TWO functions of a typical organisation. *(2 marks)*

2  Identify and explain TWO likely functions of a marketing department. *(4 marks)*

3  Explain why a not-for-profit organisation, such as a charity, might be less likely to have separate departments to carry out different functions. *(6 marks)*

4  Suggest the most important functions of a high-street retailer. Why are these functions so crucial to this type of organisation? *(9 marks)*

31

# Different kinds of working environment

YOU WILL FIND OUT:
- about the nature of the organisation
- about the needs of the organisation
- about tasks and office space

## The nature of the organisation

All organisations are different, partly because they do different things. Some manufacture products, some sell them, and others offer services to customers. Some organisations are large and on a single site, while some are spread around the country, or even the world. Others will be simple, smaller businesses with a single purpose, such as an estate agent or a travel agent.

Factors influencing the way a business chooses to set out its offices might include:

- The organisation mainly manufactures products, so the bulk of the space will be given up to this, and offices will tend to lead off the main production area.
- The organisation regularly receives customers, so the offices themselves need to be separated from the customer area.
- The organisation has different **departments** or functional areas, so they may have a range of open-plan or cellular offices.

Some organisations will have more need for offices, and some less. Some will be very administration-based. This means that they handle lots of paperwork, or need to have access to plenty of computers in order to access databases and make electronic records.

The greater the need for these types of activity, the more likely it is for the business to have to seriously consider how it organises its office space. An organisation like a **call centre** will need to have large, open-plan offices. Each employee will have access to a computer and a telephone. In order to supervise the large numbers of call centre operators, the offices need to be open-plan. It would not be easy to manage the whole operation if the employees were scattered over several cellular offices.

For many manufacturing organisations the office layout is a second thought, as the main effort will go into production. Offices will be needed for the sales, marketing, finance and administration staff, but these may be small, cramped spaces, situated off the main production area.

Some organisations will establish an effective way to set out their offices, and then copy this format at every site they operate from.

To cut costs, many organisations, including banks, have moved their call centres to countries such as India. They can use educated and well-trained staff but pay them less than a third of the wages they would have to in Britain.

## The needs of the organisation

Every organisation has its own particular procedures and ways of working, which will directly influence the office layout it chooses. All organisations will need to consider:

- The health and safety of their employees
- The situation of machinery and equipment where it will not cause danger or injury to employees in terms of noise and **emissions**
- A smoking policy
- Space for personal belongings, and eating and drinking policies. This is all part of 'clean desk' policies and designing work areas where there is only enough space to work
- Emergency procedures including regular fire drills and evacuation practices. Office layout needs to take this into account so that main routes to exits are kept clear.

32

## Tasks and office space

We have seen that a business may organise its office space according to departments or functional areas. Tasks carried out by employees are often an extension of this. Larger, open-plan offices allow teamwork to happen easily.

Some jobs will also require individuals to have more than the basic minimum (11 cubic metres). For example, employees in a design department need a relatively large amount of space to carry out their tasks, and anyone using a wide range of equipment and machinery as part of their job will also require a lot of office space. Many employees have computers, scanners, printers and a host of other electronic equipment that can take up considerable space.

Many offices also need to accommodate multiple workstations and provide a larger table for team tasks and meetings.

--- **K E Y   T E R M S** ---

**Departments** ▶ named and separate parts of an organisation that carry out a particular series of tasks for the organisation, such as the accounts department, which deals with financial matters.

**Call centre** ▶ a place where employees answer the telephone and deal with customer queries, or make phone calls to existing and potential customers.

**Emissions** ▶ in an office environment this means radiation from computer monitors, heat from photocopiers and particles in the air from fans.

▶▶ Businesses will also organise their working environments to maximise the flow of work. It makes sense for an organisation to position departments or individuals who regularly work together close to each other. For example, Sales might be placed near Accounts so that credit checks and queries relating to customer accounts can be handled in an efficient way. Larger businesses will find this more difficult as it requires considerable planning of the office space. Proximity of departments needs to be considered alongside the need for computer networking and access to telephones.

## QUESTION TIME
*12 minutes*

JCM Plastics Ltd has outgrown its factory and office units. It has decided to rent a larger unit on the same industrial estate. This will give greater opportunity for expansion over the next three to five years. The larger unit will also enable the company to organise its departments and separate the production area completely from the office area.

33

1 The sales department wants to establish a call centre. What does this term mean? *(2 marks)*

2 Why is it important for the office space to be separate from the production area of the business? Explain your reasons. *(4 marks)*

3 Suggest and explain the purpose of at least THREE functional departments of a business such as this. *(6 marks)*

# Different kinds of office layout

YOU WILL FIND OUT:

● about office layouts
● about open-plan offices
● about cellular offices
● about influences on working environments
● about planning office space

## Office layouts

Nearly every working environment is organised in a different way. Each has its own particular demands. Sometimes there is a need for quiet working space. At other times people need to interact so they can discuss and make decisions.

There has been a move towards more open-plan offices, mostly to make the best use of the space the business has available to it. Open-plan offices allow much more interaction and reduce the number of individual offices.

## Open-plan offices

### Advantages

The first major advantage is that both employees and managers can work together as a team. This means that information can be passed backwards and forwards with the minimum of fuss. There are a number of other advantages, including:

- People feel much more a part of the business.
- People can share telephones, printers, faxes and other equipment.
- People can see others doing their jobs.
- Managers can move around and supervise and help as needed.
- There is the potential for better communication.
- The working environment is more light and airy.
- Managers can actually see work being done.
- It is cheaper to construct, as there is no need for partitions.
- Lighting, heating and cleaning are cheaper.

### Disadvantages

Open-plan offices can be noisy and there is little privacy, which is difficult if something is **confidential**. Some people feel that they are being watched, which can make them uncomfortable. Others just like their own space and do not like it being invaded by others. There are other disadvantages, including:

- the increased possibility of losing or mislaying things
- things could get stolen
- illnesses can spread throughout the whole office
- there might be less warmth or light in some places than others
- the office does not really belong to anyone and it can feel impersonal.

## Cellular offices

A more traditional way of organising the working environment is to separate people off into small offices. This is known as a cellular office system, and even in open-plan offices there will be cellular offices for senior managers and for meetings.

### Advantages

The main advantages of using cellular offices include the following:

- They are a quiet and more private environment to work in.
- Meetings can be held in private.
- A person's work and documents or equipment can be kept in one office.
- The office can be made more personal.
- Security is better, particularly if the office can be locked.
- Confidential information can be kept secure.

### Disadvantages

There are some major disadvantages to cellular offices, these are:

- Employees or groups of employees in the office cannot be constantly supervised.
- The business may have to buy duplicate equipment for use in each office, so this might not be **cost-effective**.
- People get possessive about their own work space.
- People can tend to be isolated and out of touch with what else is going on in the business.

34

## Influences on the working environment

The working environment is influenced by the needs of the organisation and the demands of the tasks carried out by the employees. The idea is to make everything as efficient as possible. This means that people need to know:

- how work is planned and by whom
- how work is organised and scheduled
- how each employee's work area is organised
- where other employees with whom they work regularly are situated
- where the necessary machinery and equipment are
- whether there are any health and safety concerns.

Businesses have certainly recognised that in most cases employees work far better as a team than when left to carry out work alone. Team members drive one another. Each of them has different skills and can contribute towards getting the job done better and faster.

Teams will always need someone in charge, but if they have the resources and the space to do the job they are always more effective than individuals.

### ——— K E Y   T E R M S ———

**Confidential** ▶ something that needs to be kept private because it contains sensitive information.

**Cost-effective** ▶ something that is worth buying because its benefits outweigh the costs involved in purchasing it.

## Planning office space

Organisation charts can be used to outline relationships between employees, including who reports to whom. This helps in placing individuals and parts of the organisation physically close to one another. Communication is also important and the business can identify whether individuals or departments need face-to-face contact with one another.

Businesses will also be concerned with how many private offices are needed. Larger, general or shared offices are more economical as they will be used more often by more people. A business will also try to estimate the number of employees it will need in the future, and plan space requirements accordingly.

> **Efficient office layout can give businesses significant benefits:**
> - It can improve supervision.
> - It can allow for expansion and rearrangement of work areas when needed.
> - It can provide efficient productive work areas.
> - It can make most efficient use of the available floor space.
> - It can identify specific work areas.
> - It can give employees a sense of ownership of their specific work space.
>
> Businesses will look at the flow of work between individuals and departments when they design their office layouts. They need to come up with a way in which work can proceed logically.

## QUESTION TIME
### 16 minutes

Cellular offices are often referred to as cluster workstations. They can be imagined as having a hub and spokes, like a wheel. The 'spokes' are either modular workstations or what is known as 'landscape'. The office landscape is likely to incorporate plants, and each of the work areas is set up at a different angle to provide a more interesting environment. Most organisations that use this landscape approach allocate 80% of their space to open-plan offices and 20% to private offices.

**1** What are the advantages of cellular offices? *(4 marks)*

**2** Suggest THREE reasons why a business might require private offices. *(6 marks)*

**3** How might a business be able to predict what space it might need for employees in the future? *(6 marks)*

35

# Developments in working practices

**YOU WILL FIND OUT:**

● about new working practices

● about hot-desking

● about home and teleworking

● about flexible working

## New working practices

The traditional way of working was to get into the office or your place of work at around 9am and leave at about 5pm, five days a week. In recent years this has all changed.

Businesses have begun to adapt to new ideas in order to balance workloads, help to keep and attract employees and to ensure that the business has staff for longer opening hours.

New working practices can provide great benefits to businesses. They are often referred to as smarter working practices, as they have been seen to provide improvements in productivity and competitiveness. In addition, the wellbeing of employees is improved and this has a positive impact on their relationships with employers. It is not always about working harder, but working more productively, so that employees can have a good work-life balance and employers can be more competitive and more productive, and can save money.

## Hot-desking

This is the way of working popular at the moment. It is sometimes called 'hotelling', 'virtual office' or even 'location – independent working'.

Employees are not given their own desk space; they are expected to keep their work documents in filing cabinets or lockers. They share the available desk space and equipment as and when they need it. Most of the employees will not spend all their time working in the office. They will just be given a desk, equipment and a telephone when they come in.

Many of the employees work from home or are out visiting customers on a daily basis. The employer may provide office space for them for meetings only. The idea is to make the best use of the office space and to cut down on **costs**. If the employees are usually out of the office, there may be no need for them to have a permanent desk space. The office will have regular support staff to help the hot-desk employees.

## Home and teleworking

Home-working is a major part of a business's move over to flexible working practices and to other systems, such as hot-desking.

With computers dropping in price, and laptops being as powerful as, and more mobile than, desktop computers, some employers think that it makes sense for employees to do their work without having to **commute**.

Some businesses think that office and customers can keep in touch effectively enough by using telecommunications.

Teleworking means using either the telephone or broadband services to work at home. Customers calling a business can have their calls re-routed to a person working at home, just as they would be connected to a traditional extension number in an office.

### KEY TERMS

**Costs** ▶ spending by a business to carry on its operations.

**Commute** ▶ to travel from home to the office and back each day.

## Advantages and disadvantages of home-working

There are many reasons why home-working is a good idea. These include:

*   greatly reduced commuting
*   less impact on the environment
*   fewer distractions from colleagues, meetings, etc.
*   employees can concentrate on complicated jobs
*   no need to wear formal work clothes
*   fitting in work around other commitments, such as childcare.

There are also several disadvantages:

*   employees might be lonely
*   it can be hard to work at a constant pace
*   there can be many distractions at home
*   it is easy to lose touch with colleagues
*   employees might not know what is happening in the office
*   it is hard to know when work time should begin and end each day.

## Flexible working

This covers a wide range of different types of working practices:

*   *Flexi-time* – employees work a core time (usually 10am until 4pm) then organise the rest of their hours as they please each week.
*   *Job sharing* – two or more people divide the working week between them. This allows people to arrange their working hours around their family or other commitments.
*   *Shift working* – some businesses need to operate 24 hours a day. Shift workers still work a regular eight or ten hours each day, but could start work at 2pm, 8pm or even 2am.
*   *Multi-skilling* – not so much a flexible working practice, but involves training employees to carry out a wider range of tasks, which gives flexibility both to the business and to the employees.
*   *Peripheral workers* – employees that can be brought in at short notice or to cover seasonal work. They work when the business is busy and needs extra help, and can be laid off when work is scarce.

Many of the largest and most successful businesses in Britain use flexible or new working practices, including Microsoft, the Nationwide building society, British Telecom and the Ministry of Defence. Flexible working allowed Microsoft to be able to fit an extra 400 people into its existing office space. British Telecom had over 12,000 people working from home, which has saved them over £200 million in office costs. The Ministry of Defence carried out a survey of those taking part in flexible working and 8 out of 10 said they were more motivated, had a better work-life balance and that it had had a positive impact on their family life.

## QUESTION TIME
*15 minutes*

Stuart used to work from an office and mainly dealt with computer support problems for the whole business by telephone. He really only needed to be in the office for the two days each week when he was available to repair the computers.

Now Stuart is a home-worker for three days a week. The trouble is that he has re-routed calls to his mobile and often answers queries in the park, the supermarket or even the pub. Sometimes he does not even answer the phone.

1   What is the other term used to describe Stuart's type of working practice? *(1 mark)*

2   Was it a good idea to switch his working practices? Explain your answer. *(6 marks)*

3   If Stuart is working from home and unable to answer the phone, what should he do to alleviate the problems people are experiencing in communicating with him effectively? *(8 marks)*

37

YOU WILL FIND OUT:
- what ergonomics is
- how to identify an ergonomics problem

# Ergonomics

## What is ergonomics?

Ergonomics is a science that looks at how people actually fit with their working environment. It recognises that everyone is different: individuals have different capabilities and limitations. Managers often take ergonomics into account when considering the tasks employees have to carry out, the equipment they use and the general space they work in.

The typical things looked at by ergonomists (experts in ergonomics) are:

- the actual job being done
- the demands on the employee
- the equipment's size, shape and weight
- whether the equipment is ideal for the job
- the physical environment (including temperature, humidity, lighting, noise, vibration)
- the social environment (for example whether there is teamwork and whether management is supportive).

### The individual

As well as looking at the working environment, ergonomics also takes individuals into account and considers:

- body size and shape
- fitness and strength
- posture
- senses (in particular vision, touch and hearing)
- stresses and strains on the body (such as muscles, joints and nerves).

## So what does it mean in practice?

Taking ergonomics into account in the workplace can lead to:

- a reduction in the number of accidents
- a reduction in injury and illnesses
- greater productivity and performance by employees.

Ergonomics does not just apply to desks, chairs and computer equipment. It applies to any equipment used by staff, or tasks carried out that could cause long-term difficulties.

## How to identify an ergonomics problem

There are several ways to discover whether there is an ergonomics problem in the workplace. Usually the following questions are asked:

- What do the employees think and feel about it?
- Are the employees sitting in comfortable positions?
- Are there many employees taking time off for aches, pains, fatigue and stress?
- Is the equipment regularly maintained?
- Are there frequent errors and problems?
- What kinds of accidents have taken place?
- Is there a high **staff turnover**?

### For example Practical solutions

Ergonomics is used to solve real and practical problems, such as making sure that desktops are far enough off the floor for people to fit their legs under. Another example would be working out the best use of a computer screen (also called display screen equipment) by making sure that:

- the screen is correctly positioned so that it is not too high or low or too close or too far away
- the screen is at the correct angle to the user
- the mouse is within easy reach of the user
- the chair is properly adjusted for the user
- there is no glare on the screen from overhead lights or windows
- both the hardware and the software does the job required
- there are enough breaks from the screen.

38

## Solutions

Wherever there is a problem, there is usually a solution. Minor things like making a job easier to do are the quickest way of solving the problem. Here are some examples:

- Provide height-adjustable chairs so that desks fit everyone.
- Remove items from under desks for leg room.
- Arrange things on shelves so that those used most are closest.
- Let the employees do **job rotation** so they can have a break from their normal work.
- Make sure alterations in one area do not cause problems somewhere else.
- Encourage employees to come up with better ways of doing things.

Expensive changes might not be necessary; simple solutions are often better. Money spent on ergonomic considerations will be made back very quickly as employees spend less time absent from work.

Employees can suffer from aching feet and back problems, which are known as musculoskeletal disorders. These are created or aggravated by workplace conditions. Individuals can also suffer from repetitive strain injuries. These are created by continual use of a particular set of muscles. Typically, the finger next to the thumb can suffer, as it tends to be used for mouse-clicking. To offset many of the potential injuries even staplers and ink pens should be cushioned versions to avoid strain and potential injury. Office workers should take a break every 15 minutes just to stand up and look away from the computer screen. Employees should also wear appropriate clothing; tight shoes can create circulation problems. The desk should fit the individual and both feet should be firmly on the ground without dangling. The flooring should be cushioned to avoid leg injuries and pains.

## QUESTION TIME
*12 minutes*

Jack works on an engine assembly line, which makes over 2000 engines a day. Jack's job is to tighten an adaptor on each engine. An engine passes his workstation every three seconds. He used a handheld impact wrench to do the work. The wrench vibrates when he uses it, and he often has to stretch to tighten the adaptor. Jack had begun suffering from neck and back pain. On a tea break, his supervisor saw him rubbing his neck and shoulder, and realised that there was a problem. The supervisor immediately called the health and safety representative to see if she would look into the problem.

The health and safety representative suggested:

- replacing the vibrating wrench with a better one
- changing the workstation, so that Jack could move around the engine instead of stretching to reach it
- bringing in job rotation so Jack would get a chance to do other things on the production line.

**1** What would be the result of the modifications? *(8 marks)*

**2** Suggest and explain another repetitive job that could present similar problems for an employee *(4 marks)*

39

---

## KEY TERMS

**Staff turnover** ▶ the number of employees joining and leaving the business over a period of time. A large number of employees leaving regularly is known as high staff turnover.

**Job rotation** ▶ a system that allows employees to do different tasks and jobs from time to time to give them a break from their regular work. It also helps make them skilled at doing other things.

# Sustainability

## Social costs and benefits

Business activity brings a number of benefits, such as providing products and services, creating employment and contributing to the economy. However, there are also social costs, such as environmental damage.

A further complication is caused by new technologies, such as robotics or automation, or even by more widespread use of ICT. As businesses adopt new technologies, this creates unemployment, which is a social cost. But there may be better working conditions for the remaining employees, which is a social benefit.

### Social benefits

Businesses:

- provide a range of products and services for all consumers, which would not otherwise be available
- create new ideas, inventions and information
- put money into the economy, both directly and indirectly, through wages and spending
- contribute to the wealth of the countries in which they operate
- support organisations, groups and charities through donations.

### Social costs

However, businesses also:

- contribute to climate change or global warming by producing emissions
- create water pollution
- overuse chemicals or antibiotics in food production
- overuse resources that are difficult to replace, or use up resources that cannot be replaced
- contribute to congestion on roads and damage to roads

- carry out damaging activities that others may have to pay to put right
- push up prices through anti-competitive behaviour, so that the consumer suffers
- sell products or services that can have a negative impact on consumers.

### Tackling social costs

There are generally four ways in which social costs can be tackled by society. Society can:

- make the practice a criminal offence, which has happened with many environmental and public health issues
- carry out investigations and bring charges against businesses whose products and services cause harm
- tax businesses that create social costs, and provide subsidies (give money to) businesses that provide social benefits
- provide the service itself.

## Ethical and environmental aims

Many businesses recognise the importance of incorporating ethical and environmental aims and objectives in order to show that they are socially responsible. Businesses will aim to improve their environmental record, to make sure that their employees – and other businesses and groups that they deal with – are treated fairly, and that they support local communities.

Building ethical and environmental aims and objectives into the business brings enormous benefits. Customers are increasingly choosing businesses that are socially responsible to buy products and

services from, instead of basing their decision purely on cost. Investors are attracted to ethically responsible businesses. Employees are more motivated if they are treated fairly and allowed to develop. Customers, suppliers and other groups will trust the business, and they will enjoy better relations. The business can also save money, because being socially responsible and environmentally aware is actually cheaper than the costs of waste management.

### Being greener

Businesses aim to address environmental problems by:

- replacing toxic substances with less harmful ones
- making their products multifunctional and reusable
- reducing their energy consumption
- making sure that many of their resources and materials are renewable and recyclable
- ensuring that employees receive environmental and health and safety training.

### Community commitment

Businesses also like to stress their commitment to the community because it shows that they are socially responsible. The business can rely on the support of the local community. It can attract employees, and it can attract ethical investors and customers.

Businesses support local communities by:

- working with charities in particular areas
- sponsoring specific projects
- contributing to wider initiatives, such as literacy projects
- offering employment to disadvantaged groups.

## For example
## Fairtrade

**FAIRTRADE**

The Fairtrade Mark can be awarded to products that have been certified by the Fairtrade Labelling Organisation. It means that the product conforms to standards that have improved the development of disadvantaged people in developing countries. Fairtrade sales are growing by around 20% per year and the Fairtrade Mark can bring benefits to both small and large businesses.

## Social responsibility

Social responsibility needs to focus on:

- the market itself and how the business promotes itself, where it obtains supplies of products and services, and how its products and services are sold
- the employees, including the wages paid, working conditions and equal opportunities policies
- the community – whether the business is a good neighbour to its community and what the business puts back into the community
- the environment, including waste, use of resources and emissions
- human rights, which extends to ensuring that all suppliers are socially responsible.

In assessing whether it is socially responsible, a business needs to look at how far it goes beyond fulfilling its minimum legal obligations. Being socially responsible does not just mean staying within the law; it means being more socially responsible than is legally required. The United Nations has nine principles of social responsibility, focusing on human rights, labour and the environment.

## QUESTION TIME
### 35 minutes

In 2007, the clothing chain Gap was linked with using children as young as 10, working up to 16 hours a day, to hand-embroider GapKids clothes in India. The business was condemned for exploiting children.

The business reacted by saying it would eradicate this practice and provided money to improve working conditions in India. It suspended orders with the textile workshops concerned.

Many people claimed that Gap had a responsibility and should have checked all the way back to where the cotton is produced in the fields.

1 Explain the difference between a social cost and a social benefit. *(4 marks)*

2 Identify TWO social costs and two social benefits. *(4 marks)*

3 The charity Save the Children believes that customers should be willing to pay more for products and services, and that cheap prices always mean exploited employees, probably including children. Is it reasonable for a business to expect customers to pay more because they are socially responsible? Explain your answer. *(6 marks)*

4 Some 60 million children work in India. How might Gap have checked that all of its suppliers were socially responsible? *(6 marks)*

5 Gap has provided money to improve working conditions in India. What strategies could the company put in place for this to be achieved? *(6 marks)*

6 Do you consider Gap to be socially responsible by suspending orders with the Indian textile workshops? *(9 marks)*

# Health and safety at work

## Health and Safety at Work Act (1974)

Organisations have to comply with health and safety legislation. If they are found not to be doing so they stand the risk of court proceedings or closure. It is important to appreciate what this legislation actually covers and the number of laws that relate to someone who works as an administrator.

The legislation was initially brought into force in the early 1970s in order to try to reduce the number of accidents occurring in the workplace, and it has done this effectively over the years.

The Health and Safety at Work Act, 1974 (HASAW) is probably the most well-known and important act and it applies to all work premises, whatever the size of the business or number of employees. The duties of the employers are based on the principle of, 'as far as is reasonably practicable'. This means that risks need to be balanced against the costs of reducing a risk. The Act requires employers to use common sense and take suitable measures to tackle potential risks. It also requires employees to take reasonable steps to ensure their own safety and that of others. The Act applies to all workplace environments, however large or small, and to anyone who is on the premises, including employees, managers, customers and even contractors who are involved in maintenance or temporary work.

The Health and Safety at Work Act states that:

**A** All employers must ensure the health, safety and welfare of all their employees at work as far 'as is reasonably practicable'. Specifically this includes:

- All entry and exit routes must be safe
- There must be a safe working environment and adequate facilities for the welfare of staff (somewhere to make a drink, toilet facilities, a quiet area)
- Safe and well-maintained equipment
- Safe transportation and storage of all articles and substances
- The provision of protective clothing
- Clear information, instruction and training on health and safety with adequate supervision of issues in this area

**B** Where the business has five or more employees, there should be a written statement on health and safety policy for the business. The statement should be written by the employer and continually updated to include any changes. This document must be circulated to all employees.

**C** The business should allow a trade union to appoint safety representatives who must be allowed to investigate accidents or potential hazards and follow up employee complaints. Safety representatives should be given time off from their normal duties to carry out their H&S duties.

All employees must:

a Take responsibility for their own health and safety
b Take responsibility for the health and safety of others who may be affected by their activities or actions
c Cooperate with their employers to meet health and safety requirements

## The Health and Safety (Display Screen Equipment) Regulations (1992)

These regulations are specifically related to work with visual display units (VDUs) or computer screens.

Key aspects of the regulations are outlined in the box below.

All employers must:

- Ensure that all workstations, related furniture, computer software and the working environment of VDU users meet the minimum requirements of the Regulations.
- Ensure that all users have regular breaks or changes in activity – it is illegal to work continuously at a computer all day.
- Offer eye examinations, on request, to employees who use a VDU for more than one hour a day, and provide special spectacles if the tests show that these are needed.

- Provide users with relevant health and safety training

All equipment must conform to the following standards

- Display screens must have clear characters of adequate size, a stable image, and adjustable brightness and contrast, and must be able to tilt and swivel easily. There must be no reflective glare.
- Keyboards must be able to tilt and separate from the screen. There should be space in front of the keyboard to

# Employee rights and responsibilities

Because employers are paying their employees to represent the business in the best possible way, it is the employee's responsibility and in their best interests to assist in ensuring that the organisation is providing a healthy and safe environment for:

- all employees, whatever their job role within the business
- any visiting workers (such as those repairing, servicing or maintaining machinery or equipment)
- all the customers of the business
- any visitors or representatives from other organisations
- the general public.

It is important to remember that the health and safety regulations do not just apply to the business premises themselves, but also relate to any work undertaken by the business in other locations. This means that representatives of the business who may be carrying out repair work in another organisation also have to comply with the legislation. For example, maintenance workers carrying out repairs on a building site would have to wear hard hats and comply with legislation relating to construction sites.

Just as the employer must take heed of the requirements of the important series of Acts regarding health and safety, so must the employee. Employees may suffer harm from injuries which are not necessarily the fault of the employer.

If the employee is negligent and causes injury to him/herself or to another person, then the employer may be in a difficult position. The employee may claim that it was not really his or her fault. As long as the employer provides safe working conditions, it is up to the employee to work in a healthy and safe manner. Should an employee not comply with the legislation, or even worse, do something deliberately which could put someone else's life in danger, they could find themselves not only dismissed from their job, but also the subject of criminal or civil court proceedings.

> **According to the British Safety Council, British businesses lose £250 a second in costs and payments as a result of avoidable accidents in the workplace. Businesses now face even greater penalties under the Corporate Manslaughter and Corporate Homicide Act (2008). Senior managers are now more likely to face gaol sentences if their safety policies fail and lead to a fatality at work.**

## QUESTION TIME
*12 minutes*

**1** **Does the Health And Safety At Work Act apply to all types of businesses? Explain your answer.** *(6 marks)*

**2** **To what extent is it true to say that health and safety is as much an employee's responsibility as it is an employer's?** *(6 marks)*

43

provide 'rest' space. The keyboard surface should be matt and it should be easy to use and clear on the keys.
- Work surfaces must be large enough for the work being done and must have a low reflective finish. The equipment must be flexible so that it can be arranged to suit the needs of the user.
- Work chairs must be stable and allow easy movement and a comfortable position. The user must be able to adjust the height of the seat and the seat back – which must provide good back support. A footrest must be provided if requested.
- Working environments for VDU users should provide satisfactory lighting to minimise glare. Windows should have blinds and workstations should be positioned to avoid reflections. Noise and heat levels should be comfortable. Radiation levels must be negligible, and humidity controlled so that it is constantly at a satisfactory level.
- Software and systems must be appropriate for the task, user-friendly and appropriate to the level of knowledge of the user.

# The importance of health and safety in the workplace

**YOU WILL FIND OUT:**

- about an employer's responsibilities under health and safety legislation
- about the importance of being alert to potential hazards

## Employers' responsibilities

Health and safety legislation is important to both the employer and the employees of a business. The local council or authority has the right to inspect the business premises at any time to ensure that adequate and appropriate health and safety procedures are in place. In addition, the Health and Safety Executive also has inspectors who visit business premises to examine equipment and machinery. The Council also has the power to enforce the requirements of the different Acts of Parliament concerning health and safety.

Employers have to contact the local authority when the business begins operating, and inform it of the organisation's intention to trade in the premises. Employers also have to:

- contact either the Environmental Health Department and/or the Health and Safety Executive (depending on the type of business activity)
- take out employer's liability insurance and obtain a certificate of this insurance
- display the insurance certificate within the premises of the business
- draw up a health and safety policy for the business
- display a Health and Safety at Work poster within the business premises.

The main requirements of the different health and safety legislation require the employer to, at least:

- provide a safe working environment (safety)
- provide adequate welfare facilities for employees (health)
- ensure all entrances and exits to the business premises are safe (emergencies)
- ensure all equipment and systems used within the business premises are safe (protection)
- ensure all equipment and systems used within the business premises are regularly serviced (maintenance)
- ensure that all items needed for the handling or storage of the business's products are safe (warehousing)
- ensure that any dangerous or toxic materials used by the business are housed in safe containers (secure storage)
- provide instruction, training and/ or supervision to all employees regarding safe working practices and the use of all materials (educational programme)
- investigate and deal promptly with all accidents by identifying their causes (accident prevention).

Many employers assist employees in ensuring a healthy and safe environment by:

- setting practical goals to reach health and safety standards
- encouraging employees to work together and cooperate in a safe manner
- encouraging employees to accept responsibility for health and safety matters
- identifying key members of staff to deal with health and safety matters

- regularly addressing health and safety issues and encouraging staff to improve
- ensuring all staff are aware of health and safety issues through an initial induction programme and suitable training courses.

The employer has to take the responsibility of ensuring that employees have all the information they need to work in a safe manner and eliminate risks to themselves, their colleagues and visitors to the organisation. This information could take several forms, including ensuring that staff:

- are familiar with all equipment being used
- are trained in health and safety
- have access to manuals or handbooks relating to equipment or machinery being used
- are clear about safe working practices
- are familiar with the health and safety policy of the business.

Depending on the size of the business, employers will give training in:

- how employees should act in the event of an emergency
- how employees should act in the event of an accident.

They will also give all staff the following information:

- a list of trained first-aid personnel within the business
- the location of the first-aid room
- a list of named safety representatives or members of a safety committee.

44

# Being alert to potential hazards

Piles of books, filing cabinets, computers and their associated cables all add to the chance of an accident occurring in an office. But what is the difference between a hazard and a risk? A hazard is something that is likely to cause employees, or a visitor to the business some potential harm. A potential hazard only becomes a risk if there is an increased chance of an accident occurring.

Obviously it is in everyone's best interests that the risk of injury from potential hazards is reduced to the absolute minimum. An employer would carry out regular risk assessments, relying on the employees to report any new hazards or an increase in the degree of risk involved.

There are a variety of areas within the office environment that are a potential hazard, these include:

- The use of any machinery or equipment – because these are run by electricity, which is a potential hazard in itself. It could develop a faulty plug, the cable could be inappropriately trailed across a room, or there could be a problem with the electric supply itself.

- The use of materials or substances such as items with sharp edges, heavy or bulky items, or poisonous substances, such as ink or cleaning fluids.
- Unsafe working practices and behaviour – if accidents are to be prevented, then the right approach and attitude to safe working must be important to all employees.
- Dealing with accidental breakages and spills – all spills or breakages should be immediately dealt with to reduce the risk of an accident.
- General office environment – the overall level of hygiene within the office environment, for example adequate ventilation, general cleanliness and toilet/washing facilities available to employees.

Although the main responsibility for ensuring safe working practices is on the employer, via safety committees, officers or representatives, ultimately it is up to the individual employee. In most offices a variety of electrical equipment, such as photocopiers and fax machines, is used on a regular basis by a number of different members of staff. Something as simple as removing a paper-jam from the photocopier could place an untrained individual in some danger.

## QUESTION TIME
*16 minutes*

**1** **What is the role of the Health and Safety Executive?** *(2 marks)*

**2** **Explain how a newly set-up office environment could be made both healthy and safe for employees.** *(8 marks)*

**3** **Explain why it is important for employers to provide information to employees to work safely and eliminate risks.** *(6 marks)*

45

Working with a computer on a daily basis can also be demanding and potentially hazardous. The following should be addressed when using a computer:

- The temperature of the room – this can affect the performance of the computer as well as the user.
- No food and drink should be allowed in the computing room.
- A variety of tasks should be undertaken during the course of the working day.
- The posture of the user should be monitored – adjustable chairs should be provided with footrests and correct back support.
- The angle and the height of the screen – if these are not positioned correctly, the user becomes tired more quickly and errors can result.
- A variety of tasks should be undertaken during the working day.

# ICT data systems in business

## Data systems

Data systems are a business's network of communications channels. In effect they are the business's information-processing facilities. Sometimes the term is also used to describe the physical location of those systems. In modern businesses these can be highly complex networks, consisting of a number of networked computers, supported by external hard drives and a range of **peripherals**, such as printers, scanners, large display screens and more specialist hardware.

The business's own network, or data system, is usually a self-contained structure that is fully supported by all the necessary hardware and software. In turn, however, this data system has access to a far larger data system, which it shares or accesses remotely either by wireless or cable. In fact we could consider the Internet to be one massive data system. It holds information, it allows communication between businesses and it allows transactions to take place.

A data system is basically a computerised record-keeping and exchange system. It consists of data, hardware, software and users.

By having a centralised system, businesses can ensure that data can be stored and shared. It is also a way for the business to ensure that there is a standardised system for storing the information, by using the same forms, templates and software. A centralised system also enables access to information to be restricted to authorised users. It means that security checks can be set so that only certain individuals can retrieve the information, while others can modify it and others again may delete it when necessary. This stops the data from being changed incorrectly or shared with those who should not have access to it.

A business may want to share:

- product or service data
- customer records
- supplier records
- costs and income data
- stock data
- employee records.

Having a data system means that regardless of the location of employees or departments, all information placed on the system can be accessed by all authorised staff. It is important for different parts of the organisation to have access to the same data.

## Data sources

Data sources are documents, electronic communications, individuals' views and observations and market research. Collecting, collating, analysing and acting on information is vital to businesses. They need to be aware of the latest situation, developments, opportunities and threats. By continually looking for information from different sources of data they are better positioned to make the right decision at the right time.

Access to sufficient information gives the business the data it needs in order to assess the situation and to choose the right alternative each time. Businesses will always ask:

- Is there data that exists on this issue?
- If not, where can we get it from?
- What is the most efficient way of gathering the data?
- Is the source of the data reliable?

Reliability is very important. Businesses need to be sure that the data has been properly gathered and that it is of the same quality as the data that they would have collected themselves. It is important that they do not take facts and figures at face value without knowing exactly where they have come from.

### For example   Information sharing

A sales department may receive a phone call from a customer who wants 1,000 units of the latest product. Before Sales can confirm the order, they need to check with the warehouse to see if sufficient products are in stock. If not, they need to check with Production or Purchasing to find out how long it will take to make or to order those products. Only then can they confirm the order with the customer. The order information is then passed onto the accounts department, which needs to know the name of the customer and how many products have been purchased so that it can send the customer an invoice.

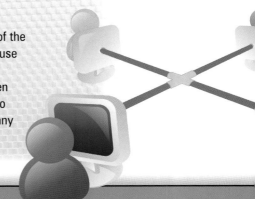

46

It is not sufficient to collect data and store it safely. It needs to be sorted (collated), analysed and then used for a specific purpose. Often businesses will try to work out trends, fashions or patterns so that they can predict or forecast what might happen in the near future. This forecasting helps them to prepare for changes and be in a position to respond to them as quickly and as efficiently as possible.

Businesses will use a wide variety of different data sources; some will scan the media, such as newspapers. Others will use their own records; some will rely on the views and opinions of experts in their area of work.

Internal and external sources of data are outlined in the following table:

### KEY TERM

**Peripheral** ▶ a hardware device such as a printer, a scanner or an external hard drive, connected to a computer or a network.

## QUESTION TIME
*14 minutes*

**1** Why is it important for a business to have a common and foolproof data system? *(8 marks)*

**2** How can a business be certain that the data sources it is using are to be trusted? *(6 marks)*

| INTERNAL SOURCE | EXTERNAL SOURCE |
|---|---|
| **Accounts can provide details of:**<br>• transactions<br>• profit or loss<br>• sales trends<br>• spending on salaries and wages<br>**Human Resources can provide:**<br>• employee personal details<br>• salaries and wages<br>• training records<br>• employee skills and experience<br>• productivity<br>**Marketing can provide:**<br>• information on competitors<br>• information on customers<br>• effectiveness of advertising and other publicity<br>**Purchasing can provide:**<br>• costs of raw materials, finished goods, components and consumables<br>• details of suppliers<br>• spending patterns<br>• status of outstanding deliveries and orders<br>• stock levels<br>**Sales can provide:**<br>• sales figures<br>• sales per sales person<br>• customer buying patterns<br>• information received about competitors<br>• level of complaints and problems<br>• sales trends<br>**Production can provide:**<br>• time taken to make products and services<br>• costs<br>• employee needs<br>  • production time required<br>    • status of current orders<br>      • delivery dates | *Government information:*<br>• data on the economy, population and society from the Office of National Statistics<br>• data from other government departments and from government-funded organisations<br><br>*Trade or industry information* – there are many trade groups that collect information specifically about their industry, such as the Association of British Travel Agents (ABTA) – an organisation for travel agents and tour operators.<br><br>*Commercial data* – there are many businesses that trade in collecting data and then selling it on to businesses. Some of these are subscription services, while others offer reports that can be bought individually. They guarantee to be valid, accurate and good value.<br><br>*Databases (government)* – the European Union and the British government have accessible databases with information – some are free, while others require a subscription.<br><br>*Databases (commercial)* – these are large databases where information is collated and made accessible by subscription. Some are provided by trade associations.<br><br>*Research* – many universities and other educational centres carry out ongoing research that can be accessed, usually for a fee, by businesses. A good example is the Centre for the Sociology of Sport at the University of Leicester, which collects information that is useful to football clubs and other sports organisations. |

47

# Data sources and input devices (1)

YOU WILL FIND OUT:

- about keyboards and mice
- about scanners
- about digital cameras
- about web cams

## Data input devices

Data input devices are computer hardware, supported by software called drivers. The drivers are designed to enable the communication between the piece of hardware and the computer. Data input devices are the means by which information or instructions are passed by the user to the computer. Some are simple, straightforward and common. Others are more complex and specialised.

## Keyboards

Computer keyboards are one of the most versatile input devices. They are very much like typewriter keyboards, but they have additional keys, including:

- shortcut keys (to make text bold, italics or underlined)
- a numeric keyboard for typing in figures
- scrolling keys (up, down, left, right, page up, page down, end and home)
- special character keys (a wider variety than a typewriter)
- backspace and delete keys.

Selecting particular keys also allows the user to save and print documents.
Keyboards can be attached to a computer in the following ways:

- A standard round pin socket (less common in modern computers)
- A **USB** connection
- Wireless connection
- Infrared, keyboard-less keyboard (the latest technology is able to project a virtual keyboard onto the desktop via an infrared device on top of the monitor).

### How keyboards work

When a user hits a key on the keyboard, an electrical signal is sent to a microprocessor. This sends a scan code to the computer's input/output system. In turn, this adds letters or numbers to the document, spreadsheet or database, or executes the command.

## Mice

A mouse is an example of a pointing device. The mouse tends to be used to move a **cursor** on the computer screen. A mouse can be used to carry out various operations, including:

- typing (by highlighting text for deletion or movement)
- drawing (using the mouse as a freehand drawing instrument)
- graphics (selection of graphics for re-sizing)
- opening files
- closing files

A mouse is vital when surfing the Internet, as it allows a one-click movement from page to page on a website or to another website by clicking on a **hyperlink**.
Like keyboards, mice have been transformed from having round socket connections, to USB connections and now to wireless infrared.

### More on mice

All mice were originally of the type with a rubber ball underneath to allow movement and a tail-like wire coming out of them (hence the name). By moving the mouse over a mat (a flat surface), the cursor on the computer screen is made to move. Mice have two buttons – left and right. Their function depends on the work being done by the user.

### Other pointing devices

There are others with different functions, used for different applications. These include:

- *Stylus* – acts like a pen or pencil. The stylus is moved (or written with) on a flat surface and the actions and movement appear on the computer screen. A stylus can also be used to touch command buttons.
- *Touch pad* – this operates like a flat keyboard with fewer keys, and is often used for graphics and design.
- *Pointing stick* – can be used for lectures and demonstrations to focus on particular parts of an enlarged (projector) screen.
- *Track ball* – an ergonomic basic version of the mouse, with integrated clickable buttons.

All pointing devices are designed to move the cursor on the screen.

48

**USB (Universal Serial Bus)** ▶ allows you to connect other equipment (such as printers and scanners) to the computer quickly and easily.

**Cursor** ▶ flashes on-screen, usually in the form of an arrow, and is controlled by either the mouse or the keyboard.

**JPEG** ▶ a standard picture or graphic file format.

**Hyperlink** ▶ an electronic form of cross-referencing that appears in a document or on a web page as text or graphics that can be clicked on by the user to take them directly to another location.

**Compact flash card** ▶ a small, removable data storage device. It is mainly used to store digital camera images.

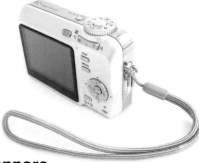

## Scanners

A scanner 'reads' text and images and converts the data into digital signals. It can have two basic functions:

- As a text scanner it uses optical character recognition software to read the text and produce documents that can be edited.
- As a graphics scanner it reads the photograph or drawing, digitises it, and produces editable graphic images (so you can change colour, size, etc.).

Text is usually converted into a Word document (or similar) and images are readable in a number of formats (chosen by the user), including:

- JPEGs
- Gif files
- Tiff files
- Bitmap files

The difference between these file types is the size (in storage terms) and the resolution (clarity of the image at large sizes).

Most scanners are now incorporated into all-in-one systems. Businesses needing scanners larger than A4 use dedicated machines capable of scanning large images at high resolution.

## Digital cameras

Digital cameras take photographs without the use of film. They record the photographic image either onto a built-in hard storage drive or a removable drive, such as a **compact flash card**.

The photographs are stored on the camera and can be downloaded onto a computer. The camera software needs to be installed onto the computer and the camera connected by a USB cable.

Most digital cameras save their images in **JPEG** format. Usually at least three size options are available when taking photographs (small, medium and large). The larger the image, the more storage space it requires. Digital images can be edited on the computer, sent by email or posted onto websites.

## Web cams

A web cam is usually mounted on top of a computer monitor and connected to the computer by a USB cable. Once the software has been installed on the computer, the web cam can take live, moving images of the user or whatever is in front of the monitor. A microphone then allows sound to be added. Web cam software allows communication with a remote computer. On the computer screen at the receiver's end, the images and sound recorded by the web cam and microphone can be seen and heard. Usually it is a two-way connection, with another web cam at the remote end also sending images and sound.

## QUESTION TIME
*15 minutes*

**1** Suggest FIVE keys found on a computer keyboard that are designed to aid Internet surfing. *(5 marks)*

**2** Why might a stylus be useful to an artist? *(4 marks)*

**3** How might a business use a web cam to aid teleworking? *(6 marks)*

49

# Data sources and input devices (2)

## Voice recognition systems/software

This software application uses a microphone as the input device. The user must 'train' the software to recognise the voice by going through a series of training drills. The software becomes increasingly reliable as it learns exactly how the user speaks and becomes able to predict certain words.

Using the microphone, the user can give the computer commands, for example to open applications, or, when used with applications such as Word, to create documents.

The system can recognise speech delivered at a speed of nearly 200 words per minute. Every word does have to be spoken separately for the system to understand.

Voice recognition technology is continually improving but there are still some quality issues:

- it may insert incorrect words as it has not heard the word correctly
- it will not deal with grammatical errors
- it may predict wrong words and substitute new phrases.

## Bar code readers

Bar codes can be seen on almost every product you buy (including this book). Bar codes are patterns of bars of varying widths and with varying spaces between the bars. They can be printed onto paper, labels or directly onto boxes. A scanner, using a laser beam or a **photocell**, can recognise a unique bar code to identify a product, along with associated information, such as price.

Bar codes are used by the Post Office to encode mail. Supermarkets and retail outlets use them with the UPC (Universal Product Code) system to scan products at the checkout. This eliminates having to manually input product codes and prices. The UPC system means that each unique product has its own unique bar code.

## Optical mark reader

Optical mark readers (OMR) are scanning devices that can read marks made on documents by pencil. They are ideal for reading data on multiple-choice questionnaires or multiple-choice examinations.

The system is set up so that the optical mark reader knows where to look for pencil marks on the document. In the case of multiple-choice examinations, it will register each correct placement of a mark in a box and add up the score to give the overall mark. For questionnaires with multiple-choice answers, the OMR can add up the numbers of responses in a batch of questionnaires and print out a report of the scores allocated to each questionnaire. This is much faster and more accurate than manual marking.

The major problem with OMR is that it can read mistakes on the document. Those completing the documents need to avoid putting responses in one box and then changing their minds. Even erased pencil marks might still be read.

## Optical character recognition

Optical character recognition (OCR) is a feature of most scanners that enables it to 'read' text characters on a document, book page, magazine page or newspaper cutting. OCR is used when a hard copy of the text already exists and the user wishes to convert that text into editable text on the computer.

Text scanned by OCR does lose some of its **formatting**. This means that the text will appear on the screen in blocks, mirroring the way it appeared in the original. Sometimes, when text characters are blurred in the original, the OCR will make mistakes. The latest OCR technology can even read handwritten text.

## Magnetic ink character recognition

Magnetic ink character recognition (MICR) was developed especially for use in banking. It is a standard character recognition system used to read bank cheques, which are printed with special ink and use specialised characters on the front. Both of these can be magnetised for automated reading. The MICR system reads the bank account number, sort code and other details. It also reads the value of the cheque. It can then automatically **debit** the cheque payer and **credit** the person to whom the cheque has been made out. This is done by matching the name on the cheque with a database of account holders.

━━━━━━━━━━━━ **K E Y   T E R M S** ━━━━━━━━━━━━

**Photocell** ▶ a light-sensitive device.

**Formatting** ▶ erasing any saved data and blanking a media device so that it is ready to receive new data.

**Debit** ▶ to take money from an account.

**Credit** ▶ to put money into an account.

**Customer loyalty cards** ▶ a reward system that gives regular customers special offers and discounts.

The system also relies on:

- the cheque envelope being coded by the cashpoint machine, or
- the cashier in the bank or building society running the cheque through a till to print a readable code on the cheque.

## Magnetic strips

A magnetic strip is a short length of magnetic coating printed onto the surface of a card or a ticket. Typical examples include:

- credit and debit cards
- **customer loyalty cards**
- season tickets
- library tickets
- phone cards.

They are very easy to make and they can store quite a lot of data. They can, however, be damaged by magnetic fields or if they are scratched.

The strip stores details such as name, address, account number and other information and is used to check if the correct user is presenting the card. At a cash point or till, a PIN confirms the user's identity.

## Electronic point of sale

Electronic point of sale (EPOS) is used in retailing. At a till, the bar code on a product is read in one of two ways:

- by a flat-bed bar code reader, in the till desk itself
- by a handheld bar code reader, used by the cashier.

The bar code reader reads the bar code and sends the information to the store's computer. Instantly, the store's computer relays back the price details and a description of the item

to the till. The customer can receive a fully itemised bill, and the store's computer can update stock levels.

EPOS has streamlined purchasing for both the customer and the retailer in the following ways. It:

- enables efficient stock control
- prevents incorrect charging
- helps employees work efficiently
- cuts down on queuing time
- provides instant sales data, hour by hour, day by day.

EPOS is used in most retail outlets as it has proved to be valuable to both the business, in terms of efficiency, and to the customer, in terms of speed of service and accuracy.

## Electronic fund transfer point of sale

Electronic fund transfer point of sale (EFTPOS) is an electronic magnetic or chip-reading system used to process debit or credit cards. It now uses the chip-and-pin system if the cardholder is present at the transaction.

The retailer can initiate an immediate transfer of funds from either the user's credit or debit card account into their own account. There are mobile EFTPOS handheld systems that can be brought to the customer, for example in a restaurant. EFTPOS offers great advantages:

- all payments are immediately approved by the bank, credit card company or building society.
- less cash has to be carried by customers or kept in tills in stores.
- it is easy to operate.
- bank charges can be lower.

The EFTPOS network is designed to be absolutely secure and reliable.

## QUESTION TIME
*16 minutes*

**1** **How might an OMR aid the collation of market research data?** *(4 marks)*

**2** **Suggest and explain the value of the type of information that could be stored on a magnetic strip on a customer loyalty card.** *(6 marks)*

**3** **Why might handheld EFTPOS devices be more secure for banks and users?** *(6 marks)*

51

# Data storage and output devices (1)

YOU WILL FIND OUT:
- about internal and external hard drives
- about high-capacity storage devices
- about memory sticks

## Data storage

Every business needs to keep records and have the ability to retrieve them. For many businesses this means shelves of folders and box files, filing cabinets and storage boxes. For other businesses, using ICT rather than just paper documents, this means hundreds or thousands of computerised files and folders.

These records need to be kept in a secure place, perhaps in a database, which can be accessed when needed. Businesses may find that they need to instantly retrieve files and folders, regardless of how long they have been in storage.

### Data storage options

Data storage actually goes beyond backing up files and folders. It is a longer-term solution to ensure that:

- all files and information can be accessed
- no information or files are lost
- computers being used on a daily basis by the business are not overloaded with files and folders not in constant use.

One of the latest developments in data storage is to send all files to a remote storage system. This storage system is managed and maintained by another business. The business acts as a storage area for the data, by in effect hosting a dedicated hard-drive storage device for the client company. This ensures that if the worst were to happen, and the business lost all its data due to a fire or theft, all the files and folders would still be safe in another location. Data storage needs to be

simple and safe. There are several ways in which it can be done:

- immediate saving of documents, files and folders that are in use
- **backing-up** of current documents, files and folders
- filing of recent documents, files and folders
- **archiving** of documents, files and folders that may not be needed immediately and do not have to be stored on computers being used each day.

### Data storage types

Data storage types tend to fall into the following categories:

- backing-up data on the hard drive of the computer on which the document, file or folder was created or received
- backing-up data on, or copying data to, a removable storage device, such as a CD drive
- the archiving of the data on either the business's back-up hard drive storage or at a remote location by another business working for it.

## Hard drives

Hard drives are digitally encoded storage devices. They store data on rapidly spinning platters with magnetic surfaces. Hard drives work in the following way:

- They record data by magnetising the magnetic material in a pattern to represent the data.

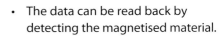

- The data can be read back by detecting the magnetised material.

The platters are made from a non-magnetic material (glass or aluminium), and then coated with a very thin layer of magnetic material.

The platters spin at very high speeds past 'read and write' heads that are very close to the surface of the platter. The heads are on a single arm, with one head for each platter.

### Features of the hard drive

Hard drives are in sealed protectors because the disc surface must be kept free of contamination. A typical hard disc drive will rotate at up to 11,000 rpm (revolutions per minute). Computers are routinely fitted with hard drives of up to 250GB of storage.

Some computers will have even more storage, with ¾ terabyte (equal to 768GB). At the current rate of development, the average new computer has 40% more hard-drive capacity than a similar machine produced just one year earlier.

## KEY TERMS

**Backing up** ▶ making a copy, either onto another computer or onto a removable storage device.

**I/O operations** ▶ opening and closing files and devices, reading data from and writing data to devices, setting the state of devices, and reading and writing system data structures. I/O stands for input and output.

**Archiving** ▶ removing any non-current data and storing it for later use.

**Transfer rate** ▶ the speed with which data, instructions, and information transfer to and from a device.

**Miniaturisation** ▶ the process of manufacturing progressively smaller and smaller devices, which are as good as, or better than, their larger predecessors.

## Hard drive characteristics

There are several ways in which hard drives can be described, including:

- capacity in gigabytes (GB)
- physical size (3.5 inch in desktops and 2.5 inch in laptops)
- reliability
- number of **I/O operations** per second
- power consumption
- noise levels
- shock rating (ability to withstand impacts)
- **transfer rate**.

## Disc drive families

The IDE/ATA (Advanced Technology Attachment) is the most common and also known as PATA (Parallel Advanced Technology Attachment). These are connected by a bank of pins and, via a cable, to the motherboard. Serial ATA is becoming the more common standard and does away with the ribbon cables. Instead it uses a thin cable with a small connector.

Around 98% of hard drives are made by only a handful of companies, including:

- Seagate
- Maxtor (now owned by Seagate)
- Western Digital
- Samsung
- Hitachi

## High-capacity storage devices

These are external hard drives, connected to a computer or a computer network by a USB cable. The key advantages are that they can:

- add extra storage to any computer
- allow common files and folders to be stored by several computers
- allow the transfer of data from a computer not on a network
- provide an instant back-up system
- prevent the heat of the hard disc drive inside the computer from damaging the computer hardware
- offer a simple way to recover data if a computer goes down.

External hard drives are now freestanding devices, needing only a power supply and a USB connection to operate. They are extremely affordable and provide essential back-up for data.

Dedicated storage devices, such as these, are called either direct attached storage (by USB), or network attached storage (to network).

## Memory sticks

USB flash drives, or memory sticks, have become an indispensable part of modern-day computer work. They can hold several gigabytes of data, even as much as 2TB, and are a far more effective way of transferring data than burning CDs. USB flash drives are plugged straight into a USB and used just like any other external drive. They are often referred to as memory pens, pen drives or memory sticks.

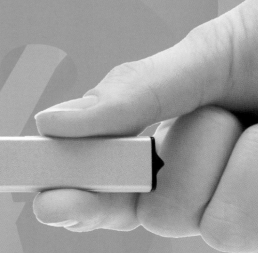

## QUESTION TIME
### 15 minutes

1 What do you understand by the term 'miniaturisation'? *(2 marks)*

2 Identify and explain FOUR ways in which hard drives can be described. *(8 marks)*

3 USB memory sticks have made CDs, DVDs and zip drives virtually obsolete. To what extent do you agree with this statement? Explain your answers. *(8 marks)*

53

# Data storage and output devices (2)

YOU WILL FIND OUT:

● about floppy disc and zip drives

● about compact discs

● about DVDs

● about Blu-ray discs

## Floppy discs

A floppy disc is a small data storage device. In its current form it is a thin dish of flexible, magnetic material, protected by a 3.5-inch square plastic case. The floppy disc can be read and written using a floppy disc drive (FDD). Until quite recently FDDs were a part of nearly every computer.

Floppy discs are now very rarely used, as they have given way to better storage devices, with considerably greater capacity. Most current floppy discs are capable of storing only up to 1.44MB of data. There was an attempt in the 1990s to save the floppy disc from near-extinction, by the introduction of the 120MB floppy disc which ran on normal FDDs, but it never really caught on. Apple was the first manufacturer to drop the FDD. Dell now offers the FDD only as an optional extra.

It is possible to buy external FDDs that can be connected to the computer via a USB cable.

## Zip discs

Iomega introduced zip drives in 1994. They are classed as medium-capacity removable disc storage items. Zip discs require their own dedicated zip drive to read, write, erase or rewrite. Originally, zip discs could hold up to 100MB of data, but later discs could hold 250MB or even 750MB.

Although for a while zip discs threatened to take over from floppy discs, they were overtaken by CD-Rs and DVDs. The zip drive system still has some strong supporters, who prefer it to other options, but its popularity has now faded dramatically.

## Compact discs and CD-ROMs

The first compact discs (CDs) were available in 1982 and were originally designed to store audio data only. They still remain the most common and popular physical medium for audio recordings. They are optical storage discs, about 1.2mm thick, and made of **polycarbonate**.

### CD-ROM

CD-ROM (Compact Disc Read-Only Memory) is the original standard data storage CD. In their current 80-minute **format** they can hold around 700MB of data. At first, users of CD-ROMs were restricted to reading them or downloading information or software from them onto their computers. Information could not be written to them. This was the next logical development.

### CD-R

Phillips and Sony invented the CD-R (Compact Disc Recordable) storage device. They are 'write-once', 'read-only' CDs. The bulk of CD-Rs on the market have a capacity of 80 minutes or up to 700MB, but others have:

- 90 minutes (790MB)
- 99 minutes (870MB)

Some special disc drives can allow 1.2GB of data to be stored on a 99-minute disc.

CD-R blank discs have groove tracks into which the data is written. The CD-R writer writes data using lasers to physically burn an organic dye in the disc. If you look at a blank CD-R you will see it reflects well, but when you look at a 'burned' CD-R it is less reflective.

### CD-RW

This version of the CD was introduced in 1997. Unlike CD-Rs, they can be written, erased and rewritten repeatedly. Otherwise, they work in exactly the same way as the CD-R. Most have a capacity of 80 minutes or up to 700MB of data. On average they will cope with being rewritten 1,000 times.

CD-RWs are not as popular as CD-Rs, mainly because they are more expensive. They have lower recording and reading speeds than CD-Rs. They are also not as flexible and useful as some other types of rewritable media, such as zip drives.

The CD-R is considered by most businesses to be a better alternative for data storage than the CD-RW. An important consideration is that once the CD-R has been burned, the data can be read, but it cannot be modified or erased.

## KEY TERMS

**Polycarbonate ▶** a hard plastic that is resistant to impact and scratching.

**Format ▶** to erase any saved data and blank a media device so that it is ready to receive new data.

**Write-protected ▶** locked to prevent data from being written onto it.

## Digital Versatile Discs (DVDs)

These are optical storage devices that were originally designed to store films with high video and sound quality. They look very similar to CDs. Originally they were called Digital Video Discs.

There are four different types of DVD:

- single-sided, single layer (DVD5)
- single-sided, dual layer (DVD9)
- double-sided, single layer (DVD10)
- double-sided, double layer (DVD18).

The number of each DVD refers to the storage in gigabytes (GB) rounded up (a single-sided, single layer DVD5 can actually store only 4.7GB of data).

### *Recordable DVDs*

These were developed so that users could make use of the higher storage capacity on each disc to save data other than video and audio. Three versions of the recordable and rewritable DVD have been developed:

- DVD-R / DVD-RW (dash)
- DVD+R / DVD+RW (plus)
- DVD-RAM (Random Access Memory).

Recordable DVDs can hold up to 4.7GB of data. The DVD-R and DVD-RWs can be used only in drives that support DVD-R or DVD-RW recording or multi-format recording, while DVD+R or DVD+RWs are compatible with most DVD drives.

### *DVD security*

Ready-recorded DVDs are copy protected, but this can be worked around on a PC if the user has the necessary knowledge.

## Blu-ray discs

Blu-ray discs can hold substantially more data than DVDs: they have a single-layer capacity of 25GB and a dual-layer capacity of 50GB. In 2003, a similar high-capacity disc was produced – the high definition, or high density DVD (HD-DVD). This was not compatible with the Blu-ray disc but was in direct competition with it. But in January 2008, Toshiba announced it was stopping manufacture of the HD-DVD, so that just one format would be universally available.

## QUESTION TIME
*13 minutes*

**1** Suggest FIVE different types of removable data storage device. *(5 marks)*

**2** What is polycarbonate and why are CDs made of this substance? *(2 marks)*

**3** Why might it be important for a business to write-protect documents and data? Explain your answer. *(6 marks)*

55

# Data storage and output devices (3)

## Monitors

The computer monitor is not only a data output device, it is the main interface between the computer and the computer user. The monitor is attached to the computer via a video adaptor. This converts the computer's instructions into a form that can tell the monitor exactly what to display on the screen. Most computer monitors are either:

- Cathode Ray Tube (CRT), or
- Thin Film Transistor (TFT).

The CRT version of the monitor is a large device, resembling an old television. The TFT is a flat screen – a more modern version of a monitor, like a plasma television. TFT-LCDs are often referred to as flat panel displays. They use the TFT technology to improve the quality of the image. In effect they are variants of LCDs.

### Monitor performance

The performance of a monitor can be measured in many different ways, including:

- luminescence (brightness)
- size (e.g. 17 inch or 19 inch)
- dot pitch (lower dot pitch = sharper picture)
- V-sync rate (smoothness of image of screen if you swap between applications)
- response time (how long it takes for the monitor to show the results of your commands)
- refresh rate (the number of times per second the image is illuminated).

### CRT monitors

CRT monitors are now the cheapest type of monitor available. They have large monitor cases, with either a flat or funnel-shaped tube. The image on a CRT monitor is created by pixels (made up of phosphors). Electrons hit the pixels. The electrons make the pixels glow at various levels of intensity. In turn this provides the bright image on the display screen.

Modern CRT monitors have a range of **resolutions** from 320 × 200 to 2560 × 2040 pixels. One of the major concerns about CRTs is that if the same image is left on the screen for a long time it becomes embedded. This is called screen burn-in. Screen savers with moving images prevent this problem.

### LCD flat panel monitors

LCD stands for Liquid Crystal Display. These monitors are far more common, mainly because the price has fallen very sharply.

A liquid crystal solution is between two partitioned panes of glass. Altering the amount of light allowed through the solution creates the image.

Additional features, such as digital or **Super Video Graphics Array (SVGA)**, will mean that the monitor is more expensive.

Early LCDs were blurred, but later technology and improved manufacturing have dealt with this problem.

### TFT Monitors

TFT monitors are fast becoming the standard monitors for businesses and for the home. They have a high level of screen resolution and sharpness of image. They are similar to LCD monitors, but have a thin transistor added to the screen. This allows greater control over the pixels.

### Choosing the right monitor

For a business, the choice of monitor is very important. It needs to be able to do the required job well and with the minimum of health and safety issues for the user. Key considerations are:

- ease on the eyes with prolonged use
- good level of brightness
- ability to display true colours
- good contrast (how it looks in low light)
- high resolution
- low level of emissions (radiation)
- low amount of 'screen flicker'
- appropriate size and weight
- the availability of monitor accessories.
- reliability and price.

---

## KEY TERMS

**Resolution** ▶ number of pixels on the screen that affect the sharpness of the picture.

**Super Video Graphics Array (SVGA)** ▶ a screen with a resolution of at least 800 × 600 pixels (now 1024 × 768 is available).

**Warm-up** ▶ the time it takes a device to reach its ideal operating temperature.

---

# Printers

A printer is an output device that produces hard (paper) copies of documents or other electronically stored data. Some are designed for specific jobs, such as printing photographs or graphics, and some are even more specialised, such as those used by designers and architects to print huge plans or drawings.

Printers are connected to a single computer or to a network of computers by using either a cable or a wireless connection.

## Multi-function printers

Many modern printers do much more than just print out black (mono) or colour copies of documents. Typically they can also:

- work as a scanner
- work as a photocopier
- send and receive faxes
- have slots for electronic storage devices, like compact flash cards or memory sticks.

Most printers used by businesses and at home are designed for fairly low-volume printing.

## Printer speeds

Early printers were differentiated by the number of characters they could print per minute. Today it is the number of pages printed per second that defines the quality of a printer.

There can be difficulties with this classification as some manufacturers take into account the number of text-only pages that a printer can produce in a given time. This can be unrealistic, as colour pages (with graphics and pictures) are slower to print than those with black text only.

## Inkjet printers

Inkjet printers were introduced by Canon in 1977. They work by spraying tiny amounts of ink onto the paper. They are the most common type of printer used at home and by businesses.

Most inkjet printers are actually thermal inkjets. They have a print cartridge with a series of heated chambers. A pulse of current passes through the heating elements. The steam in the chamber creates a bubble, which propels a tiny drop of ink onto the paper (some printers are called bubble jets). The ink itself is water-based, dye-based or pigment-based.

Inkjets favoured by business are called piezoelectric inkjets. These have an ink-filled chamber that is squeezed by pressure to put the ink droplet onto the paper. They are considerably more expensive than conventional inkjet printers.

The advantages of inkjets are that they:

- are quieter than older printers
- can print finer, smoother detail
- have a short **warm-up** time
- have a lower cost per page than laser printers.

The main disadvantages are that:

- the printer heads are prone to clogging
- they are comparatively expensive ink cartridges
- ink can be carried sideways, resulting in poor print quality
- a small drop of water will cause documents to 'run'
- highlighter pens cause blurring.

We will look at laser printers next, on page 58.

## QUESTION TIME
*16 minutes*

**1** Printer manufacturers make virtually no profit from the sale of their printers. Where do they make the bulk of their profits? Explain your answer. *(6 marks)*

**2** Identify and explain THREE key properties of an ideal monitor. *(6 marks)*

**3** What is the other term used to describe a bubble jet printer and why is it described in this way? *(4 marks)*

57

# Data storage and output devices (4)

## Laser printers

Laser printers can produce high-quality text and graphics at rapid speeds. They are considerably more expensive than inkjet printers. Their major advantages are that they:

- use powder, rather than liquid ink
- do not need special paper
- do not smear
- have a faster print speed.

The slower laser printers produce around four pages per minute. These are relatively cheap. The fastest models can achieve around 200 monochrome pages per minute, which is a staggering 12,000 pages per hour.

Colour laser printers are more expensive, but they can still be very fast. The highest specification printers can manage 100 pages per minute (6,000 pages per hour).

### Key issues

Laser printers differ from inkjet printers in the following ways:

- Paper costs are cheaper as any paper can be used.
- The printers are more expensive but toner needs replacing less often.
- The drum does not need replacing so frequently.

### How it works

The key stages of the laser printing process are:

- charging
- writing
- developing
- transferring
- fusing
- cleaning.

## Communications hardware

Communications hardware is at the heart of a computer user's ability to connect with a network or the Internet. In using communications hardware, such as modems or Ethernet cards, the user is able to:

- access the Internet
- access their mail box
- receive emails
- send emails
- transfer documents and files
- receive documents and files
- use a 'Skype' style Internet telephone.

Both modems and Ethernet cards allow communication to take place by:

- telephone line using **dial-up**
- telephone line using broadband
- connection via a mobile telephone
- connection via cable, such as NTL.

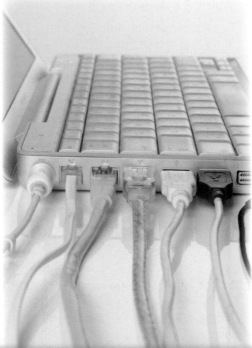

## *Modems*

A modem is a device that modulates an analogue signal in order to encode digital information. It can also demodulate the signal to decode the information that has been transmitted.

The most common type of modem uses the telephone line to transmit and receive data. Usually the quality of a modem is measured by the number of bits per second (bps) that it can handle. This is the amount of data it can receive or transfer in a second. These older types of modem are called voice band modems, but Internet users now use two other types – cable modems and ADSL modems.

We will look at these two types of modem in more detail, but it is worth considering the following differences:

- Cable modems are provided by cable television companies as part of the subscriber package.
- ADSL modems are effectively 'dial-up', where the Internet connection is not permanent and the user pays per minute or per hour.

---
### KEY TERMS

**Skype** ▶ an Internet telephone system using an Internet telephone and Skype software. Calls can be made at no cost to anyone who also has Skype, or to landlines at cost.

**Dial-up** ▶ connection to the Internet takes place when the user instructs the modem to call an 0800 or 0845 number, given to them by the ISP.

**Bandwidth** ▶ the amount of data that can pass through a network.

---

## Cable modems

Cable modems are very popular in the United States. Many homes receive their television stations via cable networks. It is popular in Great Britain, with Virgin Media being the largest provider of the service. As most British homes have either digital television via an aerial or are Sky subscribers, the cable modem has never been the dominant force in Internet connection.

Cable modems do not tend to be the choice of businesses. The typical **bandwidth** for business cable systems is in the range 3–30 megabits per second.

The key disadvantages are:

- As all users share the same cable, speed depends on how many are using it at the same time.
- Taken as a TV/Internet package it is relatively cheap. As an Internet service alone, it is expensive.

## Asymmetric digital subscriber lines (ADSL)

This system uses a modem capable of sending and receiving data over standard telephone lines. It achieves this by using frequencies not usually used in a voice telephone call. In using ADSL, it is possible to be connected to the Internet and make a telephone call at the same time.

## Dial-up

Broadband connections are, in effect, always connected to the Internet unless the user chooses to disconnect. This is not the case with dial-up users, who may have:

- a Freephone number to make their Internet connection (they pay a monthly fee for this)
- a cheap-rate number to make their Internet connection
- a standard pay-per-minute connection.

Dial-up is necessary in areas that do not yet have broadband, i.e. where the local exchanges have not been converted to digital. Dial-up is considerably slower than broadband, relying on the quality of the copper wires connecting the telephone line to the local exchange and beyond.

A conventional telephone cable is connected to the back of the computer and directly to the telephone socket. As more broadband-ready exchanges are created, the need for dial-up connections is gradually disappearing.

## Ethernets

Ethernet cards were originally used to connect two or more computers to a network. They can now be used to make the connection with the Internet.

Typically, users will have broadband connection. Instead of using a modem they will use a router as their connection device. The router is connected directly into the telephone socket and a telephone cable. It then runs from the router to each computer on the network. It is possible to purchase wireless routers that connect with the networked computers and any printers in the network.

Ethernet cards are now very small and no longer have a thick cable to connect them to each computer. Ethernet cards can also connect, via a router, straight to the Internet, without being part of a network. Business Ethernets are capable of handling at least ten gigabits of data. New developments suggest that the 100-gigabit Ethernet is not far off.

# QUESTION TIME
## *12 minutes*

**1** Why is dial-up connection to the Internet still necessary in certain parts of the country? *(2 marks)*

**2** What is the function of a router and where is it used? *(4 marks)*

**3** Explain why a business would be more likely to opt for a laser printer rather than another printer option. Explain your answer. *(6 marks)*

59

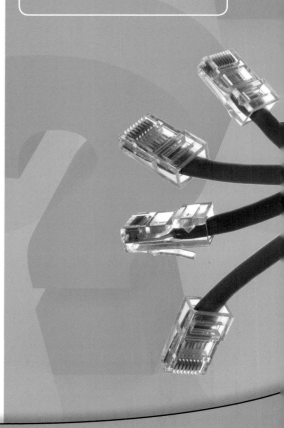

# Security of data

## The importance of security of data

### Spies and thieves

All businesses will have data that they would rather remained confidential. Some of this data will be kept in document form, in lockable filing cabinets. Other data will be kept on the computer network.

Both formats of data are equally vulnerable to theft, either by criminals or by people wishing to find out more about the organisation. They would sell it to **competitors**.

During working hours all offices are vulnerable to intruders. Many businesses have resorted to having code-locked doors, **swipe cards** or security personnel. After office hours, businesses can be protected by burglar alarms, motion sensors or patrolling security personnel.

### Keeping it safe

Businesses can try to keep their data safe and secure by:

- locking rooms when they are not being used
- providing a secure storage room for data
- marking keyboards, monitors, desktop units and laptops with ultraviolet codes, so that they can be identified if they are found by the police.

There is always a threat from virtual intruders. Highly experienced computer experts can try to gain access to a business's computer network. Not many networks are completely secure, and often these intruders will find what is known as a 'back door'. This means that there is a way into the network that bypasses any passwords or user names that are usually required. Not only can the intruder steal files, but they may also delete or **corrupt** the entire system.

In these cases, when information is stolen, simply having a back-up provides little protection. It also does not provide any protection even if the data is lost or corrupted. Sometimes it is difficult to tell whether anyone has actually been accessing the network without authorisation. If the business has not protected its systems and vital information, such as customers' details, has been accessed, this could have a severe impact on the business.

### Data at risk

All data is potentially at risk, including:

- customer details
- deals and arrangements with suppliers
- the business's financial information
- personnel records
- personal details about owners and shareholders
- sales figures
- the business's future plans
- details of any problems that the business may be experiencing.

It is not only the business's data that is at risk. It is the data held about customers, such as their credit card details, that intruders are trying to find.

## Protecting personal and financial data

In order to protect personal and financial data, a business will limit access to authorised employees only. Many businesses have several layers of security on their networks, for example:

- general data access for all employees via a password
- selected data access to a limited number of named employees
- restricted data access to a handful of senior employees
- confidential data access to usually single named employees.

There are many layers of data, and each layer is more confidential and harder to access than the last. The network system will be able to alert the network administrator if an unauthorised access attempt has been made.

Similarly, creating a **firewall** to protect the network from outside intrusion can restrict remote access. Once beyond the firewall, the multiple layers of protection come into effect.

### PINs

Passwords work in exactly the same way as PINs (personal identity numbers). Employees will swipe their access card through a card reader beside a computer. A screen will prompt them to type in their password. The network will then know which individual has accessed which computer and when. The system can log any documents or files accessed by that user.

## Physical hazards to data

There are three main threats to data. These are:

- A fire that destroys the computer network.
- The theft or corruption of data by an employee or an intruder.
- The accidental damage to data by an authorised user who has mistakenly overwritten or deleted a file.

All these problems can be dealt with and offset. A business would deal with them in the following ways:

- The data will have been backed-up and stored either physically in another location or virtually in a remote location.
- Back-ups taken on a daily basis will usually enable the business to restore the stolen or corrupted data.
- A mixture of training, automatic file saving and back-ups should restore overwritten or deleted data.

It is important to remember that networks log access to files and documents. Physical loss of computer files can therefore be traced using this **audit trail**.

 Businesses need to ensure that their data is fully secure at all times. They will usually take the following steps:

- **Install a firewall and virus-check their computers.**
- **Upgrade their operating system to the latest version.**
- **Protect their network by downloading the latest patches or security updates.**
- **Do not let employees share passwords.**
- **Encrypt all personal information held.**
- **Only allow employees to access the information they need to do their job.**
- **Take regular back-ups of the information on the network and keep them in a separate place.**
- **Be careful about disposing of all equipment (ensure data has been wiped before disposal).**
- **Install anti-spy software.**

## QUESTION TIME
*16 minutes*

**1** **Explain why a business would be interested in the data held by a competitor.** *(6 marks)*

**2** **Why is it likely that, despite all precautions, most networks are not totally secure?** *(6 marks)*

**3** **What is the purpose of encryption and how does it work?** *(4 marks)*

61

### K E Y  T E R M S

**Competitors** ▶ organisations that sell similar products and services.

**Swipe cards** ▶ a card the size of a credit or debit card that passes through a slot on a door. The information contained on the card allows access.

**Corrupt** ▶ to make data useless by making it impossible to open or read.

**Firewall** ▶ software that acts as a gateway to limit access to a computer network.

**Audit trail** ▶ a computer-generated means of tracking a series of events on a network.

# Methods of protecting data

## Computer viruses

Computer viruses are **self-replicating** computer programs. They alter the way in which a computer operates, without the knowledge or consent of the user of that computer.

Some viruses are deliberately destructive because they destroy data. Others are simply aggravating, as they slow down the computer.

In effect, a computer virus behaves just like a biological virus by infecting the computer program. Sometimes the viruses spread so quickly that entire email systems have to be shut down. Examples are the Melissa Virus in 1989 and the ILOVEYOU virus in 2000.

## Different types of infection

There are many different sorts of computer virus. Some are more dangerous and more common than others. Viruses are only one part of what is known as 'malware'. This word is a shortened version of 'malicious software'. In addition to viruses, malware includes **Trojan horses** and **worm**s. Other true computer viruses include:

- Boot sector viruses – that hide in the bootable disc or hard drive.
- Companion viruses – that are increasingly rare because Windows XP works in a very different way from previous versions.
- Email viruses – that travel with an email and copy themselves automatically by mailing themselves to everyone in a computer user's email address book.
- Logic bomb viruses – that print messages or delete files when certain programs are used.
- Macro viruses – that infect Word documents and Excel spreadsheets.
- Cross-site scripting viruses – that spread between web applications and web browsers.

## What do viruses do?

Sometimes viruses are designed to damage programs, format a computer's hard drive or delete files. Some are not designed to do any damage at all, but simply to replicate themselves. Replicating viruses use up a lot of computer memory and can cause the computer to crash.

Many of the viruses will also cause data loss and system crashes because of the way in which they have been designed.

Anti-virus software can usually handle most viruses. However, as viruses change, it is important to constantly update the anti-virus software to handle them.

## Why are computers so vulnerable?

Computers using Microsoft software, such as Outlook and Internet Explorer, are the most vulnerable to computer viruses. Virus writers seem to target these users because they know that their viruses will infect huge numbers of computers.

Not all businesses use Microsoft software, as they may use Macs or Unix systems. Any computer system that allows other programs to run on it is vulnerable to viruses. Some operating systems are less secure. A Unix system tends to allow users to run programs only within a protected area of the network.

Another operating system called Linux also found itself attacked by viruses around ten years ago. The virus, called Bliss, only attacked Linux systems, so Windows users were safe from it.

## Problems in software development

It is often the way that computer programs are designed that leaves them open to attack from viruses. Companies such as Microsoft therefore develop their programs in secret, and rely on their own developers to make sure that their programs are not vulnerable to attack. Other operating systems, such as Linux, encourage users to look for and fix security problems, so this makes it more difficult for viruses to exploit weaknesses.

62

## KEY TERMS

**Self-replicating** ▶ a virus that can reproduce itself and infect other computers.

**Trojan horse** ▶ a virus that can find a way through the security system of a computer, so that a hacker can gain access to personal information. It can also erase files.

**Worm** ▶ a virus that will look for security flaws in the network and replicate itself using the flaw and continue to look for new computers to infect.

## About protection against virtual intruders

### Anti-virus software

The most common way of detecting a virus or malware on a computer system is to run anti-virus software. The major problem with this type of software is that it can only detect and protect against viruses that were known before the last update of the anti-virus software. Unless the anti-virus software is regularly updated then newer viruses will not be detected.

Anti-virus software can eliminate most known viruses. It searches the computer and compares the files against a database of known virus signatures. A virus signature is a distinct pattern, like a fingerprint, that can be used to detect and identify viruses.

Users need to regularly update software to 'patch' any security holes in their system. This is in addition to running anti-virus software. This means that, having been exposed to viruses, the creators of a software program would then plug the problem that allowed the virus to affect the software in the first place.

Vulnerability is the term used to describe weaknesses in a computer system that might allow an attacker to violate the integrity (safety) of the system. Vulnerabilities have been found in all operating systems. There is a constant battle between the software designers and the attackers. The attackers look for vulnerabilities in the system and try to exploit them to steal or corrupt data. The software designers then have to react to deal with the vulnerability and to try and look for other vulnerabilities that they can close before the attackers find them. Constant vigilance, regular updating and creation of patches and system maintenance are the only ways to keep the attackers from exploiting the system.

## QUESTION TIME
*18 minutes*

The personal details of around 4.5m people were stolen by hackers from the job seekers' website Monster in January 2009. The hackers did not manage to steal CVs, National Insurance numbers or financial data, but it was a serious breach of the security of the website.

**1** Identify FOUR pieces of basic personal data that the hackers could have stolen in this attack. *(4 marks)*

**2** How might Monster take action to secure the personal details of the site users? *(6 marks)*

**3** The hackers used the personal details to launch a phishing campaign. What personal data would have been needed and what is a phishing campaign? *(8 marks)*

# Data protection legislation

## Computer law

There are two major laws that have been introduced to try to protect individuals whose personal details are stored on an organisation's computer system. The laws provide strict guidelines as to what can be stored and how it can be used.

Personal details could be stored by any of the following:

- Banks and building societies
- Employers
- Government departments and agencies
- Doctors and dentists
- Hospitals
- Local government
- Credit card companies
- Supermarkets and retail stores
- Gas, electricity and water companies
- Clubs, sports centres and leisure centres, or any organisation that requires you to have a membership card
- Any other business or organisation that you have contacted or given your personal details to for any reason, such as a travel company you have obtained a holiday brochure from.

## *Why data is held*

When you call a business you have dealt with before, you may find that they know who you are. Their database contains your telephone number and, when you call, your name and address will appear on the screen of the operator.

There are various reasons why organisations want to compile information about people. It is usually that they want to:

- try to sell you something
- track your buying habits
- know what your **credit rating** is
- register you for tax or legal reasons
- keep you updated on new products, special offers or the end of your membership period.

## *What data is held?*

The type of data held can vary, but it will include some of the following:

- Name, address and telephone numbers
- Age
- Gender
- Bank account details
- Credit card details
- Number of purchases made
- Type of purchases made
- Average amount spent on each transaction
- Any medical issues
- Email address

Many businesses will store information about you if you give it to them. They may also sell that information to other businesses. Your personal details are valuable!

## The Data Protection Act (1998)

The original Data Protection Act came into force in 1984. It requires any data user to register their activities and to follow eight principles of good practice relating to the data collected including:

- obtaining and processing it in a fair and legal way
- only holding it for specified, lawful and registered purposes
- making sure that the data is adequate, relevant and not excessive for its use
- ensuring that data is accurate and up-to-date if possible
- keeping it for no longer than is necessary
- respecting the individual's right to know that data is being held on them, giving access to it, and correcting or erasing it if an individual requests it
- securing data against unauthorised access, alteration, disclosure and destruction
- not transferring the data to other countries outside the **European Economic Area**.

Companies must register with the Information Commissioner. The list of companies that have registered will include the following details:

- what type of information the business holds
- what the data is used for
- where the data came from
- who might see this information.

64

**Credit rating** ▶ a score given to each individual so that an instant judgement can be made about whether or not they should be given a loan, be able to buy on credit, or to take out a mortgage.

**European Economic Area** ▶ this came into being in January 1994, and is designed to allow countries to be part of a single European market without joining the European Union, including Iceland and Switzerland.

## The Computer Misuse Act (1990)

It is an offence if someone uses a computer to secure access to a program or data that they are not authorised to view. This means that it is an offence to gain unauthorised access to a computer system. It is an offence whether the motives were well-meaning or malicious. It includes:

* altering and arranging data
* copying data
* moving data
* using data
* printing out data.

This could even extend to using someone else's password. Under the act it is also illegal to modify any data found on a computer and the maximum prison sentence for doing so is five years. Modifying data means:

* deleting other people's files
* modifying system files
* introducing viruses, Trojan horses or worms
* deliberately making someone else's computer system crash.

For even the most basic offence someone could be given a six-month prison sentence and/or a £2,000 fine.

## QUESTION TIME
*16 minutes*

**1** Identify TWO organisations that would hold your personal details. Explain why they want that information. *(4 marks)*

**2** Why it is necessary to have laws that protect the use of personal data? *(6 marks)*

**3** How would a business ensure that none of its employees illegally access and modify personal data that they should not have access to in the course of their work? *(6 marks)*

65

In January 2009, the Information Commissioner launched a Personal Information Promise initiative that asked businesses and organisations to promise to:

* Value the personal information entrusted to them and make sure they respect that trust.
* Go further than just the letter of the law when it comes to handling personal information, and adopt good practice standards.
* Consider and address the privacy risks first when planning to use or hold personal information in new ways, such as when introducing new systems.
* Be open with individuals about how information is used and who it is given to.
* Make it easy for individuals to access and correct their personal information.

* Keep personal information to a necessary minimum and delete it when no longer needed.
* Have effective safeguards in place to make sure personal information is kept securely and does not fall into the wrong hands.
* Provide training to staff who handle personal information and treat it as a disciplinary matter if they misuse or don't look after it properly.
* Put appropriate financial and human resources into looking after personal information.
* Regularly check that the above are being adhered to and report on progress.

Many major businesses and organisations signed up to the initiative, including the Royal Mail, British Gas and T-Mobile.

# What have you learnt?

This section explained the importance of business and communication systems and how they contribute to the success of a business. These systems are vital in helping businesses achieve their objectives. In this first section of Unit 8 we looked specifically at administration and how it aims to support the key functions of a business. Setting up good administrative systems from the beginning helps ensure that the business survives and grows, and is able to thrive in a competitive environment.

Firstly we looked at aims and objectives, how a business judges whether it has been a success or not and how businesses are affected by the influence of their stakeholders. We then moved on to look at business administration, its role, how it supports the company function and why it is important that accuracy underpins everything a

business does with its information. This part also looked at job roles, tasks and decision-making, as well as prioritising and planning.

The next part of the section investigated the workplace organisation. This involved how offices are laid out, the impact of new working practices, ergonomics and the environmentally friendly use of resources. Health and safety at work was the next key area, before we moved on to look at ICT data systems. In this section we examined the different types of data sources, as well as input, storage and output devices. Finally we looked at the important issue of data security. We examined how businesses protect their data and the key laws that exist to govern the use and access of personal details.

If you have tried all the Question Times on the spreads you will be getting a good idea of the kind of thing the examiner is likely to ask on the examination paper. You will

not be asked to do complicated calculations and neither will you need to know how equipment is installed or other technical matters, but you will need to know how businesses use the equipment. Your teacher or tutor will also be able to give you a copy of the Unit Revision Pack from the Tutor Support Pack. It will help you identify all the key areas to revise.

It is important to understand this unit, as it is all very well to know how to use software and hardware, but it is of equal importance to know why businesses use them.

## Section 1 integrated questions

Try these exam-style questions. They bring together all six parts of this Administration section. Remember the mark-a-minute approach, as it will help you plan your time so that you can use it in the most efficient way.

# CALL THE REPAIR MAN

**M**ark Tyler runs a computer, game console and mobile phone repair service. He works with his son and both of them have small vans. They operate from a unit on an industrial park. Mark does the majority of his repair work back at his unit, collecting faulty equipment from the customer. He can also carry out some repairs on site at his customers' business or home. Mark is very strict about not compromising his customers' personal data and he always stresses the importance of virus protection software, firewalls, passwords and encryption to his customers.

## QUESTIONS
*24 minutes*

**1** What does Mark mean by the term encryption? *(2 marks)*

**2** Identify and explain TWO routine tasks that Mark and his son would have to perform. *(4 marks)*

**3** Identify and explain TWO non-routine tasks that Mark and his son are likely to have to handle. *(4 marks)*

**4** Identify and explain the uses of THREE peripherals that Mark is likely to have to service or repair for a small business. *(6 marks)*

**5** Mark has been asked to speak to the employees of a small business about health and safety issues regarding computers. Suggest and explain what should be part of his speech. *(8 marks)*

67

# Recruitment and selection of staff

## What is recruitment?

All organisations wish to employ the most appropriate individuals as employees. To achieve this, they need to have a series of processes and procedures in place, to ensure that candidates will meet the requirements and needs of the organisation. This is known as recruitment.

The organisation's human resources department usually manages the recruitment process. It works together with the line manager (the manager to whom the new employee will directly report), deciding on the type of candidates it is looking for and identifying the key responsibilities and duties of a vacant position. For smaller businesses, this is usually the job of one of the owners or managers, who may not have the specialised skills to deal with the recruitment process.

Applicants will be sent documents that have been prepared by the organisation, laying out the requirements and challenges of the post. These are integral to the recruitment process.

Once a candidate has been shortlisted, they usually have a face-to-face interview. The impression they make at the interview will have a direct impact on the interviewers' choice.

The entire recruitment process must take into account various legal obligations, as well as any regulations laid down by the business itself.

## Full-time workers

Full-time employment means that the employee works a full week – usually up to 40 hours, but often as much as 60 hours or more. The employee does this every week, apart from the time they have off for holidays. Typical full-time jobs include some teachers, local government officers and office workers.

Full-time employees are usually paid on a monthly basis, but sometimes full-time employees such as factory workers might be paid on a weekly basis. Factory workers have traditionally been paid in this way.

The contract of employment for full-time workers will state the number of hours that they are expected to work, the availability of **overtime** (and how much pay, or time off instead of pay, they will get for working overtime), and their holiday entitlements.

Around 60% of people in work in Britain have full-time jobs. Not all of them work standard hours from 9am to 5pm. Many work **shifts**, at home, at night, or even for three or four 12-hour days each week.

An increasing trend is for employees to work **flexi-time**. This means that they can work around their other commitments, perhaps dropping children off at school or looking after elderly family members. For example, instead of starting work at 9am, they can start at 9.30am or 10am and perhaps finish work later. Employers are encouraged by government to allow employees to organise their time to suit their outside commitments, as long as they do their full weekly hours.

## Part-time workers

Part-time employment is common in the UK. It ties in with many employees' needs for flexible working arrangements. Traditionally, part-time work has allowed employees with outside commitments, such as childcare, to balance their working life and home life. The majority of part-time workers are women.

Normally, part-time work is no longer than 25 hours per week. Part-time workers have the same rights as full-time employees. They tend to work either part-days, such as mornings, afternoons or the middle part of the working day, or they may work evenings or weekends. Some may only work two or three whole days per week.

### KEY TERM

**Overtime** ▶ additional hours worked by employees, usually at a higher hourly rate of pay than their normal pay.

**Shifts** ▶ periods of non-standard hours worked by employees, such as starting at lunchtime and working through into the evening, or beginning earlier in the day and finishing at lunchtime.

**Flexi-time** ▶ employees can choose what hours they work within certain parameters, as long as they meet daily, weekly or monthly required totals of hours.

## Temporary and permanent workers

When an employee begins working for an employer, their contract of employment will state whether the job is temporary or permanent.

If the job is temporary, the contract will state that the employee has been taken on to work for a specified period of time, such as six months or a year. At the end of the period, the contract has been completed and the employee leaves the job. In many cases, temporary contracts are given to employees to cover long-term sickness, maternity leave or the short-term needs of the employer to take on more staff. Both the employer and the employee enter into a temporary contract knowing that the relationship is for a limited period of time, although in many cases a temporary contract can lead to a permanent post. Typical temporary jobs include secretarial work, catering, and seasonal work when employers take on extra staff (for example in a shop during the busy run-up to Christmas).

The majority of jobs are classed as permanent, as there is no definite period of time that the employee is expected to work for the employer. The contract only ends when the employee chooses to leave the job or, for disciplinary reasons, the employer terminates the contract. However, permanent work is not necessarily secure. An employer may wish to terminate the contract because the skills or job of the employee are no longer needed, or perhaps because the business is about to close down.

> Deciding on the exact mix of full-time, part-time, temporary and permanent workers is a major issue for start-up businesses. While many can benefit from permanent, full-time employees, they cannot be sure whether there will be sufficient work for them once they have taken on this commitment to pay wages and other benefits in the longer term.
>
> Start-up businesses often decide to opt for part-time, temporary workers. This gives them more flexibility, but it is not seen as an ideal situation for the employees, who can be discarded easily and may look for more secure work elsewhere. Part-time, temporary workers may have little loyalty towards the business, which could be a major problem for the owners.

## QUESTION TIME
### 22 minutes

**B**ased in Swansea, Wheelies Direct is a cycle replacement service. They have 75 employees and two retail outlets, a workshop, a warehouse, a call centre and an online shop.

They favour a diverse workforce. They select older people for their call centres and younger people for the more physical roles in the warehouse, workshop and retail outlets. They are firmly in favour of equal opportunities and anti-discrimination, and believe that they have a competitive advantage by recruiting skilled employees.

1 **Wheelies Direct has a mix of part-time and full-time employees. Explain the difference between these two types of employee.** *(4 marks)*

2 **Suggest TWO reasons why Wheelies Direct might hire temporary staff.** *(4 marks)*

3 **What benefits do older employees bring to businesses like Wheelies Direct?** *(6 marks)*

4 **Wheelies Direct has identified that skilled staff provide a competitive advantage. Discuss whether skilled staff are a benefit to a business like Wheelies Direct.** *(8 marks)*

# Contract of employment

YOU WILL FIND OUT:

- about contracts of employment
- about employer and employee promises
- about legal contracts

## Contracts of employment

A contract of employment is a legal document. It aims to set out the basic rights and responsibilities of the employer and the employee. Legally, the employer is supposed to provide this written statement within thirteen weeks of an employee starting work for them. It will usually include:

- both the employer's and the employee's names and addresses
- the actual place of work if this is different from the employer's address
- the job title and a very brief version of the **job description**
- the date on which the employment will begin
- details of pay and pay-scales
- when wages, salaries, bonuses or overtime will be paid
- **fringe benefits**
- normal hours of work
- holiday entitlement and holiday pay
- pension schemes
- arrangements for sickness and maternity leave
- notice period required to end the contract.

In addition to this the employer and the employee will sign and date the contract of employment.

From the list it seems that the contract of employment would be a very long document. There is an enormous amount of information included. But much of it would not actually be covered in detail in the contract itself. Businesses will try to keep the contracts as brief as possible. General company policy that

is relevant to all staff, such as holiday benefits and holiday pay, could be included in a **staff handbook**.

There are a number of laws, which we look at later in this section, which have a bearing on employment rights and responsibilities. The general rule is that the contract of employment covers the absolute minimum amount of information and detail. If something is a part of employment law it will still be legally binding even if it is missed out of a contract of employment.

Some employees work without a written contract. This may be for several reasons, including:

- part-time work
- jobs with odd hours
- self-employment.

These employees will have to rely on a verbal agreement with their employer. Verbal agreements are no less important than written ones, but if problems arise it might be difficult if there is no proof of what has been said.

A contract of employment may not mention key rights of employees, but the rights will still be legally enforceable.

## Employer and employee promises

The contract of employment will contain a number of statements, which bind the employer to carry out the following:

- to pay a wage or salary
- to provide work
- to pay back any reasonable expenses the employee has incurred in carrying our their work
- to provide a reference if required
- to provide safe working conditions
- to provide necessary information about work, pay, conditions and opportunities
- to act in good faith, which means to trust the employee and treat them with respect.

The contract is a two-way agreement and therefore employees undertake the following when they sign a contract:

- to act in good faith to their employer
- not to take bribes from any other organisation
- to keep their employer's secrets confidential
- to obey instructions and give faithful service.

---

### KEY TERMS

**Job description**
▶ a detailed list that identifies the nature of the job, including its tasks and responsibilities.

**Fringe benefits**
▶ also often called perks. These are additional advantages to doing the job, including company cars, expense accounts and private medical insurance.

**Staff handbook**
▶ a complete manual outlining all the rights and responsibilities of employees, and the policies and procedures of a business.

## Legal contract

Once an employee accepts an offer of a job, they have entered into a legal contract with their employer. The terms of the contract itself can be oral, written or implied. Sometimes it is a mixture of all three.

The implied terms of a contract include:

- the employer's duty to provide a secure, safe and healthy environment
- the employee's duty to be honest and to provide loyal service
- for both parties to have mutual trust and confidence in one another.

Some parts of a contract may be as a result of a business always doing something in the same way, such as paying an additional cash bonus before Christmas. Another practice might be for employees to be at work half an hour before their normal start time, so that they are ready to start without delay.

In the last list, keeping the business's secrets confidential is one of the employee's promises. However, new laws do allow employees to break their silence if they think that the employer has done something very wrong or illegal. This is called whistle blowing and is designed to alert the government to serious issues, such as pollution, criminal acts and other activities that are against the law.

## QUESTION TIME
*15 minutes*

Louise used to work a 35-hour week. One of the days was a Saturday, but she always took Monday off instead. She did not mind; Saturday was busy and the time went quickly. But everything changed three months ago when another business bought the company she worked for. A few days after they took over the business, Louise was given a new contract of employment. It was explained to her that it was really good and flexible: a zero hours contract. It does not say in the contract how many hours Louise has to work each week. The business is very quiet in September and October and Louise is hardly ever there and has earned very little money. Her employer rarely calls her in for duty during these quiet months.

1 From the description of Louise's new contract, what do you think is meant by a zero hours contract? *(2 marks)*

2 Explain ONE advantage to the business of having a zero contract with employees and ONE disadvantage to employees like Louise. *(6 marks)*

3 Louise used to be paid £278 per week but now she is paid £7.66 an hour and on average works around 19 hours per week. Calculate her weekly wage and explain whether she is better or worse off. *(7 marks)*

# Recruitment methods

**YOU WILL FIND OUT:**

● about internal and external recruitment

● about personal recommendation

● about advertising

● about interviewing

## Internal recruitment

Internal recruitment means filling vacancies from within the business. In other words, existing employees are either encouraged to apply or are selected for a vacancy. The business may choose this course of action because it believes it already has employees with the right skills for the job.

Details of the vacancy may be:

- advertised on a staff notice board
- placed on the organisation's intranet
- included in the organisation's in-house magazine or newsletter
- announced at a staff meeting.

There are advantages and disadvantages to using internal recruitment.

## External recruitment

External recruitment is probably the most common method of recruitment. It means filling job vacancies with individuals from outside the organisation.

A business may choose to do external recruitment itself, by advertising a vacancy and then carrying out the selection process. By advertising the post, it will hope to attract the widest possible audience, including suitable candidates.

Most businesses tend to use external recruitment agencies on a regular basis. Sometimes this is a necessary feature of recruitment and selection, as many companies have a high turnover of employees – a large proportion of employees are constantly leaving the organisation for opportunities elsewhere. Therefore, to take the strain off the organisation's human resources department, external agencies are used as a constant source of new employees.

> Using internal recruitment means that fewer new ideas, attitudes and perspectives are brought into the organisation by new employees.
>
> With external recruitment, the choice of the media, the type of advertisement, the acceptable costs and the use of external agencies depend very much upon the nature of the post in question.

## Personal recommendation

As a start-up business gets busier, it may decide to approach its part-time employees to see whether they would be prepared to work full-time. If this does not deal with the immediate need to fill a vacancy, then employees, business colleagues, friends and family can all be asked whether they could recommend someone to approach.

For some businesses, personal recommendation is a slightly less risky way of taking on a new employee, as they are known to someone who is trusted by the business owner. They may have the talents that the business is looking for, particularly if such skills are hard to find.

| ADVANTAGES |
| --- |
| • Existing employees have greater opportunities to advance their careers and gain promotion and additional skills and experience |
| • The employer will know much more about the aptitudes and abilities of the internal candidates, reducing the chance of selecting an inappropriate candidate for the post |
| • Internal recruitment tends to be a far more rapid process than external recruitment, and is far cheaper |
| • Restricting the vacancy to internal candidates can also help retain employees who may otherwise have left |

| DISADVANTAGES |
| --- |
| • The number of potential candidates for the post is limited to only those in the business |
| • There may be far better external candidates, who have more experience and better qualifications |
| • Employees, whether they are competent or not, will feel that they have an automatic right to be given a more senior post |
| • If an internal candidate is selected to fill a vacancy, a new vacancy instantly arises |

72

## Advertising

External advertising for vacant posts normally takes place when the business has exhausted its search for a suitable internal candidate. While many businesses write and place advertisements in the media themselves, others use agencies to do this for them.

Recruitment advertisements in local or regional newspapers can be relatively straightforward, featuring simply the job title, a brief description of the role, the closing date and necessary contact details. While these small advertisements – known as 'display' advertisements – may be suitable for recruiting relatively unskilled workers, something more is required to attract experienced and potentially key employees. The advertisement must intrigue and maintain the interest of a suitable candidate who would be attracted by the prospect of working for the business. This can mean that large display advertisements are required, often with images and an indication of salary ranges and future prospects.

The increasing cost of media advertising in newspapers and magazines has caused a shift to online recruitment. More and more organisations are using online employment sites and special pages on their own websites as a means of attracting potential candidates.

There can be a great deal of competition for good candidates. Increasingly, in key job roles it is the candidate rather than the potential employer who can pick and choose. Organisations are also discovering that the proportion of key job roles being filled by internal and external recruitment is falling, and that recruitment consultancies are becoming particularly important for senior posts.

## Interviewing

Face-to-face interviews are still popular with many businesses. They give the business a chance to meet qualified candidates, and the candidates can get a taste of the business. The interviewers can ensure that the candidates have the right kind of attitude, experience and characteristics for the business.

Businesses also use a number of other interviewing techniques:

- **telephone interviews** – an initial screening interview on the telephone is useful in helping the interviewer and the candidate to get a feel for whether there is a mutual interest in pursuing the application. It is a faster and more cost-effective way of creating a shortlist
- **computer interviews** – these are becoming more common. The potential candidate is asked to answer a series of multiple-choice questions online or to fill in a brief summary of their skills and education. Computer interviews can be used before shortlisting takes place
- **assessment websites** – these are particularly useful if the business is looking for individuals with keyboard and mouse skills. Responses can be timed and the candidates' computer proficiency assessed.

## QUESTION TIME
### 16 minutes

Online recruitment site www.jobsite.co.uk believes that small and medium-sized businesses in Britain waste £69 million per year on poor recruitment decisions.

Jobsite favours: competency-based interviews; offering training to existing employees, so they can be more motivated and productive; and promoting internally, to use existing talent to its full potential. Businesses should also be more flexible, and communicate with their employees to help prevent them from leaving.

Finally, businesses should think carefully about where they advertise their vacancies. Small ads in national newspapers and using the Internet are ways of reaching the broadest possible selection of potential employees.

1 What is meant by 'competency-based interview'? *(2 marks)*

2 Explain the difference between internal recruitment and external recruitment. *(4 marks)*

3 Explain ONE advantage and ONE disadvantage of internal recruitment. *(4 marks)*

4 Discuss TWO reasons why a business might choose to advertise a job vacancy on the Internet, rather than in a national newspaper. *(6 marks)*

73

# Job description and person specification

## Job descriptions

A job description aims to explain exactly what a particular job post will entail. It is extremely useful to create a job description, as it will allow the organisation to match the right person to that job.

A typical job description would include:

- the job title
- the job's position or grade within the business
- the tasks, activities and duties involved in the job
- the roles and responsibilities of the job holder.

Some job descriptions will be very detailed, but they will really depend on how complicated the role is, particularly if it is a **technical job**.

More senior posts will have more complicated job descriptions, while fairly straightforward and low-level jobs will have simpler job descriptions.

Most job descriptions will also end with a statement saying that the post-holder may be given additional or alternative duties if necessary.

It should be possible to match the tasks and duties of a job description with the aptitudes, skills, knowledge and experience outlined in a person specification.

## Person specifications

A person specification describes the qualities that an individual should have in order to do the job to a satisfactory level. Typically, it is a checklist, identifying essential or desirable qualities. The qualities may be banded into categories, usually including:

- any previous experience the person needs
- the skills that a person should have
- any physical characteristics the person will need
- the qualifications required
- the ideal personality or temperament of the person
- the level of **motivation** required for the job.

The department or functional area that needs a new member of staff usually draws up the job description and the person specification. If there is a person doing a similar job then they are a useful source of information. The managers of the department seeking to recruit are the best people to tell Human Resources exactly what the job will involve and what qualities will be most useful in the person required to do it.

By creating a job description and a person specification, a business can compare the qualities of individual candidates with the qualities of the ideal kind of person they are looking for. The business will be able to rapidly reject any candidates who fall seriously short of the minimum requirements.

### A SAMPLE JOB DESCRIPTION

POST TITLE: Administration Assistant

DIVISION/DEPARTMENT: Installation and Facilities Management

REPORTS TO: Installation and Facilities Manager

GRADE: 7

AIM: To provide administrative support. The post holder will be required to work flexibly, in a rapidly developing office environment. It may be necessary to assist, or cover for, other administrative staff from time to time.

RESPONSIBILITIES: The key duties of the post are as follows:
- Filing of correspondence in/out.
- Setting up and maintaining filing systems as and when required as work progresses.
- Preparing document transmittal forms based on a list of drawings/documents.
- Upkeep of the document/drawing register of all the Group contractors.
- Typing – Word skills for general preparation of letters/forms that the Group will issue, along with logging into the Group records system.
- User notifications for statutory/routine/unplanned-for inspections/testing/repairs, etc.
- Arranging meetings, booking and preparing meeting rooms and providing/arranging hospitality.
- Once operational – helpdesk assistance.

Plus other duties consistent with the grade as directed.

74

A person specification is not a legal requirement, but it is particularly useful for a business when it is devising a job advertisement and trying to define the qualities it is looking for. Usually the business will identify essential skills that are needed for the job and those that are desirable. This will assist the business when it comes to looking through the job applications and shortlisting those candidates that match the person specification. The person specification provides a set of criteria against which the business can objectively measure applicants. It may include:

- skills and abilities, e.g. ability to use Microsoft Office or to speak a foreign language fluently
- knowledge, e.g. up-to-date knowledge of employment law
- experience, e.g. having managed people in the past
- qualifications, e.g. 5 GCSEs at grade C or equivalent
- personal attributes and circumstances, e.g. ability to work flexible or unsocial hours.

## KEY TERMS

Technical job ▶ one that probably involves specialist, scientific or professional knowledge, e.g. a laboratory technician or a legal specialist.

Motivation ▶ the drive to get on with things without being told to by a superior. To work without supervision and to take pride in one's work and be conscientious.

## QUESTION TIME
16 minutes

Read the following mystery job description and then answer the questions:

### Mystery job description

Outline duties:
1  Answer a high volume of calls and maintain a rapid response rate according to agreed standards.
2  Log information on calls received, where required, and maintain detailed and accurate records.
3  Maintain and update continuously, by local knowledge and by local means, a log of the availability of staff likely to receive inbound calls.
4  File data and perform other routine clerical tasks as assigned, and for other departments as needed.
5  Order and maintain relevant office supplies for effectiveness of personal duties.
6  Operate a variety of standard office machines, including a personal computer and a variety of computer software, phone, fax, calculator, shredding machine and photocopying machine.
7  Communicate and liaise verbally and in writing between: customers/suppliers/visitors/enquirers and relevant staff, and interpret and respond clearly and effectively to spoken requests over the phone or in person, and to verbal or written instructions.
8  Establish and maintain effective working relationships with co-workers, supervisors and the general public.
9  Perform reception duties in an efficient, professional and courteous manner.
10 Maintain regular consistent and professional attendance, punctuality, personal appearance, and adherence to relevant health and safety procedures.
11 Pursue personal development including skills and knowledge necessary for the effective performance of the role.

1  **Identify the likely job title.**
*(2 marks)*

2  **What other, more obvious duties would this role require?** *(4 marks)*

3  **Devise a person specification to match the job description.**
*(10 marks)*

# Training

**YOU WILL FIND OUT:**

● about developing people

● about training process ideas

● about work-related training

## Developing people

Most organisations face the challenge of developing their employees. Organisations want their employees to be resourceful and creative, and to have the ability to make their own reasoned judgements and decisions. This means that training often goes beyond simply giving employees the opportunities to learn how to carry out tasks. This part of training is still very important because businesses recognise that although employees join them with basic skills, for example computer skills, these abilities need to be developed. They also need to be adjusted so that they match the precise needs of the business itself.

Businesses have begun to realise that the best way to develop employees is to enable their learning and personal development. This means that once employees have been taught the basic work-related skills they need, everything else needs to be individual – tailor-made to each employee. This makes it more exciting and challenging and, above all, more relevant to each employee.

Businesses have moved away from simply providing training. They now use phrases such as:

- enabling learning
- facilitating personal development
- helping people identify and achieve their personal potential
- Continuing Professional Development (CPD).

## Training process ideas

Businesses prefer to have some kind of formal way in which they identify, design, deliver and then evaluate their training. Each business will have a slightly different way of doing this, but the following table outlines the five key steps:

**KEY TERM**

**Appraisal** ▶ a regular meeting between an employee and his or her manager, to discuss the employee's performance and identify training needs.

| TRAINING PROCESS | WHAT THE BUSINESS WOULD DO |
|---|---|
| Assess and agree training needs | The process begins by the business identifying the training that is necessary. Sometimes this can happen in the **appraisal** process. Individuals will be identified, and relevant training needs will be agreed. |
| Create training or development | Having identified who needs to be trained and what they need to be trained in, the business needs to break down the training into manageable parts. It also needs to have specific objectives, or a purpose, which can later be measured. |
| Decide on the learning style | The right kind of way to deliver the training needs to be considered. Sometimes businesses will choose workshops, presentations, demonstrations or courses of study. The choice will depend on the subject of the training and also the skills and knowledge of those being trained. |
| Plan the training and evaluation | The training now needs to be broken down into a series of activities, exercises, workshops, meetings or presentations. In order to assess how well the training works, it is a good idea for the business to check the skills and knowledge of those being trained before and after to assess its effectiveness. |
| Design the materials, methods and deliver the training | Delivering training is an important communication and it needs to be relevant and interesting to those being trained. It also needs to get the main points across. Everything should be prepared in advance and, if possible, it should be tested. It is also important to make sure it is up-to-date and relevant. |

⏩ With work-related training it is not always a good idea to assess its effectiveness against a job description. A job description really only focuses on responsibility and does not necessarily focus on skills. A person specification is probably better as a guide. Some businesses do like to establish a 'behaviour set', but this is difficult to assess and develop and it can also mean that employees are unable to react in situations that are out of the ordinary.

# Work-related training

Most work-related training is about passing on necessary job- or work-related skills or knowledge. This is different from personal development. However it still needs to be well planned. Ideally the business needs to:

- set training objectives
- be aware of how many people need to be trained
- decide on the methods that will be used
- decide when and how long the training will last
- decide where it will happen
- figure out how it will be measured in terms of its effectiveness
- check to see how the trainees react to the training.

In order to deliver skills training, a business can again use a five-step approach, but this is a different process from the personal development one, as we can see in the following table:

| PROCESS | WHAT IS INVOLVED |
|---|---|
| Prepare the trainee | Make sure that they are as relaxed as possible because many people find learning stressful. |
| Explain why they need to do the training | They should be shown the method and explain why things need to be done in this way. Any equipment, systems or tools need to be shown to the trainees. |
| Demonstration | Show the trainees a step-by-step demonstration of what they will need to do. Complicated tasks need to be broken down and the step-by-step demonstration needs to be repeated if there is confusion. |
| Let the trainees practice | Most people learn better by actually doing something. Now the trainees have had a demonstration they should be allowed to try it out themselves. |
| Monitor progress | The trainers should encourage and give positive feedback and should be prepared to repeat parts of the training because people learn at different speeds. |

The idea behind work-related training is to ensure that all employees in particular job roles have the relevant 'skill set'. This means that they all have the same basic skills necessary to do their job. The training can also help develop a standard set of behaviours. This might mean ensuring that employees all answer the phone in the same way, handle complaints using the same process or carry out tasks in the same order.

Tesco, the supermarket giant, has a 'Tesco Academy', which is designed to train and develop their key managers and potential leaders. Tesco prides itself that it has well trained and highly motivated staff throughout the organisation, and recruitment and training is very important to them. Their training is based around the slogans: 'No one tries harder for customers', and 'Treat people how we like to be treated'.

**1** What might be the primary aim of basic Tesco training for new employees? *(2 marks)*

**2** New managers have 12 weeks to get to know the store business before they are placed in a particular store. Identify what type of training this is and its advantages to both Tesco and the new employee? *(8 marks)*

**3** Tesco uses a management recruitment centre to ensure it has the right people in the right roles. Other positions are dealt with by the separate stores. Why might the recruitment process be different for these? Explain your answer. *(10 marks)*

# Methods of training

**YOU WILL FIND OUT:**

● about formal training

● about distance or Internet-based training

● about informal training

● about training providers

## Formal training

Formal training courses can either be run by the business itself or provided by an external training company. Businesses will often use the expertise of some of their key employees to write and design formal training courses for other employees. The problem is that they need to find someone who is able to teach these skills, as the individual will need to have:

- good presentation and speaking skills
- the ability to deal with difficult employees
- the ability to plan a course or session
- the means to set up support for the employees after the training
- the ability to evaluate, monitor and feed back the skills.

Obviously, using existing employees to devise courses is a cheaper option, but it will require the individual to be taken out of their normal work, which could cause disruption to the business.

External trainers can provide either **off-the-shelf** or **tailor-made** training programmes. They can be very targeted and cost-effective, particularly if they are held within business hours and at the place of work. Courses can cover a variety of different areas, including:

- managerial or supervisors' skills, such as communication, leadership and presentation
- computer packages
- sales and marketing
- accounts and finance
- legal requirements.

## Distance or Internet-based training

These two options offer flexible, workplace-based training. Employees can complete the training at the convenience of the business. There is of course no travel or accommodation cost involved.

Often these are referred to as e-learning courses, which are designed to take from between one hour and several weeks to complete. They can be bought off the shelf or tailor-made. They are also ideal because they are broken down into topics and can actually lead to a recognised qualification. Many of these e-learning courses are completely Internet-based, with presentations, multiple-choice questions and other interactive learning activities. Some of them are also live Internet-based events. The trainer has a web cam and provides the training live. The trainer can interact with the trainees.

There are also online presentations, **e-book**s and other ways to learn. The courses also offer discussion forums, so that trainees can communicate with one another and discuss the topics.

### For example
### Learn Direct

Learn Direct (www.learnthroughwork.org) has a range of government-backed online learning and information services. Many of them work in cooperation with universities, through the Learning Through Work Scheme. They include online learning and one-to-one tutorials.

## Informal training

Informal training has the advantage that it can be organised by even the smallest businesses that do not have a budget set aside for training. It can involve an employee showing another employee how a particular job is carried out. This is known as job shadowing and is often used during induction. For more about induction, see pages 80–1.

More generally, an employee that has been on a training course can come back to the workplace and pass on what they have learned. This is ideal for teaching ICT skills. Some businesses also identify coaches or mentors. These are individuals who are experienced in a particular job role and can guide new employees through the various difficulties that they might face in their new role. It uses the experienced employee's expertise.

## Training providers

Finding a good training provider can always be a problem. There are literally thousands of individuals and organisations that offer training services. All of them differ in terms of their methods and their quality and, of course, their costs.

Once a business has identified exactly what kind of training is needed, the first thing for them to think about is whether or not there is an existing employee who could carry out the training. If this individual does not exist, then the business needs to look for a training provider. Typically the business will ask:

- Does the trainer understand what is needed?

## KEY TERMS

**Off-the-shelf ▶** ready-made, general packages that can be adapted in some way for a specific business.

**Tailor-made ▶** designed specifically for the business and its particular training needs.

**e-book ▶** short for 'electronic book'. A digital version of a printed book.

- Is the training at the right level?
- Will it lead to a qualification?
- Has the trainer had experience of this type of business?
- Can the training be tailored?
- Is it up-to-date?
- Where would the training take place?
- When would the training take place?
- How will the training be assessed?
- Is it possible to gauge the quality of the trainer?
- Have they had many satisfied clients in the past?
- Does the training represent good value for money?

Broadly speaking, businesses will be able to identify four different types of training provider, as can be seen in the table below.

Another way of finding valuable training contacts is to either use a business consultant, who can point a business in the right direction in finding suitable training, or for the business to network. Networks are informal contacts made with educational establishments, trade associations and other businesses. The business can find out how other businesses organise their training and get feedback from them about particular trainers and methods that they have used.

# QUESTION TIME
*16 minutes*

**1** How might a business decide what training needs it has? *(6 marks)*

**2** 'In-house training is far more focused, is cheaper and can be monitored more easily than any kind of external training'. To what extent do you agree with this statement? Explain your reasons. *(10 marks)*

79

| TYPE OF TRAINING PROVIDER | EXAMPLES OF TRAINING PROVIDERS |
|---|---|
| Public sector | The Learning and Skills Council has a Train to Gain Service, which runs in England. Learn Direct offers flexible online learning. The Department for Employment and Learning offers similar services in Northern Ireland. Local schools, further education colleges and universities also offer training opportunities. |
| Professional bodies and trade associations | Some of the best training comes from organisations that best understand the business. There are a number of professional bodies, such as those that focus on areas like accounts or marketing. Trade associations are also linked to particular areas of work, such as the Catering Equipment Suppliers Association that represents businesses that manufacture and supply commercial kitchen equipment. |
| Private sector | Many businesses will use the Train to Gain Service to find a suitable private trainer and then draw up a shortlist of the most appropriate ones. |
| Mentors and coaches | The local Chamber of Commerce is a good place to start to find an experienced individual. Mentors can come from outside the business and these individuals may be recently retired, but still highly experienced and of value to the business. |

# Induction

## Induction

A new job means a new start. It also means having to learn about a new business and its **policies and practices**, and how to do the new job.

Good employers organise well-planned induction sessions for new employees. The induction sessions are designed to be an introductory training programme to help new employees become familiar with the business and how it operates.

### An induction programme

The induction programme is important because it can often take a long time and cost a great deal of money to find ideal employees. The main idea behind the induction is to help the new employees settle into the business as quickly as possible.

If an employee is going to have second thoughts about the new job then it is likely to happen in the first few days. The induction programme can ease any doubts. A typical induction programme includes:

- a welcome meeting on the first day
- a guided tour of the organisation
- copies of, or the opportunity to see and read business documentation, including departmental manuals, health and safety documents and staff handbooks
- accompanied introduction to new work colleagues
- initial introductions, training, or the promise of training for any new software, hardware or machinery not known to the new employee
- an opportunity to sit in on team meetings and a general opportunity to become familiar with the working environment.

### Length of induction

Induction programmes can last for anything from a single day to several weeks. It will depend on the job itself and the challenges ahead for the new employee.

Usually the induction programme will be followed by additional training and a review, to see how well the new employee is fitting into the working environment.

The better the induction programme, the more likely the employee is to be able to adjust and fit in with the new business. Induction sets employees off on the right track. As a result they should:

- feel valued
- be trained
- be more motivated
- be more productive.

Induction is usually the first type of training given to new employees. Additional training will be identified later.

## Training opportunities

An induction programme is just the first of the training and development opportunities that could be offered to new employees. Increasingly, jobs are becoming more complicated and require a broader range of skills. This is particularly true of jobs that involve information technology.

A new employee may know how to use common software, but businesses will often prefer to use specialist software, including databases and specialist spreadsheet packages. These are quite different. It is in the best interests of the business to train its employees to the highest possible standard in order for them to do their jobs to the highest standards.

Untrained or badly trained employees can make mistakes. At worst they can be a danger to themselves and those around them. They can also cause customers and suppliers to become dissatisfied.

It is the responsibility of the human resources department to make sure that all employees attend basic training sessions. After that, specific departments will identify training needs for their employees. This is a process called **training needs analysis**.

Once the need for training has been identified, the department will contact the human resources department to arrange the necessary details. It can then be decided whether several employees would benefit from this training or whether it is training specific to that individual employee.

## Evaluating training

It is one thing for an organisation to provide or to pay for training and development, but it needs to be assured that these are effective. Once training needs have been identified, processes need to be put in place for the business to be informed of the value of the training. The business will want to review training that was given to its employees, usually through **feedback** from those undertaking the training.

The review and feedback should provide enough information for the business to see whether the training was adequate and positive. It enables an employer to find out whether the employees actually achieved or learned what was intended.

There is always competition for the money available for training in a business. Managers will want to secure as much of this money as possible for their own staff. They will therefore request training at the earliest possible opportunity, but will usually have to justify the need for training and the expense involved. Completing Training Needs Analysis Forms, supported by details about the training requirements, usually achieves this.

> Induction training is far more than simple skills training. It is about teaching new starters the basics. New employees are told about dress codes, the routine to book holidays, what to do if they are sick and even where the toilets are located. They also need to know about the business's goals, objectives, practices and health and safety rules. Induction programmes need to be properly planned to allow new employees to settle in and begin to do their job.

## KEY TERMS

**Policies and practices** ▶ the business's general approach to work and the ways in which it prefers duties and tasks to be carried out.

**Training needs analysis** ▶ a process by which the business identifies the training requirements of its employees.

**Feedback** ▶ opinions and an evaluation of something that has taken place.

## QUESTION TIME
### 22 minutes

**V**alerie is the Human Resources Manager at Silver Computers Ltd. She has spent the morning listing all the possible areas to cover in an induction programme that she needs to run next month. Twelve new employees are starting on the first day of the month and she has two days to cover the following:

- Essential 'visitor level' safety and emergency procedures
- Toilets
- Food and drink
- Smoking policy
- Timings and induction training overview
- Organisational history and background overview
- Ethics and philosophy
- Mission statement(s)
- Organisation overview and structure
- Local structure if applicable
- Departmental structure and interfaces
- Who's who (names, roles, responsibilities)
- Site layout
- Other sites and locations

- Dress codes
- Basic communications overview
- Facilities and amenities
- Pay
- Absenteeism and lateness
- Holidays
- Sickness
- Health insurance
- Pension
- Trades Unions
- Rights and legal issues
- Personnel systems and records overview
- Access to personal data
- Time and attendance system
- Security
- Transport and parking
- Crèche and childcare
- Grievance procedures

- Discipline procedures
- Career paths
- Training and development
- Appraisals
- Mentoring
- Awards and Incentives
- Health and Safety, and hazard reporting
- Physical examinations, eye test etc.
- Emergency procedures, fire drill, first aid
- Accident reporting
- Personal protective equipment
- Use, care, and issue of tools and equipment
- Other housekeeping issues
- General administration
- Restricted areas, access, passes

All the job roles are in customer service. The new employees will be answering calls from customers and using computers to access customer information and record the details of their conversations with the customers.

**1** Choose FOUR of the areas Valerie needs to cover and explain why they are important. *(6 marks)*

**2** Suggest the order in which the areas could be delivered to the new employees. *(10 marks)*

**3** How might Valerie vary the way she explains the information to make the induction programme interesting? *(6 marks)*

81

# In-house training and off-the-job training

**YOU WILL FIND OUT:**

- about staff development
- about in-house training
- about off-the-job training

## Staff development

In most organisations staff development needs are identified in a process known as **appraisal**. Every six or twelve months an employee will meet with his or her manager or supervisor. The purpose of the meeting is to discuss the employee's performance during the period since the last appraisal. During the appraisal meeting, the strengths and weaknesses of the employee will be discussed in a positive way. The process aims to identify any training or development needs the employee may have that could improve their performance.

The suggestion for staff development or training can come from either the manager or the employee. During the appraisal any particular gaps in skills or knowledge can be identified.

Some larger businesses will have ongoing training, which the employee can slip straight into. Other training will require more thought and organisation. It is sometimes left to the employee to suggest when, where and how training could be provided. Sometimes the training can be done within the company. More specialist training may require the employee to take time off from work to attend an outside organisation.

Many training programmes can either be done online or at home, with the employee meeting with course tutors at regular intervals.

### Importance of staff development

Businesses recognise that their employees are their most valuable resource. Not only do businesses want their employees to be confident and competent in their roles, but they also want them to feel motivated.

By assisting them in pursuing training or development opportunities, the business will make an investment in its employees. This not only improves the employees' performance but cements the relationship between employer and employees.

Development opportunities and new skills open doors to employees. The employer would hope that those doors are within the organisation and not with another business. An employer will aim to earn commitment from an employee to remain with the business, in return for funding additional staff development.

New practices and procedures, as well as new technology, may require the business to push all employees through staff development. In other cases staff development takes place on an individual basis.

## In-house training

It used to be the case that in-house training, carried out in the workplace, did not come with nationally recognised certificates of achievement. This is generally no longer the case, as it is as easy to obtain qualifications such as **NVQs** at work as to attend a course in a college or training institution.

In-house training simply means carrying out a training programme specifically designed for the business. These are still very common and are used to help update employees on policies and procedures. The problem is that the qualification may have no practical value to the employee should they change their place of work.

In-house training could be provided by:

- the human resources department
- project leaders
- management or supervisors
- external specialists.

On-the-job training is training that takes place in the working environment. Typical forms of on-the-job training include:

- shadowing or following around an experienced employee to learn from them
- mentoring of a new employee by an experienced employee
- coaching a new employee to learn new tasks.

The purpose of each of these types of training is useful in the following situations:

- When the new employee has lots of different things to learn.
- When the new employee would benefit from reassurance in the first few weeks.
- When the new employee might need to know about new equipment or machinery.

There are disadvantages to in-house training, and it is important that businesses try to minimise it. The disadvantages could include:

- passing on inefficient ways of working or poor practices
- employees not taking it seriously and not attending

82

- the need to provide training facilities and rooms
- employees not being honest about any problems or difficulties they are encountering

## Off-the-job training

Off-the-job training involves attending training courses outside the working environment. Typically, they would include:

- management training
- sales and customer service training
- health and safety training.

There are literally thousands of different training courses available. Larger organisations have a rolling programme of their own training, which may be at a remote location, away from the normal working environment.

Organisations that encourage or provide training can apply for an Investors in People Award, which recognises their commitment to training and staff development.

A wide range of different training organisations, including colleges, specialist training providers and training agencies, can provide external training. One of the big advantages of external training is that it comes with a certificate. Many of the training programmes are ongoing and employees can be given the necessary time to attend the courses outside the business.

The vast majority of the training programmes are not organisation-specific, but are based around particular skills, abilities or knowledge. Examples could include health and safety or new software training.

> **In order to make the best use of in-house training, a business needs to:**
>
> - **analyse its business needs**
> - **involve employees in identifying training that would improve their productivity**
> - **plan the training**
> - **set objectives for the training**
> - **select the most appropriate type of training**
> - **carefully choose the trainer (if necessary hiring someone to do it)**
> - **evaluate the training using feedback forms**
> - **analyse the feedback to improve the training next time.**

### — KEY TERMS —

**Appraisal** ▶ a regular meeting between an employee and his or her manager, to discuss the employee's performance and identify training needs.

**NVQs (National Vocational Qualifications)** ▶ practical qualifications that require a candidate to display actual skills against a list of requirements for the course.

## QUESTION TIME
*14 minutes*

**K**nowsley Safari Park, near Liverpool, is a 200-acre attraction with half-a-million visitors per annum. It uses formal and informal in-house training to develop customer care skills. It has have 35 full-time staff and 150 temporary employees over the summer season. The business decided that it was not practical or cost-effective to bring in external trainers or to send people out on courses each time a new employee joined. They decided to focus on in-house methods.

**1** Why was it the case that it was not practical or cost-effective to use external trainers? *(2 marks)*

**2** How was the situation complicated by the fact that 150 temporary workers all needed training? *(4 marks)*

**3** Suggest and explain FOUR areas of customer care that could be included in the in-house training programme. *(8 marks)*

# Rewarding staff

YOU WILL FIND OUT:

- about rewarding staff
- about training
- about greater responsibility
- about financial rewards

## Rewarding staff

As we will see in this section, rewarding staff is not just about paying them a competitive wage or salary. In fact, pay itself does not provide sufficient reward for valued employees, they often look for more. This is why training, responsibility and other non-financial rewards are important.

## Training

Offering training and development opportunities is a key way in which even small businesses can motivate their employees. It benefits both the employee and the employer.

Many jobs need a broad range of skills. It is in the interests of employers to train their employees to the highest possible standards, to help them do their jobs to the best of their ability. At the same time, offering training to employees reinforces the fact that they are valued by the business.

Untrained or badly trained employees make mistakes. They can become a liability, as customers and suppliers can be dissatisfied by the level of service or the communications they receive.

A business will usually carry out a process of training needs analysis, which identifies the training requirements of its employees. This helps the business to identify which employees would benefit from particular types of training, and can also be seen as a reward for an employee's efforts and willingness to learn new things.

In a small business there are no huge training budgets and money is always tight. But training is often seen as a two-way investment. It improves the quality of the employees, by ensuring that they are up to date with the latest technology and ideas and that they have acquired additional skills. At the same time, employees welcome the opportunity to learn new skills and broaden their expertise.

## Greater responsibility

Techniques such as **job enlargement**, **job enrichment** and **job rotation** can all contribute towards giving employees greater responsibility and decision-making power in their day-to-day tasks. The same can be said for encouraging teamwork. Natural leaders or experts usually emerge from teams, taking the lead in tasks that they feel particularly confident or competent to handle.

Encouraging employees to take on more responsibility allows them to broaden and improve their levels of skills and expertise, cope with more complex jobs, and take the strain off hard-pressed managers and supervisors. Again this is particularly important for small businesses with only a few employees, who may be constantly under pressure to perform more and more complicated and exhausting tasks to ensure that the business continues to grow.

Small businesses often suffer from employee shortages, because they cannot necessarily predict which parts of their business will come under pressure as the business grows. There is often a time-lag between increased workloads due to business growth and a business taking on extra employees to handle the additional pressures. It takes time to find the right employee, even when the need to take on someone extra has been identified.

Again, rewarding existing employees with new, more senior positions is a great motivator. It also means that when the business is looking for additional employees, it can search for less experienced candidates, as the more senior positions will have been taken up by employees who know what is involved and have been willing to take on the extra responsibility.

**Job enlargement** ▶ encouraging employees to extend the range of tasks involved in their jobs, particularly to move away from repetitive or boring ones.

**Job enrichment** ▶ improving an employee's job role by encouraging them to move beyond what is strictly their role, aiming for greater variety, challenges and stimulation.

**Job rotation** ▶ switching from one job to another.

## Financial rewards

Although financial rewards are not the whole answer to keeping employees motivated, linking financial rewards with performance and business success can work well. Like any business, a start-up will have set a series of objectives or targets, which it aims to reach and hopefully exceed. Employees will have played an important role in ensuring that these objectives or targets have been met, so a business should reward them for their contribution. This can be done in a number of different ways, for example a broad-based bonus system, paid as a lump sum to all employees.

A more precise way is to link additional payments to individual performance, but this often means having to set up some kind of appraisal system, where individual targets and goals are compared to actual performance. This is not always possible for a start-up business, as setting up the appraisal system – let alone running it – takes too much time and effort.

Commission can also work as a means of rewarding employees, but it relies on each employee being in a selling role. Commission is paid as a percentage of the total value of sales that an employee has achieved. It is not a system that can be easily applied to those who do not make direct sales to customers, and could be a problem if they are rewarded on a different basis.

An increasingly popular way of rewarding employees financially is to make them shareholders of the start-up business. Instead of paying them cash, they are given a number of shares. This makes them part-owners of the business. From that point on, they have a direct interest in every aspect of the business, as the value of their shares and any dividends they may receive are directly linked to the success and profitability of the business. It can also help to retain employees, as part-ownership gives them a stronger bond with the business and they may view their job role in the longer term as a result.

As start-up businesses become more established, they will be able to bring in many of the systems and innovations used by larger, more established companies.

Paying bonuses is still one of the simplest financial rewards that a start-up business can offer. The business will simply set aside a certain amount of the profit made and distribute it among its employees. However, this means that highly motivated and key employees, who have worked consistently over the year, may be rewarded with precisely the same amount as an employee who has not been very useful or productive, which could lead to difficulties.

## QUESTION TIME
*15 minutes*

According to Learn Direct Scotland, pay can be a demotivator. It believes that pay packets send a message to employees:

- If a business is paying less than the competition, then employees may be demotivated.
- If a business only pays more when employees threaten to leave, then it is rewarding disloyalty.
- If a business offers higher rates of pay to attract new employees, current employees will be angry.
- If a business uses its end of year profits as a basis for its bonuses, employees do not always see the link between their personal efforts throughout the year and the bonus they receive at the end of the year.

Source: adapted from www.learndirectscotland.com

**1** Explain the meaning of the term 'bonus'. *(2 marks)*

**2** Identify two reasons why a business will train employees. *(2 marks)*

**3** Why might employees who have been given more responsibility be motivated? *(3 marks)*

**4** Advise a small business on whether its bonus reward scheme should be based on individual performance or not. *(8 marks)*

85

# Methods of remuneration

### YOU WILL FIND OUT:

- about wages and salaries
- about skills
- about time rates and piece rates
- about overtime, bonuses and commission

## Wages and salaries

The term used to describe all types of pay is 'remuneration'. This is payment by the employer in return for the hours worked by employees. It is the most expensive part of most businesses' outgoings.

Depending on the type of job, an employee will be paid either a wage or a salary. Wages are usually based on the number of hours that have been worked in the previous week. Salaries, on the other hand, tend to be a twelfth of the annual payment to an employee. In other words, the employee is paid a twelfth of their total salary each month.

In both cases, payments are often made in **arrears**. The employees will have worked for either several days or several weeks before they are paid for their labour.

### Payment methods

There are four usual ways in which employees are paid:

- **by cash** – usually paid on a Friday to part-time or casual workers on wages rather than salaries
- **by cheque** – either handed to the employer or posted
- **by credit transfer from a bank** – this is an example of **electronic data interchange**. Payments are guaranteed on a particular day of the week or month
- **by Bankers' Automated Clearing System (BACS)** – where money is transferred directly from a business's bank account straight into an employee's bank account.

### Deductions

Employees do not receive all their wages or salaries. The money that is given to them has already had money deducted from it, including:

- income tax
- National Insurance
- pension contributions
- trade union subscriptions.

Wages and salaries are calculated using the PAYE – or Pay As You Earn – system. This means that employees pay their income tax and National Insurance as they earn their wages or salary.

### Pay slips

Regardless of how an employee is paid, they will always receive a pay slip that summarises the payments made to them and any deductions that have been made. It usually includes:

- the hours worked
- the pay before tax and other deductions
- itemised deductions
- the pay after tax and other deductions
- how much income tax has been paid in this **tax year**
- how much National Insurance has been paid in this tax year.

## Skills

The term 'human resources' is used because employees are seen as a valuable resource. The better the employee, the more valuable they become. There is a direct link between skills, experience, qualifications and pay. Employees with rare skills and good experience are often more difficult to attract and cost more.

A start-up business trying to find skilled and experienced employees needs to balance the risk of taking on someone with less experience and ability, against the greater cost of recruiting someone with more experience.

Older employees, particularly if they have been with the business for some years, will cost more, as they will have had a number of pay increases over time. However, pay is always connected with age. A start-up business needs to match or better the pay offered by more established businesses; otherwise it could not possibly attract experienced employees away from other businesses.

## Time rates and piece rates

Most employees on wages are paid a 'time rate'. This means that their pay depends upon the number of hours they have worked. They will have been allocated an hourly rate of pay. Their pay before deductions is equal to their hourly rate of pay multiplied by the number of hours they have worked.

Rather than being paid for the number of hours they have worked, employees on 'piece rate' are paid for the number of items they have made, or tasks that they have completed, over a given period of time. Piece-rate workers (known as 'pieceworkers') tend to be paid when a batch of work is completed.

### For example

An employee is paid 10p for every letter folded and put into an envelope. If they managed to do 1,000 of them, then they would receive £100.

Businesses now have to be very careful about setting piece rates, because they are expected to pay the National Minimum Wage to all employees.

## Overtime

Overtime is additional pay that is given to employees for working over and above their normal working hours. Overtime payments are usually higher per hour than regular hourly pay.

> ### For example
>
> If an employee receives £7 per hour, they might receive 'time-and-a-half' for overtime, giving them £10.50 per overtime hour worked.

## Bonuses

Bonuses are often paid to employees because they have achieved a goal or an objective set by the business, or because the business itself has achieved particular goals or objectives.

Bonuses are usually paid as a lump sum at a particular time of the year, perhaps just before Christmas or shortly before the end of the tax year. Alternatives to bonuses include holidays, cars or other non-financial rewards.

## Commission

Commission is usually paid to employees who are on relatively low hourly rates of pay. Commission is usually a small percentage of the total value of sales made by that employee. Commission is added to the employee's basic pay.

> ### For example
>
> If an employee receives 2% commission, he or she will receive £2 in commission for every £100 of products or services sold.

> ▶▶ Bonuses in particular are seen as a way in which a business can reward employees for their contribution towards the business achieving its aims, objectives or targets. Bonuses are usually paid on a sliding scale, with more senior employees and managers receiving larger bonuses to reflect their additional contributions during the year.

## QUESTION TIME
### 19 minutes

A business receives a rush order for £1,000 of products. The business knows that the materials used will cost £400, but in order to produce the products and sort out the order it will need ten of its employees to work 5 hours overtime each at £10 per hour. The business owner wonders whether it will make any money out of the rush order.

1 Define the term 'overtime'. *(2 marks)*

2 Why is the business willing to pay overtime to its employees? *(4 marks)*

3 Calculate the total cost of fulfilling the order. *(5 marks)*

4 What advantages and what disadvantages did accepting the order bring to the business? *(8 marks)*

---

**KEY TERMS**

**Arrears** ▶ the payment is made after the work has been done.

**Electronic data interchange** ▶ a system that links the business directly to its bank in order to make automatic payments.

**Tax year** ▶ the period from 6 April one year to 5 April the following year.

**National Minimum Wage** ▶ the lowest legal hourly payment to employees, set by the government. It is dependent upon the age of the employee.

# Other forms of reward

## Performance-related pay

Performance-related pay – also known as 'merit pay' – is additional payments made to employees who manage to achieve specific goals. Usually these goals have been agreed in individual appraisals or in team meetings, or are announced to employees across the whole organisation.

Performance-related pay is similar to a bonus, but the payment is linked closely to actual achievements, such as:

- increased efficiency
- higher profits
- lower numbers of complaints
- dealing more quickly with customer queries.

Individual employees could be awarded performance-related pay because they have achieved certain goals, they are efficient and helpful, or they have a good record of attendance. The system rewards individual employees for meeting agreed goals, which could give them a higher rate of pay than others doing similar work who have not met the goals.

### Appraisals

Many businesses link performance-related pay to appraisals – one-to-one interviews and discussions between an employee and a manager or supervisor. Appraisals review the employee's performance and form the basis for development and improvement or future training.

In an appraisal, each employee can be graded. For example:

- unacceptable (U)
- improvement needed (I)
- good (G)
- high achievement (H)
- outstanding (O).

If the employee can reach the outstanding category, then they will be awarded a 5–10% pay increase. Those in category U do not receive a pay increase – not even to keep pace with **inflation**.

### Problems

Performance-related pay was the big new idea of the 1980s. By the early 1990s, nearly 60% of businesses had adopted it.

However, by the late 1990s, businesses were beginning to realise that it did not really achieve what it set out to do. Also, it was expensive to run and was causing unhealthy rivalry between employees. Nonetheless many businesses still use performance-related pay.

The main problems with performance-related pay are that:

- it is often not generous enough to encourage employees
- it is seen as being unfair
- it damages teamwork, as one person wants to take credit for success
- it is actually unlikely that money alone will **motivate** employees. According to government research, less than 10% of employees believe that performance-related pay is the best way of improving motivation at work.

## Fringe benefits

As an alternative to extra pay or higher rates of pay, a business may instead offer a range of non-financial rewards, known as 'fringe benefits' or **incentives**. These include:

- **subsidised** meals and drinks
- free or subsidised travel
- free pick-up and drop-off to and from work

- free travel passes
- travel loan schemes
- company cars
- essential car users' allowances (employees provided with a company car and a company credit card for fuel)
- overseas travel and expenses for work
- refund of travel expenses
- discount on purchases made from the business
- loans and mortgages at reduced rates (typical for bank employees)
- health insurance.

### Pensions

As well as the State Pension (paid for by National Insurance contributions), there are two other forms of pension:

- **non-contributory pensions** – the employer (not the employee) pays into the pension scheme
- **contributory pensions** – the employer and the employee both pay into the pension scheme.

Pensions that feature a contribution from an employer are a very attractive fringe benefit for an employee, as the pension will support the employee after they retire.

Generally there are two different types of pension scheme:

- company pension schemes
- personal pension schemes.

Company pension schemes usually include a contribution from the employer. The advantage of personal pension schemes is that the pension is related only to the employee. When they move job to a different business, the pension can move with them.

88

**Inflation** ▶ a general rise in prices. As costs rise to produce products or provide services, these contribute to pushing up prices, creating inflation.

**Motivate** ▶ to encourage, particularly making an employee happy with their work so they perform at their best.

**Incentives** ▶ any kind of reward or benefit to encourage an employee.

**Subsidised** ▶ partly paid for by the business or offered to employees at the price it costs the business to obtain it.

## Gross pay

Gross pay is an employee's total pay before deductions. The monthly gross pay of an employee paid is:

$$\frac{\text{annual salary}}{12}$$

The weekly gross pay of an employee paid on an hourly basis is:

Hours worked $\times$ hourly pay rate $+$ overtime hours $\times$ hourly overtime rate

### Deductions

The two major deductions from gross pay are income tax and National Insurance.

The amount deducted depends on the person's gross pay. The higher the gross pay, the higher the deductions. Deductions may also include pension, donations to charity or trade union subscriptions (monthly payments).

## Net pay

Net pay is the actual amount of money paid to the employee after deductions. The simple formula for calculating net pay is:

Gross pay − deductions

Banks and other financial institutions offer reduced-rate loans and mortgages as a fringe benefit to their employees, while other businesses may offer discounts on the products and services they sell.

Reduced-rate loans and mortgages are seen as a way of locking the employee into the business for the longer term. If they were to leave the business, then they would no longer be eligible for the reduced rates. Unless they found a similar deal elsewhere then, despite finding a better-paid job, they might actually be worse off.

The same can be said for pension schemes, although pensions are technically portable. This means that pension contributions made while working for one organisation can be transferred into a new pension fund with a new employer.

**For example** Net pay

Suppose an employee receives £28,000 per year. The employee is allowed to earn £4,000 tax-free. After that, the employee pays 22% income tax and 15% National Insurance. The way to work out the employee's monthly net pay is:

£28,000 − £4,000 = £24,000

£24,000 − £8,800 = £15,200

$\frac{£19,200}{12}$ = £1,600 per month net pay

£24,000 × 37% = £8,800

£15,200 + £4,000 = £19,200

## QUESTION TIME
### 21 minutes

**Q** PC Limited, a customer contact centre, runs a staff incentive scheme. Initially they ran their bonus scheme based on annual financial targets. Now they have switched to a range of different goals, including revenue targets, break-even targets and personal targets based on each employee's own job role.

The new bonus scheme is designed to give employees a percentage of the available bonus, even if they do not achieve every target in each three-month period.

**1** Explain the term 'incentive scheme'. *(2 marks)*

**2** Explain the term 'bonus scheme'. *(2 marks)*

**3** Give TWO reasons why businesses such as QPC Limited run incentive schemes. *(4 marks)*

**4** When QPC Limited ran the bonus scheme on annual financial targets, why might the financial targets not have been met? *(5 marks)*

**5** In your opinion, was QPC Limited right to introduce a new incentive scheme that was not only based on financial targets? *(8 marks)*

89

# Employment rights and responsibilities

YOU WILL FIND OUT:
- what legislation is
- what employers' legal responsibilities are

## What is legislation?

Most businesses will have policies on how they handle employees, but employees also have specific rights and responsibilities that are enforceable by law. Legislation in this context means laws and regulations that impose minimum standards or requirements on a business in employer/employee relations.

The table on the right summarises the main employment issues and whether or not there are minimum legal requirements.

## What are employers' legal responsibilities?

Regulations and legislation on equal pay, minimum wages, discrimination, employment rights, and health and safety are legal responsibilities of all employers, regardless of their size.

Many of the rules and regulations are Acts of Parliament. These laws have often been created to deal with – or outlaw – particular problems that employees have experienced in the past. Other laws, often referred to as 'regulations' or 'directives', are European Union laws. They apply to British businesses, as all countries that are EU members have to abide by them.

Most businesses have staff policies, which take the legislation into account as minimum standards. Staff policies outline the rights and responsibilities of employers and employees and aim to explain how particular situations will be handled by the business. Different policies will be more or less relevant to different people who work for a business. Some health and safety issues, for example, may relate only

| EMPLOYMENT ISSUE | MINIMUM LEGAL REQUIREMENT | |
| --- | --- | --- |
| | Yes | No |
| • Maternity/paternity/adoption | ✓ | |
| • Leave and absence | ✓ | |
| • Equal opportunities | ✓ | |
| • Working hours and overtime | ✓ | |
| • Health and safety | ✓ | |
| • Pay | ✓ | |
| • Dealing with harassment, victimisation and bullying | ✓ | |
| • Conduct and disciplinary action | ✓ | |
| • Rewards, benefits and expenses | | ✗ |
| • Measures to improve performance or manage change | | ✗ |
| • Use of company facilities, eg email, Internet and phone use | | ✗ |
| • Training | | ✗ |
| • Right of search | | ✗ |
| • Patents and copyrights | | ✗ |
| • Confidential information | | ✗ |
| • Drugs and alcohol | | ✗ |

to people operating machinery or working with computers.

By setting up a policy and making sure that minimum standards are kept, a business reduces the chance that it will break one of the laws. This also helps to make employees more positive and productive, as they know they will not be discriminated against.

A start-up business has to consider:

- **Employment terms and conditions** – these include pay, contracts, working conditions, working hours, holiday pay and entitlements, and handling part-time and temporary workers.
- **Workplace disputes** – a business has to put policies in place to resolve problems. It needs to know what to do if an employee complains or misbehaves.
- **The rights of trade union members** – whether individuals have the right to join – or not to

join – a trade union, and what to do when trade union members take **industrial action**.
- **Handling overseas workers** – whether particular employees need permission to work in Britain, and how to handle references and pre-employment checks on candidates.
- **Families** – businesses need to be aware of pregnancy and maternity or paternity rights, adoption rights, parental leave and flexible working.
- **Redundancy** – a business has to be sure that it has a valid and legal reason for making them redundant. Redundancy occurs when an employee's job no longer exists, when the business decides to reduce the number of employees, or when the business is closing down or moving.
- **Discrimination** – is an important area. It includes discrimination on the grounds of disability, age,

Within two months of starting work for an employer, all employees are entitled to a written contract of employment. It has to include details of pay, working hours, holiday entitlements, sick pay arrangements, notice periods and information on disciplinary and grievance procedures. The contract of employment is an agreement between the employer and the employee. It outlines employer and employee rights and duties.

In effect, a contract of employment is made as soon as an individual accepts a job offer. From that point on, both sides are bound by its terms until it is ended, or until both sides agree to change it.

gender and equal pay. It also covers dealing with bullying at work.

- **Health and safety** – has become an important area, placing legal requirements on employers. There must be health and safety representatives, safety procedures, and methods of dealing with workplace stress, accidents at work and special health and safety hazards. It also includes drug testing and the monitoring of employees for drug or alcohol use.

### KEY TERM

**Industrial action** ▶ this happens when there is a dispute in the workplace that has not been resolved. During industrial action, employees can refuse to work (i.e. can go on strike) or will do only their basic job; trade unions can ban overtime; or an employer can lock their employees out of the workplace.

## QUESTION TIME
*17 minutes*

**A**ccording to the Federation of Small Businesses, only 20% of small businesses in Britain feel confident about employment law. Many are worried about the complicated regulations and all the paperwork. This means that many have put off taking on employees.

As a result, many entrepreneurs decide to work on their own, and the number of small businesses (defined as those with nine or fewer employees) has fallen. This means that with a decreasing number of small businesses taking on employees, some potential jobs are never even created due to the complicated regulations and paperwork involved.

Source: adapted from www.fsb.org.uk

1 **What is meant by the term 'legislation'?** *(2 marks)*

2 **Identify FOUR different employment issues that have minimum legal requirements.** *(4 marks)*

3 **Why might a small business be less confident about applying the different employment rules and regulations than a large business?** *(5 marks)*

4 **Discuss ONE advantage and ONE disadvantage of a small business offering better than minimum standards.** *(6 marks)*

# Equal opportunities

## Equal pay

Pay is a major aspect of a relationship between employers and employees. Setting the right rate of pay is necessary to attract and to retain employees. But pay rewards need to be fair. There are rules and regulations that aim to ensure that this is the case.

### Equal Pay Act 1970

Under this Act, every employment contract includes an 'equality clause', which guarantees both sexes the same money for doing the same or broadly similar work, or work rated as equivalent by a **job evaluation** study.

The clause operates unless an employer can prove that pay variation between the sexes is reasonable and genuinely due to a material difference between their cases.

In 1983, the Equal Pay (Amendment) Regulations came into force. This gives a person a right to claim equal pay for work of 'equal value' to that of a person of the other gender in the same employment, where there is no existing job evaluation scheme, and where there is no person of the opposite sex engaged in 'like work'. The Equal Pay Act 1970 (Amendment) Regulations 2004 made equal value claims even clearer.

In terms of recruitment and selection, it is therefore illegal for an organisation to offer a job at one rate of pay to a person of one gender, and a similar job at a higher rate of pay to a person of the other gender.

## Minimum wages

Most British employees have a legal right to a minimum level of pay, known as the 'National Minimum Wage'. The level is set by the government each year. The minimum pay is regardless of the size or type of business or the work that the employee does.

### National Minimum Wage Act 1998

The minimum wage is a legal right that covers nearly all employees above compulsory school-leaving age. It sets the absolute minimum hourly rates for groups of employees in different age bands.

As of May 2009, the minimum wage for those aged over 22 is £5.73 per hour. For those aged 18 to 21 it is £4.77 per hour. For all workers under the age of 18 who are no longer of compulsory school age it is £3.53 per hour.

In terms of recruitment and selection this means that employers would not be able to advertise vacancies attracting hourly rates of less than the minimum wage.

## Discrimination

Discrimination refers to situations when an employer treats one employee less favourably than others. It is illegal to discriminate on the grounds of:

- gender
- marital status
- pregnancy
- sexual orientation
- disability
- race
- colour
- ethnic background

- nationality
- religion or belief
- age.

Direct discrimination is when one employee is treated differently from others. Indirect discrimination is when the employer has a policy that disadvantages a group of people.

### Sex Discrimination Act 1975 (and later amendments)

In terms of recruitment and selection, an organisation should not:

- appoint on the basis of gender, marital status or sexual orientation
- offer less favourable terms and conditions on the basis of gender.

The law covers a broad range of workers, including contract workers. It applies regardless of length of service in employment or the numbers of hours worked. It allows for employees to take a case to an employment tribunal. If the case is successful, they will receive compensation for any financial loss they have suffered. An award for injury to feelings can also be made.

Where an organisation can prove that specific requirements are necessary in the appointment of an employee, then what is known as 'genuine occupational qualifications' apply. These include:

- **physiology** – for example a male model to model men's clothes
- **privacy and decency** – for example when care assistants of a particular gender deal only with clients of that gender
- **single-sex accommodation** – such as the crew of a submarine.

## Race Relations Act 1976 (and later amendments)

It is unlawful for a person, in relation to employment by him or her at an establishment in Great Britain, to discriminate against another:

- in the arrangements he or she makes for the purpose of determining who should be offered that employment, or
- in the terms on which he or she offers that employment, or
- by refusing or deliberately omitting to offer that employment.

Under this law, 'racial discrimination' means treating a person less favourably than others on racial grounds – which means race, colour, nationality, or ethnic or national origins.

This law protects individuals against people's actions, not their opinions or beliefs.

## Disability Discrimination Act 1995 and 2005

The Disability Discrimination Act applies to all employers during the recruitment and selection process.

Many employers have demonstrated that they have a positive policy towards employing disabled people. Employers that place advertisements in jobcentres and encourage disabled applicants will display a two ticks disability symbol on their advertisements. This means that the organisation has a commitment to employing disabled people and will give them a guaranteed job interview, provided they meet the basic criteria of the person specification.

There are good reasons for an individual to declare their disability. Under the Act, employers are required to make reasonable adjustments to working conditions to enable disabled people to work for them. It is advisable for applicants to state their disability at the earliest possible stage, rather than waiting for a medical questionnaire to be completed.

> Age discrimination is also unlawful in most situations, as is discrimination on the grounds of religion or beliefs.
> The Human Rights Act 2000 has also had an impact. It particularly applies to the public sector and is designed to protect employees' rights to privacy. It also means that employees have the right to see any information that an employer may be holding about them.

### KEY TERM

**Job evaluation** ▶ an independent review of a particular job role to determine exactly what is involved in it in terms of duties and responsibilities.

## QUESTION TIME
### 17 minutes

Businesses now need to be careful about using phrases such as 'highly experienced', 'mature' or 'enthusiastic', because they can be considered discriminatory.

Age discrimination now means that making an employee retire before they are 65 is unlawful. Employees have the right to request to work beyond 65. It is also illegal to discriminate by refusing to employ someone who is over 65 or to refuse to give employees who are close to retirement the same opportunities as younger employees.

1 What is meant by the term 'discrimination'? *(2 marks)*

2 Explain why a business would be breaking the law by paying a female employee more than a male employee for completing similar work. *(3 marks)*

3 Explain why a business would be breaking the law by hiring a male applicant for a job instead of the female applicant who was the better candidate. *(3 marks)*

4 Explain why a business would be breaking the law by employing a non-religious female applicant for a job instead of a religious female applicant who was the better candidate. *(3 marks)*

5 Identify and explain ONE advantage and ONE disadvantage to a business of age discrimination being banned. *(6 marks)*

# What have you learnt?

94

This section aimed to highlight how important people are in helping businesses to achieve their objectives. As a result we looked at recruiting, retaining and rewarding staff and ensuring that the business provides a safe working environment. This is the second of the three sections of Unit 8 and it should show that recruiting, developing and rewarding the right kind of managers and employees can help businesses operate in an efficient way and contribute to being successful.

Firstly we looked at recruitment and selection, focusing on different types of contract, the ways in which a business recruits, and the purpose of job descriptions and person specifications. The second part of the section focused on training, looking at the different methods and the importance of induction training. We also looked at in-house and off-the-

job training methods. It is important to remember that businesses need to identify training needs as soon as possible and to choose the most appropriate way to deliver this.

We then turned our attention to how businesses reward their staff. This does not just mean through wages and salaries, but through offering them training, development, fringe benefits and a host of other incentives. Finally we looked at employment rights and responsibilities. This featured current legislation that affects employment rights and responsibilities and the importance of ensuring that all employees are treated in an equal way.

If you have tried all the Question Times on the spreads you should now be getting used to the speed at which you need to work and the level of detail needed. There are some simple pay calculations

covered in this section, but you will usually be given all of the data you need. Your teacher or tutor will also be able to give you a copy of the Unit Revision Pack from the Tutor Support Pack. It will be useful in identifying all of the areas that you need to revise.

It is important to remember that businesses are only as good as the people they employ. Not only do businesses rely on their employees to interact with their stakeholders, but they also need them to work in an efficient and accurate way at all times.

## Integrated questions from Section 2

Try out these exam-style questions. They bring together the four parts of the human resources section. Remember the mark-a-minute approach, as it will help you to plan your time.

# CALL THE REPAIR MAN AGAIN

**M**ark Tyler, who runs the computer game console and mobile phone repair service has decided to expand the company. He has been offered a contract with a major insurance company that operates in his region. The problem is that the contract will provide far too much work for Mark and his son to manage. He will need to have three new employees, two of whom will have to be permanently based at the insurance company and the third will work with them and at Mark's industrial unit. Mark has never interviewed anyone before. He has no idea about recruitment or training. Mark needs to learn quickly because the contract starts in one month's time.

## QUESTIONS
*28 minutes*

**1** Suggest TWO possible ways in which Mark could attract potential candidates for the new job roles. Explain your suggestions. *(4 marks)*

**2** What steps should Mark take before he even advertises the job roles? *(4 marks)*

**3** How might Mark identify the training needs of his new employees and suggest how he might organise the training? *(6 marks)*

**4** Suggest the most appropriate way in which Mark's new employees should be rewarded. Include both financial and non-financial rewards. *(6 marks)*

**5** Briefly explain Mark's main responsibilities under current legislation as far as employment rights and equal opportunities are concerned. *(8 marks)*

# The purpose of communication

## Acquiring and disseminating information

Effective communication in business is absolutely essential, as is communication within a team of people working together. Managers and other employees have to work hard, sometimes under pressure, but they also have to work accurately and try to make optimal decisions. In order to do this there has to be effective communication.

Day after day information will flow in and out of a business. This all has to be checked, read, understood and communicated to another individual or another department within the business.

There are several advantages, but also some disadvantages to using verbal (spoken) communication as opposed to written communication. These are shown in the table at the top of the page.

The use of written communication, as opposed to verbal communication, is also common in all businesses. The advantages and disadvantages of the written method of communication are given in the table on the right.

| VERBAL COMMUNICATION | |
|---|---|
| **Advantages** | **Disadvantages** |
| • Speed | • May not be easily audible |
| • Low cost | • The person passing on the message has to be clear about what they are saying |
| • The voice can be used to emphasise points | |
| • Immediate feedback can be obtained from the recipient (person being communicated with) | • It is not ideal for long or complicated messages |
| | • The recipient could be distracted by, for example, a telephone ringing or a noisy office |
| • Body language and facial expressions can be used to help explain things | • A conflict of opinion could cause an argument or disagreement |
| | • There is no written confirmation that the conversation has taken place |

| WRITTEN COMMUNICATION | |
|---|---|
| **Advantages** | **Disadvantages** |
| • Written communications are more formal | • Can take a long time to get the communication right |
| • A record of the communication is created (which can be kept and filed) | • Needs to be accurate and error-free |
| • The communication can be re-read and referred to later | • Must not have spelling mistakes and look messy because this gives a bad impression of the business |
| • The communication can be copied for others to read | • Needs to be legible (the receiver must be able to read what the sender has written) |
| • It is ideal for difficult communications as there is a distance between the sender and the receiver | |
| • Can use diagrams and instructions to back up the words | |

## Internal communication

People who work inside the organisation are also customers of the business. They work in order to provide themselves with an income, and, in many cases they rely on the business to provide them with opportunities to gain new skills and to develop and progress in their jobs.

In a smaller business there may only be a few employees or internal customers. Everyone can answer the telephone and take messages for each another. This usually makes communication and the passing on of information very straightforward and there is not too much likelihood that problems will occur.

In a larger business, communication can be more complicated. The organisation may be divided into different departments and these may be situated on different floors, or even in different buildings. Members of one department or section are the internal customers of another department. This means that should one department require information from another, it is just as important that the correct, accurate information is passed on. After all, all the employees are working for the same organisation, even if they are working in different departments.

# External communication

In many organisations, there is a wide variety of different customer types. When we talk about customer types, the following list shows you those we are considering as external customers (in other words, those who do not work inside the organisation):

- individual customers
- groups of customers
- customers from different age groups
- customers from different cultures – this means people from different backgrounds or from different countries
- non-English-speaking customers
- customers with specific needs, for example, those who are sight- or hearing-impaired, those in wheelchairs, or young children
- other businesses, for example suppliers of the business's raw materials.

 There are a number of things to bear in mind regardless of the type of communication used:

- **Clarity** – leave no room for confusion. A reader or listener should not have to stop to figure out what you mean.
- **Conciseness** – a skilled writer will replace key common phrases with much shorter words or descriptions (e.g. 'along the lines of' could be 'such as', and 'for the purpose of' could be 'for').
- **Appropriate language** – you should always use the most appropriate words and back up what you are saying with charts, tables, graphs, icons, illustrations or drawings.
- **Brevity** – state your ideas clearly and briefly. Important ideas should have sub-headings and be the basis of a document.
- **Jargon** – use only words that everyone will understand (if you are writing for readers who will understand jargon then it is acceptable). In many cases, documents may be seen by others who do not understand jargon, so it is best either to avoid it or to provide a glossary of terms if it is absolutely necessary.

## QUESTION TIME
*10 minutes*

**W**hat method of written internal communication do you think the managers of a business would use to inform their employees about the following?

**1** To invite a manager from another branch of the business to join them for lunch after a meeting. *(2 marks)*

**2** To provide the results of some research to all the managers of the business. *(2 marks)*

**3** To inform all employees about a change to the car-parking arrangements. *(2 marks)*

**4** To tell someone they have a pay rise. *(2 marks)*

**5** To tell all employees the details of the forthcoming Christmas party. *(2 marks)*

97

# The importance of communication

**YOU WILL FIND OUT:**

● about communicating in the right way

● about clarity and accuracy

● about image and tone

## Appropriate communication

An important consideration in the way people behave at work is degree of formality. This means appropriate behaviour, particularly when dealing with colleagues or customers. The degree of formality will very much depend on the type of business and the size of the business, as well as the nature of its activities.

### For example

In your local garage, if the receptionist wishes to call one of the mechanics to the telephone, s/he may just call out their first name. The receptionist would probably do this even if there were a customer waiting at the desk.

However, some organisations expect their employees to behave in a much more formal way than this. Occasionally more senior members of staff, possibly the senior management, still expect the junior employees to call them by their title and surname, for example, Mr Saunders, Miss Foster or Mrs/Ms Blythe. This degree of formality may only be required if there is a customer present and, when alone, the employees are likely to still call each other by their first names.

The basic rule to remember regarding formality at work is that a new employee should always call someone by their surname until they are told that it is acceptable to use first names. It will become obvious to the new employee what the degree of formality is within their working environment, as well as how other members of staff are required to be addressed in front of customers.

> An organisation will have particular ways in which it wants it employees to deal with customers and with fellow employees. These are known as procedures and the employees would have to be made aware of these when they first start their job. Sometimes organisations issue booklets to all their employees containing the procedures for dealing with customers. The procedures will be about all aspects of care of the customers.

## Clarity and accuracy

Clarity means communicating in a way in which there is no room for confusion. The person receiving the message needs to be in no doubt about what is meant. This often means choosing the right kind of language, and communicating the message in the simplest possible way.

All information passed on to either a colleague or a customer should be as accurate and as complete as possible. It is not always possible for an employee to give a customer all the information they require, as they may not have that information to hand, or they may not be confident enough to convey it. In such cases it is a good idea to check with another person to ensure the facts are right. The employee, in such cases, should ensure the customer that they will call back with the information, or ask them to wait while they find out the answer to their query.

Some information can be obtained easily, but the more complex the customer's query, the more difficult it may be for the employee to find the correct information immediately, and to be confident that it is correct.

If a customer is asking a specific question there is little point in telling them about other things that they might be interested in, or giving them more information than they really need. It is often a case of deciding what to say and what not to say, what to put in and what to leave out. The more complex the information, the more chance there is that someone will not fully understand it.

It is vital that business information is accurate. This may sound an obvious statement, but one incorrect figure or a decimal point in the wrong place could cause enormous problems, not only for the business itself, but also for the customer. The same would apply to the address on an envelope. It can cause unnecessary delay and inconvenience if a document goes astray in the post because of an inaccurate address. Some businesses design their documents in duplicate or triplicate so that such inaccuracies can be spotted more easily.

All documents and information given by the business should be checked thoroughly before being passed on or sent out. The person completing the documents should do this, although it is not always as easy as it sounds. Sometimes one simply cannot see the mistakes in one's own work and it is more efficient to either get someone else to check it, or to read it to them while they check the figures and data.

## Image and tone

It is important to a business to present a good image to its customers and the general public, and it should be equally important to the employees of that business. The way we dress, the image we give, the way we write to or speak to customers, what we say and how we say it, all contribute to the impression that is given of a business as a whole.

Tone is about the approach you adopt in what you say or write. It involves putting something across in the right kind of way to get the right kind of reaction from the person you are communicating with. This means that you will adopt a different tone in different situations to match the needs of the person you are communicating with, otherwise they may not understand or appreciate what it is you are saying or writing. Different tones of voice will be appropriate in different circumstances, as outlined in the table below:

| TYPE OF PERSON | TONE TO BE USED |
|---|---|
| Person working with you, not senior to you | Friendly, familiar tone, not too formal, can use jargon if you both understand it. |
| Person working with you, senior to you | Friendly, but not too familiar. You may need to be formal, you can use jargon. |
| Customer | Friendly, polite and respectful. The customer may always be right, but sometimes they are not. You must be clear and even forceful, but not rude. |
| Supplier | Friendly, polite, quite formal. Depends on how well you know the supplier. They may expect you to be more formal, but need you to be clear. |

## QUESTION TIME
### 14 minutes

Paula has recently started work in an engineering business. One of her responsibilities involves taking the phone calls and passing on messages to her boss. Over the last three days Paula has made a number of mistakes because she has not been accurate enough. While her boss was at lunch on Tuesday, a visitor called to see him. Paula took the visitor's name, but spelled it incorrectly. The same day her boss gave her a telephone number to dial to speak to a customer. Paula copied it down wrongly and when she dialled the number she got the wrong person. Today Paula's boss has a meeting 100 miles away and he had decided to take the train. Yesterday Paula gave him the train times, but she copied the wrong time for his departure. Paula's boss has just phoned to say that he had to wait an extra hour for the train, and is now late for his meeting.

1 **What are the consequences of the mistakes Paula has been making?** *(6 marks)*

2 **Suggest how her boss might handle the situation.** *(8 marks)*

# The benefits of communication

## Benefits of communication

Regardless of the size of a business, it is vital that it maintains effective communications with any external groups. Some of these groups will be customers; others will be suppliers, government departments, **business partners** and the public at large.

Effective communication is also important within an organisation. There are constant changes in any business, and employees, working with customers or suppliers on a daily basis, need to be kept informed and to know the impact of these changes on what they say and do.

In smaller businesses it is relatively easy for all employees to be kept informed, while larger businesses need to set up systems to make sure that its employees are always up-to-date.

Conmmunication can be a problem for larger businesses that are spread across several buildings or are located in different parts of the country or the world. Regular email updates, newsletters, bulletins or noticeboards can be used to keep employees informed. Team meetings, where information can be passed directly on from managers and supervisors, are invaluable.

If employees feel that they are not being given the information they need, this can lead to their feeling **demotivated**. A lack of information can lead to rumours and gossip, and employees might be feeling insecure and concerned about their jobs.

By ensuring that employees are kept up-to-date, an employer can avoid all this concern. Sometimes it is called 'keeping people in the loop', which means informing them about all major issues and business

decisions. This, in turn, makes them feel more valued and motivated. On the other hand, effective internal communication can lead to well-informed, well-motivated staff who will work in a more efficient manner.

If employees do not have access to information that they need to do their jobs, it will be difficult for them to make decisions and to work in an efficient manner. By keeping employees informed, they will be able to do things in the required way.

Maintaining a good relationship with customers is important for any business. For many businesses the main point of contact with customers is through a customer service department or section, usually via the telephone, email or post.

Businesses will also make sure that they obtain feedback from customers by sending out **questionnaires**. These aim to discover the views and attitudes of customers. The results may show the business how to avoid mistakes and problems in the future.

If an organisation has effective communication with its customers, it should be able to strike up long-term relationships with them. Businesses recognise that loyal customers are the most valuable type of customer. Some businesses extend their effective communications by offering their customers **loyalty cards** and an obliging customer service provision.

If communication becomes confused, information may have to be sent again, which costs money. So it is most effective for a business to get its message through the first time. Sending the message will have been relatively cheap. Any

additional cost to put right ineffective communication will cut into the profits of a business.

If a business can find a cheap and effective way of getting messages to its employees, its suppliers and their customers, they can certainly reap the benefits in terms of profitability.

A business will regularly review the effectiveness of its communications and look to find not necessarily a cheaper method, but a more effective one. It may need to use different communication methods for each group it wishes to communicate with. It may need to change those methods from time to time.

## Effective communication

Effective communication in business is vital within the normal activities of a team. Even organisations not concerned with profit-making activities need to be able to effectively respond to the pressures they find themselves under. This can place enormous strains on the staff. They have to work fast, accurately and try to make well-informed decisions at all times. At the heart of this is effective communication.

Day after day information will flow in and out of the business. This needs to be checked, read, understood and, above all, disseminated to everyone who needs it. Communications can take the form of:

- telephone calls
- email messages
- business letters
- faxes
- reports
- sales documents (invoices, etc).

## KEY TERMS

**Business partners ▶** other organisations that the business may rely on, such as accountants, lawyers and banks, or contacts in foreign countries.

**Demotivated ▶** lacking in enthusiasm for work.

**Questionnaire ▶** a series of questions, designed to allow the business to judge, from answers received, the overall views of customers. Questionnaires can be written or verbal. If verbal, they can be over the telephone or face-to-face.

**Loyalty cards ▶** given to customers by a business. The customer receives points or rewards for the value of each purchase, which can entitle them to discounts and special offers.

---

Businesses will routinely have contact with the government, their bank, insurance companies, customers, suppliers, shareholders and many other groups and individuals. For the business to make the right decisions or take the right course of action, the information needs to be communicated as quickly and accurately as possible. Effective communication extends to every role. Typically, it can be described as:

- being accurate in terms of details
- making sure that the communication is understood
- preparing or presenting information in a way that the receiver understands
- making sure that you choose the most appropriate way of communicating that information (email, fax, letter, telephone call, etc.)
- making sure that the information reaches the right person when they need it.

# QUESTION TIME
## 25 minutes

In many cases, communication is ineffective. Here are some examples of ineffective communication:

1 You arrive back at your desk after lunch to find a scribbled note saying: 'Call Mr Smith Urgently'. You do not recognise the handwriting and there are nine Mr Smiths on the customer database.

2 Last night you were asked to send a fax to a customer, but other work made you forget to do it. You have faxed it this morning, but have just received a call to say that the fax has arrived too late to stop the delivery of an order that you do not need.

3 Two days ago you called a hotel in Blackpool to book a room. They confirmed the booking on the telephone. Today, after the sales representative has already left for Blackpool, the hotel has faxed you with a confirmation of the booking, but the date of the booked room is for tomorrow night, not tonight as required by the sales representative.

4 Last week you were asked to re-order some stationery. Instead of using the supplier's catalogue, you used the code numbers on the side of the stationery boxes. The order has arrived today and they have sent you the wrong stationery.

5 An hour ago a customer called and gave you his telephone number and wanted you to call back with some information. He is a new customer. The telephone line was poor and you have written down the wrong number.

---

**For each situation:**

**1** Identify what went wrong. *(5 marks)*

**2** Suggest what would happen as a result. *(5 marks)*

**3** Suggest what could be done to deal with the situation. *(5 marks)*

**4** Suggest how you would have, ideally, dealt with things. *(10 marks)*

# Communication systems

## Communication systems

A business needs a range of ways in which it can collect, share and pass on information. Communication systems are the ways in which the business achieves this aim. They need to be efficient and effective; they also need to be accurate and reliable. Above all, they need to be suitable for the type of information being processed and for the intended audience of the information.

As we will see, a business has a huge variety of options, some of which will be more useful for some circumstances, and some for others. This will depend on the speed of the communication, the distance between the sender of the information and the receiver, and the complexity of that information.

## Communication policy

Businesses do not always have a definite communication policy. Later in this section we will be looking at different channels of communication and communication types. The tables on the right outline the different types of communication and whether most businesses tend to use them.

| CHANNEL | WHAT IT CAN DO TO IMPROVE COMMUNICATION / DECISION-MAKING |
|---|---|
| **Formal** | |
| Employee suggestion scheme | Vital for improving enterprise performance – the most cost-effective communication tool. |
| Customer satisfaction survey | Vital for improving quality of product/ service offering, and new product/ new service development. |
| Corporate governance | Establishes formal rules for availability of information to a wide range of stakeholders. |
| Business plan | Informs all stakeholders of where the enterprise has been and sets clear goals for the future. |
| Annual report | Can provide clear information about company performance and future direction. |
| Review meetings | Crucial to integrate key staff into operational and strategic developments of enterprise. |
| Planning meetings with key suppliers/ customers | Improves understanding of suppliers/ customer requirements, improves integration with company operations. |
| Document storage for wide availability | Enables all staff to access information and standard operating procedures. |
| Website | This has multiple functions. Serves as online brochure, and can be rapidly updated. Provides e-commerce platform which provides service information for both suppliers and customers. |
| Noticeboard | Provides reference site for regulatory notices; social events; company progress. |
| Newsletter | Provides stakeholders/ potential stakeholders with continuing information. |
| General meetings | Difficult to manage as a communication channel – better to deal in small groups. |
| Employment contract/ code of conduct/job description | Provides employees with clear information of what is expected of them. |
| Employee manual | Provides detailed information on operating procedures in form of collection of SOP material. |
| Disciplinary and grievance code | Provides clear information on how the enterprise will manage employee problems. |
| Customer complaint system | Provides key communication on customer perceptions of company and, when properly handled, can be a positive sales tool. |
| Public relations | Provides company with a low-cost route to maintain contact with market when properly structured and managed. |
| Formal communication – email, letter, telephone, fax | Needs specific policy to ensure that communication is maximised. |
| Promotional expenditure | Part of the communication mix |

102

| CHANNEL | WHAT IT CAN DO TO IMPROVE COMMUNICATION / DECISION-MAKING |
|---|---|
| **Formal/ informal** | |
| Canteen/ coffee room | Enables all staff to meet in environment conducive to discussion. |
| Premises design | Research suggests that involving staff in premises design can create an environment that stimulates communication. |
| Teamwork | Enables staff to develop links within enterprise while completing a specific task. |
| Quality circle | Provides formal platform for informal discussions about company performance. |
| Appraisal | Permits two-way discussions between management and employees. |
| Job design/ rotation | Ideal for improving understanding and links within the organisation. |
| Motivation design | Can link with appraisal in providing individual solutions to job satisfaction – ideal communication channel. |
| Reward design | Bonus systems linked to group performance can certainly influence communication. |
| Induction training | Provides ideal platform for creating informal links within organisation. |
| Maintenance training | Provides means of developing teams |
| Development training | Provides means of developing teams |
| **Informal** | |
| Management by walking about | Very good communication channel providing that management style is appropriate. |
| Face-to-face discussions | Ideal communication channel if management style is appropriate. |
| Social gatherings | Normally poor communication channel |

Some businesses are introducing unified communications systems. These are a suite of voice, data and video products and applications specifically designed to help organisations of all sizes to communicate more effectively. The system allows businesses to integrate their communications system with their IT infrastructure, helping to streamline business processes.

**N**etwork Rail is implementing a new £1.7 billion railway communications system in an effort to provide significant performance and safety improvements to the railway. The Railway Communications System will enable:

- contact between train drivers, signallers and control centres to be quickly established in emergencies
- simultaneous broadcast calls so that all drivers in a certain area can be contacted immediately to be warned of an incident or obstacle
- signallers to have more accurate information on the whereabouts of trains
- significant train performance benefits. The number of incidents relating to signalling faults will be reduced. Passengers will receive more timely and accurate information on train movements, and performance issues will be resolved more quickly.

The system is due to be in place by 2013.

1 **Suggest and explain the main reasons behind this massive investment.** *(8 marks)*

2 **What are the key benefits to customers?** *(6 marks)*

103

# The process of communication

YOU WILL FIND OUT:
- about the communication process
- about senders and receivers
- about the message and the medium

## The communication process

The communication process is an open loop, within which you constantly send and receive messages from others. This is true of any conversation, either face to face or on the telephone. It is also true of written communications such as letters or emails. The communication process can be a closed loop too. This is when information is passed on to someone else, but the sender (transmitter) does not have a way of knowing if the receiver understands it. The receiver has to process it in their minds and then try to understand.

The diagram above right shows the basic communication process. In the diagram it is shown as a one-way system, but in fact it is a complete loop. Just imagine that the semi-circle is a full circle and that in the bottom half of the circle, the receiver becomes the sender and the sender, the receiver. This would show a two-way conversation or exchange of information.

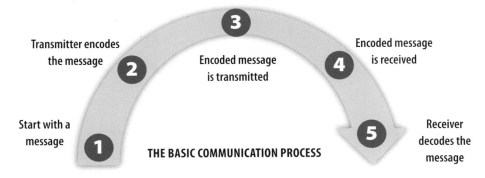

1 Start with a message
2 Transmitter encodes the message
3 Encoded message is transmitted
4 Encoded message is received
5 Receiver decodes the message

THE BASIC COMMUNICATION PROCESS

## Senders and receivers

The sender or transmitter has a major part to play in making sure that the communication process will work. The sender will decide what will be in the message, how it will be sent and its relevance and interest to the receiver. Typically, the sender will consider:

- How they will prepare the message so that the receiver can make sense of the information. It needs to be in the right kind of language for them to understand. This is all about encoding the communication in the right way.

- Whether obstacles exist that might prevent the receiver from properly understanding the communication. This is all about the decoding side of the process. Visual images and graphs can help.
- Decide the best way to ensure that the receiver is engaged by the information. This means that the sender has to choose a way to transmit the information so that the receiver takes notice of it.

The diagram on the left shows the full process. It illustrates the point that the sender's message really needs to prompt the receiver into sending back a message to prove that they have received it, understood it and are acting on it.

In this model the idea comes from the sender, who encodes the idea. The sender then chooses the best medium to send it to the receiver. When it arrives at the receiver, the receiver decodes it and reacts to it by sending feedback to the original sender of the message. The feedback of course has to be encoded, sent through a medium and then decoded when it arrives.

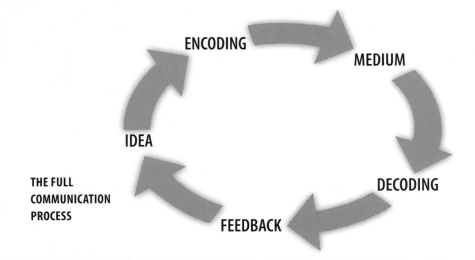

ENCODING → MEDIUM → DECODING → FEEDBACK → IDEA

THE FULL COMMUNICATION PROCESS

**For example** `Wrong communication medium`

Millie has decided to take another job. She asks her boss to come with her to the sandwich bar at lunchtime and in between mouthfuls she springs the news on him. He reacts very negatively, yelling and going red with anger, and then he gets up from the table and storms out of the bar and goes back to work without her. Millie is now sitting in the sandwich bar not knowing what to do. Where has the communication broken down?

This has resulted from a poor selection of medium. Something as personal as this should perhaps not have taken place in a public area, and during another activity (eating lunch). This could have been avoided if Millie had told her boss in a neutral place. The idea generation is not a problem here, it is the timing and the place that has caused the communication breakdown.

## The message and the medium

In the message stage, an individual develops an idea or opinion from which action or communication is needed. The communicator develops the meaning of a message before delivering it. Communication can break down at this stage if the idea generated is incorrect or muddled. Even a well-delivered, properly encoded and decoded message can prove ineffective, if the original idea was poor.

The message now needs to be encoded. At this stage an individual develops the words, images, sounds, or even gestures that will make up the intended message. This stage relies on the sender's careful selection of verbal and non-verbal signs that the receiver must recognise and understand. If the message is encoded poorly, it will be impossible for the receiver to have an accurate meaning. Saying things that come out the wrong way or sending signals (intentional or not), cause conflict and are examples of encoding problems.

During the medium stage, an individual decides the communication setting. Businesses can choose between a number of media, including: face-to-face conversations, telephone calls, memos, letters, computer reports and networks, photographs, bulletin boards, meetings, organisational publications, news releases, press conferences, and many others. Managers can also choose from a number of settings: among colleagues, friends, at home, at a neutral location, in public or private, at special occasions, on regular days, and others too. The timing of communication is closely related to the medium. Sometimes, even with the correct media and setting chosen, communication can still go awry if the communication is poorly timed. If the wrong medium is selected, the receiver risks a communication breakdown.

## QUESTION TIME
*10 minutes*

**J**ohn tells his boss that he cannot imagine staying with one company for any extended period of time if promotional opportunities do not come his way. His boss then fires him on the spot and says: 'There are no promotions available right now.' Later John tells a friend, 'I was only trying to let him know that I was committed to long-term employment and wanted to grow with the company. I had no idea he would fire me!'

**1** Where did the communication break down in this scenario? Explain your reasons. *(10 marks)*

105

The transmission model is not just an over-simplification, but dangerously misleading about the nature of human communication. In the model, the participants are treated as isolated individuals. Communication is nearly always a shared experience. Humans are social beings, and our communication is rarely about individual thoughts and feelings. Even what we call 'our' language isn't our own: we are born into it and we can't change the rules. Words have meanings that we don't choose for them.

# Channels of communication

## Formal and informal communication

Communication is all about sending and receiving messages. In a business situation, sending and receiving messages effectively is crucial to success. A message needs to be sent in the right way, to be accurate, and to be understood when it has arrived. Communications can either be formal or informal. Typical formal communications include:

- business letters
- **invoices**
- contracts of employment
- **reports**.

Typical informal communication methods might include:

- face-to-face communications
- rumours and gossip (also called grapevine communication)
- telephone conversations
- notes left on desks.

There is a place for both types of communication in a business. In the course of a day, employees and managers will have both formal and informal communications. A new employee will be given a formal letter offering the job and a contract of employment, both of which are formal communications; conversations that the new employee has with colleagues on their first day will be informal.

Within an organisation, messages take different routes. Some messages begin at the top of the organisation and are passed through layers of management to employees.

This may be an example of formal communication, as instructions and information are being passed down the business. Day-to-day communication between an employee and their manager, or an employee and their colleagues, will tend to be informal.

The type of communication method also depends on the receiver of the message. A conversation with a colleague might be informal, while a conversation with a customer will always be formal. In the second case, an employee is representing the business and must give the impression of being efficient and professional.

Most informal communications tend to be verbal. This means that telephone conversations or face-to-face conversations need not be as formal as written communications. Informal communications also make the assumption that the person you are communicating with understands as much as you do. You

do not have to explain the basics to them. Informal communications tend to be quick and efficient. They can pass on information in an effective manner.

Formal communications tend to use standardised and generally accepted methods of communication. There are formats and templates for all types of formal, written communications.

### KEY TERMS

**Invoices** ▶ written statements requesting payment for products or services supplied by a business to a customer.

**Reports** ▶ detailed written investigations into a subject or situation, suggesting solutions or recommendations to solving problems.

**Memoranda** ▶ internal communications that look either like a note or a shortened version of a letter. They are used only for internal communications.

| SITUATION | FORMAL | INFORMAL | EXPLANATION |
|---|---|---|---|
| Telephone contacts | Yes | Yes | Formal if dealing with individuals outside the organisation or with more senior employees. |
| Meetings | Yes | No | Meetings have set formal procedures. |
| Technical enquiries | Yes | No | There is a need to be clear and specific. |
| Supervisors | Yes | Yes | Depends on situation. |
| Colleagues | No | Yes | Usually informal, but professional. |
| Customers | Yes | No | Usually formal, as they expect a professional attitude. |
| Complaints | Yes | No | Specific procedures would need to be followed. |
| Presentations | Yes | No | Professional and formal approach is required. |
| Confidentiality | Yes | No | A professional approach is expected. |

| COMMUNICATION TYPE | INTERNAL | EXTERNAL |
|---|---|---|
| Letter | | Yes |
| Report | Yes | Sometimes |
| Memorandum | Yes | |
| Telephone | Yes | Yes |
| Face-to-face | Yes | Yes |
| Teleconferencing | Yes | Yes |
| Videoconferencing | Yes | Sometimes |
| Financial documents | Yes | Only if not confidential to the business |
| Advertisements | Sometimes | Yes |
| Email messages | Yes | Yes |
| Drawings, graphs, charts | Yes | Yes |

## Internal and external communication

As we look at the different types of oral, visual, written and pictorial communications, we will see that some of them are more appropriate for internal communication and others are mainly used for external communications. The table above summarises their use.

## Confidential and non-confidential communication

Confidential information is also known as sensitive information. As we already know, any employee who has to deal with confidential information will ensure that only authorised staff are able to see it.

Much confidential information is kept on computer. Customer records, for example, would be held on computer by many businesses and they would not want to let their competitors know any of their customer details. Another reason for confidentiality of customer information is the Data Protection Act 1998. This is the legislation (law) governing how organisations keep information about customers on computer.

If sensitive information is kept on computer, businesses can make sure

it remains confidential in a number of ways, including:

- Ensuring its employees have to use a password to use the system.
- Ensuring their employees have screen-savers so that they do not leave confidential material on their computers when they are away from their desks.
- Ensuring that computers are not situated in public areas of the business, for example the reception area, where the general public can see the screen.

## Urgent and non-urgent communication

Businesses will deal with tasks and communications that have different priorities. Broadly, they can be broken down into four different categories:

- urgent and important
- urgent but not important
- important but not urgent
- neither urgent nor important.

If the message is short and urgent, then it is likely that it will be dealt with either through a telephone call or a face-to-face meeting. It could also be sent as an email. If the message is less urgent and more complicated then it is likely to be sent as a letter, put together as a report, or printed and then distributed by the business.

## QUESTION TIME
*22 minutes*

**1** Suggest and explain a business communication that might fall into each of the FOUR categories of urgent/non-urgent and important/not important. *(8 marks)*

**2** Why is it essential that a business maintains confidentiality of information relating to its customers? *(6 marks)*

**3** Identify and explain FOUR different types of communication, formal and informal, that an employee is likely to deal with in a normal working day. *(8 marks)*

# Methods of communication

## Oral communication

It is obvious to say that oral or verbal communications involve some form of speech. This can be a live message, such as in a conversation, or a verbal message left on voicemail or an answer phone.

Verbal communications are used every minute of the working day by businesses around the world. The common business language of the world is English.

There is a wide variety of different situations that can involve verbal communications. These include:

- any type of discussion carried out within a business
- conversations between employees during lunch-breaks or at other times
- formal and informal meetings
- conversations with customers
- giving instructions or orders to others
- receiving instructions and asking questions to make sure you understand
- attending an interview or appraisal
- listening to or giving presentations to colleagues or customers
- telephone conversations
- teleconferencing or videoconferencing, which allows individuals in different locations to have a conversation with sound and pictures.

Most verbal communications that take place in the working environment will be face-to-face and informal. The major advantage of face-to-face verbal communication

is that the individuals having the conversation can see one another and read one another's body language. We already know that this is called non-verbal communication, and that both the speaker and the listener can read much into this body language.

You can, of course, have verbal communication with someone who is not standing in front of you. This will involve having to explain everything very literally, as the listener cannot see hand gestures or eye movements. Visual images or documents cannot be as easily shared in these circumstances. It is also hard to get feedback from someone if you are talking to them at some distance. It is difficult to know whether or not they have understood, or agreed, or have even taken note of what has been said.

An employee will be expected to carry out verbal communication in many different ways, according to the type of person they are talking to. Sometimes the communication will need to be formal, while at other times it can be informal, as it would simply be a part of a general conversation.

## Visual communication

Visual communication can add enormously to any type of communication, whether it is in face-to-face situations between people, or whether it is the use of visual images in documents. Visual communication helps to reinforce what is being said, and in face-to-face situations it allows those involved to judge from facial expressions whether they have been understood and to have an opportunity to reply.

As we will see, visual communication is distinct from graphical communication and in this sense we are focusing on videoconferencing and electronic noticeboards. As we will discover, videoconferencing brings together the convenience of being able to carry out a conversation with two or more people at long distances, rather like teleconferencing. However it has the additional benefit of those people being able to see each another. This makes it a far more realistic and useful form of communication system.

Electronic noticeboards on the other hand, are primarily text-based,

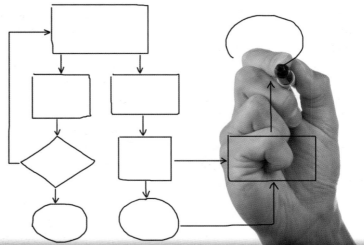

108

The best communication method will always aim to use the most appropriate human senses. The spoken word, whether it is in a conversation or an advertisement, will tend to use hearing and sight. A face-to-face communication will incorporate hearing, sight and body language. This is known as non-verbal communication. It involves interpretation of all the gestures and facial expressions of an individual and even how they are standing, as well as whether they are looking at the person they are talking to. Many people believe that non-verbal communication tells us much about the person and the message and whether they are being truthful and helpful or just trying to be persuasive.

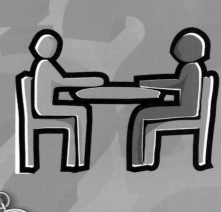

although they may have images. They can be used both internally and externally by businesses. A business may choose to have an electronic noticeboard system on their computer network, which will allow discussions to take place, ideas to be shared and suggestions to be made by a variety of employees.

Public noticeboards allow a far broader number of people to become involved in the discussions and to put in their ideas and points of view. In effect this allows an individual to read through a conversation and then pick up that discussion and add to it themselves.

## Written communication

Businesses routinely use all types of written communication. Internally they may use memoranda, emails, reports and various financial documents, such as invoices, statements of account or delivery notes. Many of the more complex financial documents are now created using software packages, such as Microsoft Excel.

External communications that fall into the written category would include letters, advertisements and email messages to customers or suppliers. Generally, businesses will have a standardised format in which they prefer all their written communications to be laid out. This will include having the business's

name and contact details and, perhaps, a business logo or slogan. Many will also have a standardised statement, particularly at the end of emails, which says that the message is only intended for the named receiver and that the content of the email, no matter what its subject, should be considered to be confidential.

## Pictorial communication

As far as pictorial communications are concerned, this would include graphs, charts and drawings. All of these can be used either on their own as ways in which information can be put across, or to reinforce written or oral communication. It is often far easier to understand information if it is presented in a pictorial way. It is easier to compare sets of figures if they are in a chart or table or on a graph. As far as new products are concerned, or designs, it is easier to visualise what is intended if a production drawing is made, rather than it being described in words.

Businesses will routinely use pictorial images so that employees, customers, suppliers and other groups can instantly recognise their logo or design. They do not even need to put the business name if they are a well-known organisation. This is useful shorthand and can again be used as an addition to standard written information.

## QUESTION TIME
*16 minutes*

**1** A business wants to test out potential customers' reactions to a new brand of chocolate. Suggest how it might do this and make use of as many of the five senses as possible to get an honest reaction. Explain your answer. *(10 marks)*

**2** Only face-to-face communication allows the sender of a message to be sure that the receiver of the message has understood. To what extent do you agree with this statement? Explain your answer. *(6 marks)*

109

# Communication media (1)

## Telephone communications

The simple telephone has come a long way over the last decade or so. Circular dials have given way to touch pads to call numbers, and it is no longer necessary to trail a long wire behind you when you walk around with the telephone. Many modern telephones are now digital, some are 'hands free' and the quality of the sound has greatly improved.

Traditional telephones are often used by businesses, but linked as an extension to a central switchboard. Switchboards have improved to the extent that it is no longer necessary to talk to an operator in order to be put through to an extension number. A voice prompt can ask the caller to tap in the extension number if it is known.

Most telephones now have the following features:

- a visual display of either the number dialled or the incoming number
- a redial button
- a secrecy button (so that when you leave the telephone to speak to somebody in the room, this conversation cannot be heard by the caller)
- a timer, indicating the length and cost of the call

- memory buttons for frequently dialled numbers
- the day, date and time
- the ability to transfer calls to other extensions
- a hands-free option, so that the caller's voice is fed through a speaker in the phone, allowing everyone in a room to hear the conversation.

**Voicemail** is a system for managing telephone messages. In effect it is rather like an answering machine, but instead it uses a centralised system. This allows it to be more sophisticated. So the voicemail system can:

- answer a number of calls at the same time
- store messages in personalised message boxes, linked to an employee's extension number
- forward messages from one mailbox to another
- play personalised messages of each extension number user.

Messages are recorded digitally and stored on hard disc drives. It is fully automated if the business is closed.

Mobile phones have voicemail as a standard feature. There were several reasons why voicemail became possible for any business. These were:

- faster processors
- inexpensive disc drives
- cheaper semi-conductor chips.

The first attempts to create voicemail in the 1970s did not work, as the systems were overwhelmed by the calls. But new digital phone sets and better private branch exchanges have made voicemail a reality.

## Face-to-face communications

As we have seen, face-to-face communications take place all the time in businesses, both between employees themselves and with employees communicating with customers or other people external to the business. Discussions tend to be informal rather than formal, but they are an important part of face-to-face verbal communications in the working environment. Discussions routinely take place, passing on information, and sharing ideas and instructions. They also form a vital part of updating colleagues on situations, calls made by customers or suppliers, or feeding back on meetings that have been attended.

Discussions, by their very nature, tend to involve a dialogue, in which the parties involved exchange ideas and points of view. Discussions take place in many different situations in the workplace and also with any number of participants.

Situations in which workplace discussions might take place include:

- at the beginning of the day to discuss the work ahead
- before a meeting to talk about the **agenda**
- after a meeting to talk about decisions that have been made
- before a customer is contacted
- after a customer has been contacted
- social discussions during break times
- discussions about how the day went at the end of the working day
- informal discussions when colleagues meet in a corridor.

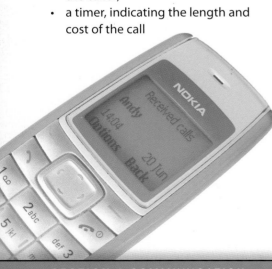

110

Meetings can involve more formal types of discussion. Both verbal and written information is used in meetings. The purpose of a meeting is to provide a forum that will promote discussion, and for those attending to make joint decisions.

The most formal meetings will have an agenda, detailing the topics to be discussed.

Individuals are invited to attend a meeting either because the topics being discussed affect them, or because they have knowledge and expertise that could prove useful in the meeting.

Informal meetings can take place when a group of employees gather together to discuss problems and seek solutions. Regardless of the type of meeting, the purpose is to use the collective skills, strengths and expertise of employees to bring ideas together.

## Teleconferencing communications

This is another way in which conversations can take place live without the participants being in the same room. **Teleconferencing** allows several people in remote locations to have a telephone conversation at the same time. Teleconferencing is more common than **videoconferencing**, but in some ways less effective, as everything relies on the voice, and no clues or additional information can be passed on by body language. It is also not possible to share documents, images or other visual material through teleconferencing in the way that videoconferencing allows.

---

### KEY TERMS

**Voicemail** ▶ a digital system on many modern switchboards that allows a personal message to be left on a telephone extension.

**Agenda** ▶ a document issued before a meeting that lists the topics to be discussed.

**Teleconferencing** ▶ a telephone system that allows several people, on different telephone lines, to have a discussion or conversation by linking them together so each can be heard.

**Videoconferencing** ▶ involves either digital web cams on top of computers, or video cameras being linked up so that sound and vision is transmitted to each location, allowing the people at each end to see and hear one another during a conversation.

---

**1** Why is voicemail affordable as a feature for business telephones and mobile phones? **(6 marks)**

**2** Identify THREE features of a modern telephone and explain the purpose of those features and the benefits to a business. *(9 marks)*

**111**

# Communication media (2)

**YOU WILL FIND OUT:**

- about memoranda and letters
- about financial documents
- about advertisements
- about email messages

## Memoranda

An inter-office memorandum can be used to communicate between different departments. Memoranda are usually referred to as memos and are shorter than letters. They tend to deal with one particular subject, but when more than one point is being made it is normal to number the points. Memos are not signed, but they are often initialled at the end by the sender.

A memo should be structured to provide any background information, followed by the main text in one or more paragraphs. Despite being more informal than business letters, memos should always be checked for accuracy, and should include appropriate information only.

Advantages of memos include:

- pre-printed headings remove the need to write out the same thing several times
- can be handwritten or typed
- pre-printed headings can be saved on computer as a template
- can be used as reminders
- can be used as a notice to a large number of members of the business
- can be sent to a number of different individuals.

Disadvantages include:

- they are paper-based and often have to be filed
- they are more formal than handwritten notes, and often require the recipient to act on them.

## Letters

Business letters may be written for a number of different purposes:

- to contact potential customers – people who are either buying or may buy the organisation's products or services
- to communicate with suppliers – other businesses that may provide items such as products, photocopy paper or office equipment to the organisation
- to answer a customer complaint
- to tell existing customers about a new product
- to contact job applicants.

Business letters need to be neat, accurate and well-presented in order to give a good impression of the business's professionalism. Businesses tend to use headed paper, so the same details do not have to be re-typed every time a letter is sent.

Business letters can be:

- personalised
- a standard format
- used to deal with a single issue
- professional if correctly formatted
- used as a simple covering letter when sending other information.

But there are disadvantages too:

- they can be rather formal
- they may not convince the reader to respond
- they can take too much time if a separate letter has to be written each time
- they may be delayed in the post
- poorly presented letters can give a bad impression.

## Financial documents

Recording business transactions is an essential operational and legal function of a business. The financial documents are used to provide proof of transactions, detailing precisely what was involved in the transaction. It is essential for the information to be kept up-to-date and for it to be accessible for the following reasons:

- the planning and control of the business's activities
- in order to keep shareholders informed of the business's performance
- to ensure creditors are aware of the performance of the business
- to ensure that legal requirements are met
- to show prospective investors, who may wish to become involved in the organisation, the current status of the business.

Eventually all of the business's transactions will be used to create a series of ledgers and then a set of accounts, which will be a summary of all the business's transactions. All businesses will set themselves a budget. Whether the business is large or small it will have a set of objectives that it will wish to meet. It would be impossible for the management to monitor the performance of the business if documents relating to the amount of money spent and the amount of money coming into the organisation were not readily available and accurate. Obviously the larger the organisation, the more documentation it will generate.

112

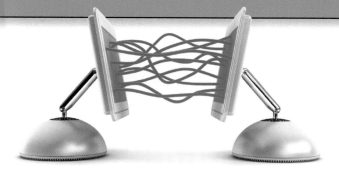

## Advertisements

Leaflets and advertisements should be simple and draw the reader's eye to the most important information. While leaflets can have more information, they should not overload the reader with unnecessary detail. Leaflets need to look eye-catching, and should provide a summary of what is being presented. Advertisements work best with few words, and thought needs to be given to what needs to be said and how it is said. Advertisements also benefit from the use of illustrations and different kinds and sizes of font.

## Email messages

Email, or electronic mail, enables people to send text messages, pictures and files via the Internet. Both the sender and the receiver need to have email software, such as Microsoft's Outlook Express. Most email software packages allow you to write, send, receive, store and manage emails. The sender and the receiver need to have an email address. Many email addresses are available free through websites such as Yahoo.

Emails can be sent to several different people at the same time. It is a fast and convenient way of getting into contact with people as the messages can be sent and received almost instantly, unlike normal posted mail which can take several days to arrive at its destination. Email allows businesses to send messages and receive messages from other businesses, or individuals, from anywhere in the world.

Email, or electronic mail, allows businesses and individuals to communicate with one another without having to use a telephone, or having to write, print and post a formal business letter. Because emails can be sent at any time of the day or night, and on any day of the week, messages can be sent and received without worrying about whether the post will be collected or delivered.

Email is not only ideal for sending simple messages, but can also be used to send complex communications and various other documents as attachments. They can be easily printed and stored.

There are many advantages of emails, including:

- they can can be sent instantly
- they save on telephone, stationery and postal costs
- they can be sent or received anywhere
- sent and received messages are stored in the email system for later reference
- email addresses can be stored and accessed without having to retype each time
- hard copies can be printed out if needed for records.

The disadvantages of email are that:

- there is usually no way of knowing whether the email has been opened by the recipient
- users need Internet access and an email account
- a computer failure could lead to the loss of email records.

## QUESTION TIME
*14 minutes*

1   A memorandum is a far better way of communicating within an organisation than an email. To what extent to do you agree with this? *(8 marks)*

2   Suggest TWO reasons why a business would send a letter to one of its employees and suggest another communication method that could have been used instead. *(6 marks)*

113

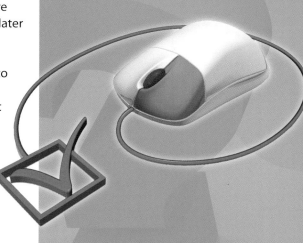

# Communication media (3)

## Videoconferencing

Videoconferencing allows two or more remote locations to connect and interact with one another. This is achieved via video and audio transmissions.

There are two basic types of videoconferencing, in terms of the systems used:

- A dedicated system with a high-quality, remote control video camera. This is connected via a computer to microphones, a TV monitor and loudspeakers. Some of these are portable, but others have to be set up permanently in a room used for videoconferencing.
- The smaller version is a desktop system, with a camera fitted to the top of the monitor and a microphone for speech.

All videoconferencing facilities use:

- a video camera or web cam for video input
- a television, computer monitor or projector for video output
- microphones for audio input
- loudspeakers or headsets for audio output.

When three or more remote locations are being used, the system needs a multipoint control unit. This connects the calls from the different sources.

There are some problems with using videoconferencing facilities, including:

- People involved in the videoconferencing are aware of the fact that they are being filmed and possibly recorded. This can

have an impact on their ability to cope with the situation.
- Eye contact is not possible, as those involved are simply responding to an image on a screen, rather than a real human being. Sometimes it appears that people are avoiding eye contact in this situation.

Videoconferencing can allow meetings to take place at very short notice. It also means that employees and managers do not have to spend time or the business's money on travel. It is possible to carry out face-to-face business meetings using this system without leaving the office. It is also a very useful tool in telecommuting, allowing employees to work from home.

114

# Electronic bulletin boards

Electronic bulletin boards are online communication systems. They are often called message boards or forums. They allow people to share, discuss or request information. They are different from emails, as the bulletin boards are public, or at least open to everyone who has access to that bulletin board. Messages can be posted on the bulletin boards, and anyone with access to them can read a message and respond to it.

Some bulletin boards are public, while others are private. The public ones are also referred to as news groups. The bulletin boards operate in a simple way; someone will start a discussion on a particular topic and then wait for replies. Each different discussion is known as a thread. In effect it is a conversation with individuals responding to the original question or discussion topic and then responding to replies. Bulletin boards can be very useful as they are highly accessible, and information can come from a wide range of sources.

Public bulletin boards can cause problems because people can access them and not actually answer the question or contribute to the discussion. Many of the public bulletin boards do not archive or save every thread or individual post and can disappear over time.

As far as businesses are concerned, they can be used to discuss the market, recruit workers, obtain technical support and share information. Bulletin boards can also cause businesses problems, as negative messages may be posted about their organisation. There is even special software that businesses can use to alert a business if a negative comment is made about them on a bulletin board. They can then request that it is removed if it is untrue and also identify who posted that message.

## QUESTION TIME
*12 minutes*

**1** How might a business make effective use of bulletin boards? *(6 marks)*

**2** How might a business working with international partners be able to use videoconferencing? *(6 marks)*

115

# Drawings, graphs and charts

Graphical communication is communication that uses maps, diagrams, sketches and symbols to record situations or information. You will recall when we looked at the communication process we saw that messages are encoded by the sender and transmitted through a medium to the receiver who must then decode the message. Using drawings, graphs or charts, this means:

- Decoding of signals can be compared with those stored in the mind from past experiences.
- A combination of mind and eye is used.
- Messages must be presented in a manner that will allow recognition and avoid misunderstanding.

There are several different ways to combine graphical images with words, as shown in the table below.

| GRAPHICAL TYPE | EXPLANATION AND EXAMPLES |
|---|---|
| Alphanumeric | The design of text, the layout of reports and other text documentation, the design of screen fonts, the design of data-entry forms and menus and road signs, warnings and information signs and labels. |
| Pictogrammic | Very useful way of communicating messages as it does not rely on language. It includes symbols, signs, icons, graphical user interfaces, map legends. It is also used on controls in a car, road signs, disabled parking spaces and corporate logos. |
| Diagrammatic | Useful in making sense of complex numerical material by showing patterns. Used in graphs, bar charts, pie charts and 3-D plots. |

# Communication barriers

## Potential communication problems

A communication barrier is where there is a problem between the sender and the receiver of information. In other words, a block of some sort exists which stops a message getting through or stops it getting through in the intended way. Some common barriers to communication are:

- *Lack of training* – if employees are not trained to use the different ways of communicating then they may either make mistakes or not be able to use that form of communication at all. Training in the use of equipment, and the ways in which communications should be written or spoken, are essential. These forms of training and ways of doing things will often be part of organisational procedures.
- *Lack of information* – one of the most common barriers to effective communication is a lack of information. If, for example, a customer calls a business to ask for the price and availability of a product and is told that it is out of stock, a sale will be lost. If the employee who takes the call knows that the warehouse has just received a delivery of that product, then the sale can be made.
- *Personal relationships* – one of the most common reasons why communications are ineffective within an organisation is that individuals either do not like one another or do not understand one another. Personal likes or dislikes may mean that employees will avoid each other, even if this means that information is not passed on between them and there is a

detrimental effect on both their own work and the business itself. This is a very difficult barrier to deal with but may be solved either by getting to the root of the problem between the two individuals, or by changing the job role of one so that the two are not in direct contact so often. Another way a business can help with this kind of situation is to give team-building training.

- *Faulty systems* – there can be a problem with organisational procedures, leading to something being forgotten, which causes a barrier. Perhaps one part of the process of dealing with an order has not been considered and this causes a blockage and the customer fails to receive the product or service.

Barriers to good communication with customers might include:

- writing something down incorrectly
- failing to hear a customer's request correctly
- losing important notes or documents
- not telling the right person about a problem
- having too many other things to do
- not realising the importance of a query.

## Other potential barriers

There are many other potential barriers, including:

- Muddled messages, where the sender leaves the receiver unclear about the message. This may be because the sender is confused in their thinking.
- Stereotyping – which may mean assuming that everybody has the same level of understanding and that they will all react in the same way to the same message. Everyone is slightly different and if the message is not ideal for them there is no guarantee that they will understand.
- Wrong channel – giving complicated messages to someone using oral communication is not a good idea; it should be written down or at least explained verbally and then backed up with a written communication.
- Language or jargon – there is no guarantee that the receiver will understand either complicated language or specialist words (jargon). This does not just mean being careful with communication if the receiver's first language is not English.

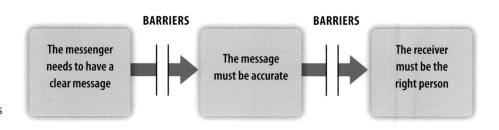

116

- Lack of feedback – without feedback from the receiver, communication is one-way. Not receiving feedback might mean that the receiver has not understood. Communication should be active and feedback makes it two-way.
- Poor listening skills – a typical speaker can say about 125 words a minute and a typical listener can receive between 400 to 600 words a minute. This leaves a lot of free time for the listener to be side-tracked. Prompting feedback by asking questions can help ensure that the receiver is still listening.
- Noise, interruptions and distractions – in businesses few days are routine and sometimes they are very hectic. Communications are often interrupted or something else is happening that distracts one of the people involved in the communication. There is likely to be other communication going on at the same time, which means that those who are communicating may not be focusing just on that conversation.

To be a good communicator an individual has to have a positive attitude and to want to work at improving their skills. Communication is a creative process that involves trying to find the best way to get messages across. Good communicators will vary their channels and their techniques, and will try to avoid miscommunication.

## QUESTION TIME
### 20 minutes

It had been a long and hard week for Hamish and it was only half an hour before he could leave and forget work for the weekend. Hamish was sorting out his desk when he looked up and saw Miss Brandish. His heart sank. Miss Brandish was a regular customer, but always arrived unannounced and took up hours of staff time. Hamish decided to ignore her, but Miss Brandish spotted him and walked straight up to his desk.

'Young man, I require some bonded envelopes, some sticky labels and some blue paperclips. I'm organising Long Norton's dog show and I will need to take these away with me today.'

Hamish grunted and reached for the customer order pad, scribbled down Miss Brandish's requirements, tore the top sheet off and thrust the piece of paper towards her without looking at her. Still without looking at her he said:

'You know where to go.'

'Well!' she replied, turning on her heel and heading off towards the warehouse.

'They can deal with her at this time of the day,' Hamish thought to himself.

Twenty minutes later, as Hamish was putting on his coat, an irate warehouse manager, being nagged by Miss Brandish, appeared. Hamish did not leave the office until quarter to six.

1 How should Hamish have greeted Miss Brandish? *(2 marks)*

2 What was wrong with Hamish's body language and attitude towards her? *(4 marks)*

3 How might simple questioning have speeded things up? *(4 marks)*

4 What impression did Hamish give Miss Brandish of his attitude and her value as a customer? *(4 marks)*

5 What might the warehouse manager say about Hamish's attitude? *(6 marks)*

# The importance of ICT in communications

YOU WILL FIND OUT:

- what ICT is
- about the benefits of ICT
- about the barriers to the use of ICT
- about ICT across the sectors

## What is ICT?

Information and communication technology is the use of computers and the Internet as a day-to-day part of a business's operations. Smaller businesses are often slower than larger ones to adopt new technology. Some smaller businesses do not see a great deal of use for ICT and only use its basic functions, such as using the Internet to check emails or computers to generate business letters.

As we will see, the use of ICT is widespread, but its importance depends on the type of business a company is involved in and also whether or not it is able to afford or access the technology.

## The benefits of ICT

With any business decision the advantages must always outweigh any investment or maintenance costs. In other words it must bring the business greater efficiency, more customers, a bigger turnover or higher profits. Larger businesses often see these benefits very quickly because they are involved in e-commerce or communications throughout the world. Smaller businesses may tend to stay with more traditional business processes and perhaps not have a website.

Most businesses, however, regardless of their size or the nature of their operations, will have at least one computer. Communication via email and the Internet helps to improve external communications; it can reduce transaction costs and speed up the transaction.

As far as computers themselves are concerned, they can make communication much faster and more efficient. Managers and employees can share electronic files through networks; data can be processed in a much more efficient way with standardised documents and purchase orders and invoices can be organised much more easily. All businesses have relationships with other organisations and once again ICT can make that coordination much more efficient.

Even a simple website can provide information on products and services and can attract new customers. All that is required is a link to an email account.

The use of ICT certainly improves a business's performance. There are of course risks and costs, but increasingly businesses simply cannot afford not to use ICT.

## Barriers to the use of ICT

Some businesses may not use the Internet because they consider their products or services not to be suitable for e-commerce. Prime examples are construction and small retailers. They simply cannot justify the expense and also traditionally their customers have come from backgrounds where they were used to either face-to-face communication or telephone and fax.

Other businesses fail to use ICT because they do not have the necessary skills and knowledge to know what to buy and how it can be used. This is improving because the government in particular is keen to encourage the use of ICT and provides free or low-cost advice through organisations such as Business Link.

Some businesses are also concerned about how much it costs to develop and maintain a system. Many smaller businesses will routinely use computers for day-to-day operations and may have a straightforward website, but they will not have seen the potential benefits of e-commerce.

There are still many areas in Britain that have relatively poor Internet connection. Broadband services are being rolled out gradually across the whole of the country, but even when this has been completed there will still be isolated pockets where Broadband will not be available. This is an even greater problem in developing countries. Added to this are access costs. Businesses, like private users, have to pay a service provider in order to have Internet access. In Britain, prices are very competitive, but in other countries where there are few providers, the prices can be relatively high.

Finally there is also the question of trust and security. If buyers do not know the name of the business and do not recognise a particular brand, they may be reluctant to do business with the company online. There is always the worry that financial data will fall into the wrong hands and that viruses could be picked up or hackers could compromise the computer system.

118

# ICT across the sectors

The use of ICT and e-commerce varies widely across the different sectors. In the following table we look at three different examples of sectors and see how they have adapted to the use of ICT and e-commerce:

| SECTOR | USE OF ICT |
|---|---|
| Tourism | Although tourism is dominated by some very large businesses, many travel and tourism services are still provided by relatively small operations. In the past, customers made their tourism purchases primarily through travel agents. Smaller businesses can now make the most of ICT by making direct sales and can specialise in particular types of tourism product. Websites are ideal because customers want plenty of information. They can view movies of the resort, read reviews by past customers and make reservations and payments. In the office, the business's ICT allows customer databases to be built up and instant access to airline companies and other travel providers, so that bookings can be made on behalf of customers. |
| Retail | ICT has allowed a large number of very small businesses to provide specialist products and services that are not normally supplied by the larger stores. They have specialised and provide services that are difficult to obtain elsewhere. The smaller businesses are able to give a higher level of service and a swift and reliable delivery. Examples include online book sales and clothing. |
| Vehicles | The biggest impact on the making of vehicles has been the development of electronic data interchange. This gives the businesses instant real-time connection with their suppliers so that they can share information about stock levels. As orders come in, the suppliers know that they need to deliver a certain number of components. ICT has also provided huge improvements to vehicle service booking, customer databases and communication between car dealers and manufacturers. It has also allowed the manufacturers to run advertisements, directing potential customers to their websites, where they can then search for their nearest dealership. |

The adoption and use of the Internet depends on the characteristics of the sector. The tourism industry sells intangible services, and customers want high information content, so they are ideal for the Internet. Vehicles, however, are far less likely to be sold over the Internet, but the ICT advantages come in along the supply chain, where improved communication and collaboration make for greater efficiencies.

## QUESTION TIME
*14 minutes*

1  A small shop buys and sells hand-printed designer T-shirts. Advise the business of the benefits of ICT, particularly e-commerce. *(8 marks)*

2  Why might a small business on a remote Scottish island have difficulty in obtaining any major benefits from ICT? *(6 marks)*

119

# Uses of applications software (1)

YOU WILL FIND OUT:

● about applications software
● about word-processing software
● about presentations software
● about database software

## Applications software

Gradually, over the years, Microsoft has come to dominate the applications software market. As the majority of computers are supplied with ready-installed **Windows** and **Internet Explorer**, most businesses and home users have opted for variations of the Microsoft Office suite of applications software.

Many computers are also supplied with a cut-down version of Microsoft Word, called Microsoft Works. This serves as a useful introduction to the more extensive Microsoft Word.

The Microsoft Office suite has become the industry standard. Most businesses will use it for their application software needs. As more businesses opt for it, it has become a case of whether other systems are compatible with Microsoft's applications.

The Microsoft Office suite includes:

- Microsoft Word (word processing, **mail merge** and graphics)
- Microsoft PowerPoint (presentation software and slides)
- Microsoft Excel (spreadsheets and calculations)
- Microsoft Access (databases)
- Microsoft Outlook (email system more sophisticated than the basic Outlook Express).

## Word-processing software

Microsoft Word can be used for a variety of word-processing tasks beyond simply typing a document. It can be purchased on its own or as part of the Microsoft Office suite of applications. A computer is obviously needed to run the software; a keyboard and mouse are used for the input devices; a printer is the output device.

### Key advantages

The main advantages of word-processing software are:

- Text can be stored and edited at a later date
- Documents can be stored and printed when needed
- Mistakes can be edited (they are highlighted as either spelling or grammar mistakes) so retyping the document is not necessary
- Documents that are well laid-out are professional-looking
- Any mistakes can be picked up (including changing the layout) before printing
- Documents can be attached to emails
- The system is easy to use.

### Spelling and grammar

Word has an integrated dictionary. It is important to make sure that the spelling is set for UK English rather than US English. The software will pick up any spelling mistakes and suggest changes. In terms of sentence structure, the software will advise about punctuation and order of words.

You will be asked by the examiner to identify the key characteristics and uses of applications software. In the practical examination you will need to use the software for the tasks.

## Presentation software

Microsoft's PowerPoint is the industry standard for presentation software. It is easy to use and can produce some very professional-looking results.

The application offers users a number of different templates (colour and layout) that can be chosen or amended. The user can also design their own layouts for each of the slides. The slides are single screen or page designs, with areas for text and graphics.

Typically, users will have text areas and graphics areas on the slide. They can also have bullet points, different fonts and sizes and the ability to insert business names and logos.

PowerPoint presentations are often displayed either on laptops or using projectors. The key advantages of PowerPoint are:

- It is easy to customise the slides.
- It is easy to update the slides.
- Customised graphics, images and sounds can be used.
- The presentation does not need to be printed out.

**KEY TERMS**

**Internet Explorer** ▶ Microsoft's Internet browsing software.

**Windows** ▶ Microsoft's computer operating system. It provides an interface for the user to access programs and files.

**Mail merge** ▶ combining lists of names and addresses with a typed letter.

# Database software

In effect, a database is an electronic filing system. Microsoft Access is the dedicated database. Excel could also be used for the same purpose, although it does not have all the features of Access.

Businesses can use a database for a host of different reasons, including:

- collecting and storing information about customers and suppliers
- as a product or service listing, with all the features and prices included
- as an internal database containing information about each employee (personnel records).

## What is a database?

A database is a series of records. Each record is stored in what is called a field. Each of the fields holds a specific category of information (name, part of an address, etc.). The database is designed so that:

- the user can design the overall structure of the database
- each field can be created to contain specific information
- the number of fields can be decided by the user
- fields can be amended or deleted as required.

Each record is a set of fields containing all the information about a person, a product or whatever the business needs.

## Templates

Access comes with several different database templates. These can be amended to suit the needs of the user. Alternatively, the user can create his or her own personalised database and set it up so that it contains a number of fields for each of the records.

Specialist databases can also be designed for database professionals. They can custom-make a database to match the specifications and needs of the business.

## Database advantages

The main advantages of a database are:

- All information on the database can be instantly accessed.
- All information can be tracked.
- It is easy to update or delete records.
- The database is not paper-based, so less storage is needed.
- The data is safe (assuming it is backed up on a regular basis).
- Databases can be used with stock control and other systems by the business.

Databases can also be locked to prevent access. This means that only authorised people can view, update or delete records from it.

> The term 'applications software' actually means software programs. These tend to have file extensions of .bat, .exe, or .com. By opening any of these files the program will be opened. Without these sorts of program, users would not be able to do much with the computer. Software programs, however, are one of the most common causes of computer-related problems, as many of them have a high number of errors or bugs.

## QUESTION TIME
*14 minutes*

**1** How might a business make use of the mail merge facility?
*(6 marks)*

**2** Explain how a database would help an organisation to organise its customer records.
*(8 marks)*

121

# Uses of applications software (2)

YOU WILL FIND OUT:
- about spreadsheet software
- about graphics software
- about desktop-publishing (DTP) software

## Spreadsheet software

All businesses need to keep track of their spending and income. Spreadsheets are designed to do this. They are most commonly used to list and order data (usually numerical data). The software can also make additions, divide, subtract and multiply.

It is possible to create spreadsheets that can add all the figures in one column and then take the total away from the total of another column. This produces a final figure. This would be extremely useful for a business to work out its **cash flow**.

### Microsoft Excel

Microsoft Excel has become the industry standard spreadsheet application software. Some businesses will have their own, or non-specialised spreadsheet software. This will be particularly true of businesses that use other non-Microsoft software to keep track of their **stock levels** and other activities.

Nearly all businesses opt for Excel as it offers huge advantages if used with other parts of the Microsoft Office suite. For example, spreadsheets and tables created in Excel can be **imported** into Microsoft Word with a single click of the mouse.

Excel is a powerful tool for businesses. It tends to be used by those who deal with the financial side of the operation, such as accountants.

### Spreadsheet capabilities

Spreadsheets have many capabilities. The key ones are:

- A grid of 'cells' into which numbers, text and formulae can be typed
- Cells can be formatted for inputting text, numbers, dates or currencies

- Cells can be sized as necessary
- Columns can be ordered alphabetically or by value.

### Modelling

Companies use spreadsheets to help them predict changes and their effect on the business. This is called modelling. It is achieved simply by changing the data that has been put into the cells of a spreadsheet.

The uses of modelling are:

- predicting sales if prices increase or decrease
- predicting changes if the **interest rate** changes
- predicting changes of temperature or other data relevant to particular products.

Modelling helps a business test the likely outcome of a decision before making it. So it helps in the decision-making process by predicting results.

## Graphics software

Graphics can include pictures, drawings, graphs and charts. They can be used in documents to illustrate the information and to make the page look more attractive. There are many different types of graphic, including:

- line diagrams (like drawings and cartoons)
- bitmap images (computer-created drawings)
- photographs
- graphs and charts.

### The features of graphics

Graphics are used by businesses to produce professional-looking documents. Magazines and newspapers use attractive layouts

to interest the reader. By using either Word or desktop-publishing software, such as Publisher, the business can make similar designs and layouts. This means that the business does not necessarily have to use professional designers or printers.

Most types of graphics can be obtained relatively easily:

- Hard copies of photographs and artwork can be scanned.
- Photographs can be taken with a digital camera.
- Graphics and clipart can be bought **royalty-free**, either on CD/DVD or from the Internet.
- Photographic libraries offer images at relatively low cost.

## Clipart

Clipart is the most commonly used type of graphic image. The images are **copyright-free** and can be dropped into pages to break up the text. There are literally millions of free clipart images, although their quality is generally low.

If used correctly, they can be useful in making the document appear more professional, but many of them will only look good if used small.

Clipart galleries are often part of a software package, with extra images available on CDs or the Internet. Clipart can be imported into documents and resized to fit.

### Vector graphics

These are higher-quality graphics images. They tend to be photographs, which are easy to change in size. They do not blur when they are enlarged on the page and printed out. Computer Aided Design (CAD) makes use of vector graphics.

─── K E Y   T E R M S ───

**Cash flow ▶** the measurement of a business's income and expenditure over a period of weeks or months.

**Stock levels ▶** the amount of products stored by a business before being sold.

**Interest rate ▶** the cost of borrowing set by the Bank of England each month.

**Imported ▶** data transferred from one application to another.

**Royalty-free ▶** the graphic can be used by anyone, without payment having to be made to its creator.

**Copyright-free ▶** the creator of the graphics has given permission for anyone to use it. Often they will ask for a credit underneath the graphic.

## Bitmap graphics

These are graphics made up from individual pixels. Colour images are much bigger files. It is difficult to change the look of them, as they have to be altered a pixel at a time. They can be easily enlarged. Many clipart images are, in fact, bitmap images.

Not all graphic images on the Internet can be used and put into documents without a copyright fee. Permission, and often payment, is required to use them.

# Desktop-publishing software

Microsoft Publisher is a standard application used by many businesses to create professional-looking newsletters and stationery. It is far better adapted to this role than Word. Desktop publishing is also carried out using the Adobe Pagemaker system, which allows the user to make completed pdf files. Another package, produced by Serif, is called PagePlus. This also allows documents to be created as Adobe pdf files if desired.

## Key features of DTP software

- Graphics can be imported, resized and edited.
- There is no need to use a designer, as several templates are available.
- Documents can combine text and graphics.
- Different fonts can be used.
- The text can be made to flow around graphics.

- Text and pictures can be put into columns.
- Text and graphics are in frames, which can be moved around the page or document.

## Hardware needed

A considerable amount of memory (or RAM) is needed on the computer to cope with the text and graphics. Other requirements are:

- a keyboard and mouse
- a high-quality printer
- a scanner for photographs/digital camera.

## Advantages of DTP

The main advantages are:

- control over the layout
- ability to combine text and graphics
- a professional look
- the document can be saved, edited and printed
- can avoid employing a designer

> Unlike Microsoft Word, Excel documents are automatically created with several hundreds of columns and rows, broken down into cells. A user can modify the cells by changing their size, format, font, colour and layout. Users can also take the data from the cells and create graphs and charts.

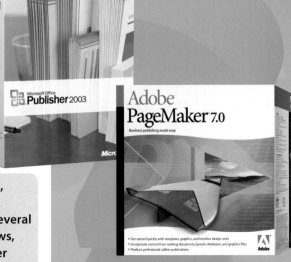

## QUESTION TIME
*16 minutes*

**1** How might a sales department in a business make use of Microsoft Excel? *(8 marks)*

**2** How might a small business that wishes to create and print a regular newsletter for its customers make use of software applications to do this? *(8 marks)*

123

# Use of local and wide area networks (1)

## Computer networks

As a business grows, it is important that information is still available to employees, and that their ability to communicate and share data is maintained. A computer network can allow the sharing of:

- common files
- databases
- application software
- company news

A computer network allows several computers to share not only data, but also **peripherals**, including scanners and printers.

A computer network can make positive improvements to internal communications in the workplace:

- Employees, customers and suppliers can share information and communication easily.
- Data-sharing can avoid duplicating work.
- Employees can deal with queries more efficiently.

Networks can also reduce costs:

- Customers can be dealt with more quickly by access to customer and product databases.
- The IT support can be centralised, cutting costs.
- There is a smaller number of peripherals needed, as they are all shared.

## Local Area Networks (LANs)

For many businesses, setting up a computer network in a single building is the first step. There are two main types of LAN, these are:

- peer-to-peer network
- client/server network.

In peer-to-peer networks, two or more computers are directly connected. This enables the sharing of applications and data. It is the most straightforward networking option and it is relatively cheap. It is ideal when several employees are working together on the same kind of work. The major problem with this type of network is that it is quite slow. The other key issue is that it does not really suit complicated networks with dozens of linked computers.

The second option is the client/server network. One computer in the network acts as the server. This is a normal computer, but it is powerful and sometimes a purpose-built server. This computer holds all the applications software and the shared files.

As the files are stored centrally, this makes the network ideal and efficient in terms of backing up. Users cannot modify the same file at the same time.

As long as the server computer is working, it does not matter if one of the client machines breaks down. This is a considerable problem in the case of peer-to-peer networks, as a single failure causes the whole network to go down.

LANs are high-speed data networks that tend to cover a relatively small area. They connect workstations, personal computers, printers and servers. They allow the users to share access to devices and applications, to exchange files and to communicate via electronic mail.

One option is a wired LAN system, in which all computers, peripherals and other pieces of equipment are physically connected to one another. Businesses might choose this approach for the following reasons:

- low initial cost
- low interference
- high level of security
- tried and tested.

The alternative is a wireless system, which links all the machines using radio frequencies. This means that no cables are required. Businesses choose this option because:

- They can move equipment around without rewiring.
- It is easy to install.
- The number of computers and other machines can be added to.
- It is generally easier to maintain.

The examiner will expect you to know about different types of network, and identify any advantages or disadvantages relating to them.

── **KEY TERMS** ──

**Peripherals** ▶ hardware devices connected to a computer or a network, including printers, scanners and external hard drives.

124

## Cable or wireless?

Most LANs are created using cables. It is now relatively easy to create wireless LANs to provide an even more flexible network for businesses.

Wireless networks effectively eliminate the need for cables. This gives the network greater mobility and flexibility. Cable-based networks require holes to be drilled in walls, and cables to be laid under floors or in special trunking to protect them.

Wireless networks actually cost less to install and less to maintain. The major problems with wireless networks are:

- The signal quality may be a problem, particularly if other networks in the same area are using the same frequency for their networks.
- Some areas of a building can be 'black spots', where it is impossible to get a signal at all.
- Wireless networks tend to be slower than cabled ones (in some businesses the main parts of the network are cables and the rest is wireless).
- It is difficult to keep the network secure, as the wireless transmissions can actually be intercepted and information can be read from the network.

A wireless network also means that all the peripherals are connected wirelessly, so they can be placed centrally for shared use. Overall, as businesses replace old networks, or install them for the first time, wireless is the usual choice.

## Intranets

If a business only chooses to share its network internally (in a LAN or WAN), it is called an Intranet. Only the business can access the information and applications.

A business may open up its Intranet to suppliers or customers, usually accessed via a password. This is called an Extranet.

Essentially an intranet is a collection of private computer networks within a business or organisation. It uses network technology to allow communication, as well as data sharing. A simple intranet will just consist of internal email and a message board service. More sophisticated ones will have websites and databases.

> Intranets use standard network hardware and software, such as Ethernet, WiFi or TCP/IP, as well as web browsers and web servers. Normally an intranet allows Internet access, but the actual intranet itself is firewalled, so that external users cannot access it from outside the network. This means that the intranet has its own extranet that provides controlled access to outsiders.

## QUESTION TIME
*14 minutes*

**1** **Why might a wireless network be far more efficient and flexible for a business than a cabled network?** *(8 marks)*

**2** **How can a business allow its employees to access the organisation's intranet if they are working from remote locations?** *(6 marks)*

125

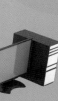

# Use of local and wide area networks (2)

## Wide Area Networks (WANs)

If a business is operating on more than one site, it is inevitable and vital that the different sites can communicate with one another. They may need to share the same data and applications that users on a LAN can enjoy.

A WAN connects different local area networks together. This is a more complex network. Usually businesses opt for client/server networks. These are based around central server computers. The central servers are then connected together over a telecommunications network. The telecommunications cables and lines are **leased** from businesses such as British Telecom.

Many WANs are designed for single organisations, but others are built by Internet service providers to provide connections from LANs to the Internet. WANs enable computers to communicate with one another, to share data, to allow videoconferencing and effectively set up a safe and secure network.

## Other networks

There are two other major types of network, Storage Area Networks (SAN) and the Internet, which we will look at here. There is also a Vertical Private Network (VPN). This is often used by businesses to make connections from a user via the Internet to their own private (Intranet) network. This means that a VPN is especially useful when connecting an employee in a remote location with the central computer network of their employer. It is able to create a secure connection. VPN is also cheaper than using either leased telecommunication lines or domestic broadband connections.

## Storage Area Networks (SAN)

These are high-speed, special-purpose networks specifically designed for storage. They differ from normal client/server LANs as they do away with the single server. The single server system in a client/server network is called Network Attached Storage. Bottlenecks and slow response often occur on these

networks, as everything is being routed through a single server.

A SAN avoids these problems by allowing the network to grow as the needs of the network grow. If additional storage is needed, the business simply adds another server.

SANs usually involve connecting the network up with optical fibre. This is a system developed by IBM called ESCON and the technology is called Fibre Channel.

The other alternative is to use copper wiring, which is a cheaper option. The main point, regardless of the connection, is to ensure that the data moves around the network at the fastest possible speed.

A Fibre Channel SAN has a bandwidth of 2Gbps (**gigabit**s per second). SANs, using copper wire, achieve about half that performance.

In the near future both types of SAN will feature far quicker transfer of data; the new generations of both systems can cope with 10Gbps.

### Network needs

Before a business orders a network it needs to look at its requirements. Questions would include:

- Do we need to produce or access information?
- What centralised tasks can a network help with?
- Can we expand the network in the future?
- What equipment do we have?
- What is our budget?
- What potential savings are there?
- Who will need access?

Storage Area Networks are more flexible than normal client/server networks.

---

### KEY TERMS

**Lease** ▶ a long-term renting arrangement with the owner. Bandwidth – the amount of data that can pass through a network.

**Gigabit** ▶ one million bits. A bit is the smallest measurement of data.

**Instant messaging** ▶ a real-time communication system. Users type a message into a box and send it to a named individual who is also online.

---

# The Internet

Most businesses are connected to the Internet via broadband or cable services. Some businesses choose to block certain areas of the Internet and searches, so that their employees can use it for work-related matters only.

A business will routinely use the Internet for emails. Emails may need to be sent to other employees, customers and suppliers. The Internet is also an invaluable tool if employees are working outside the office. It allows instant communication via Internet telephony or **instant messaging**.

In effect, the Internet is the sum total of a huge number of computer networks. They cooperate with one another and exchange data using common software standards. This allows users to:

- connect easily either through their local telephone connections or by using wireless connections
- exchange electronic mail
- post up information and update it and allow others to access it
- access multimedia.

The Internet is designed to be dynamic. Routers and servers will always try to find the best connection and to maintain that connection. In effect the Internet operates rather like a sophisticated library coupled with a postal service. It allows an almost infinite amount of information to be made available for direct access. Most importantly it allows the user to search for information (such as products or services) via search engines. It then facilitates contact between the provider of products and services and a potential customer.

## Internet security

One of the major problems with linking a computer up to the Internet is the risk of virus and other malware attacking the computer and the network. Businesses, like home users, employ a firewall to protect their machines. This sets up a virtual block between the computer and the Internet connection. It will automatically repel attempts to access the computer or the network by unauthorised individuals.

## QUESTION TIME
*14 minutes*

**1** **Why might a business choose to set up its own WAN?**
*(6 marks)*

**2** **Apart from availability of funds, what other questions will businesses ask themselves when deciding whether or not to set up their own network?**
*(8 marks)*

**127**

Over a billion people worldwide use the Internet. In just three decades it has grown from an experimental network to a vital part of the world economy. Both large and small businesses have become dependent on it. A prime example is Nestlé; all of its orders from supermarkets now come via the Internet, and the shipping company, UPS, uses its online networks to organise its delivery routes. In doing this it is able to save millions of litres of fuel each year.

# The Internet and e-commerce

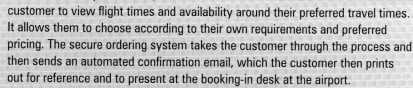

## Websites and e-commerce

For the first time, rather than having to visit dozens of shops in order to compare products in terms of features and price, it can now be done with a few clicks of the mouse. It also means that customers can demand lower prices on account of the fact that they will inevitably, after searching, discover the same product with the same availability at a lower price.

Customers will also be aware of the latest developments and be able to take advantage of immediate business offers and sales, particularly in the field of airline ticketing. Other primary benefits of Internet marketing to customers are immediate online sales and customer service. Many businesses use digital complaints services and businesses can respond to complaints and queries far faster than they could using traditional methods, such as post or call centres.

There are many price comparison websites that can be used by consumers to compare and select not only products and services, but also providers. There are, of course, many criteria to consider when comparing suppliers, including:

- key features and description of the product or service offered
- how this compares to other similar products or services
- a price analysis
- delivery costs
- ongoing cost analysis
- risk assessment – has the customer heard of the business and has it got a good reputation?

**For example** easyJet

Customers of businesses such as easyJet, have to purchase their tickets with the airline online. This attracts not only immediate discounts from conventional telephone sales, but also allows the customer to view flight times and availability around their preferred travel times. It allows them to choose according to their own requirements and preferred pricing. The secure ordering system takes the customer through the process and then sends an automated confirmation email, which the customer then prints out for reference and to present at the booking-in desk at the airport.

Businesses use a scoring mechanism when they choose suppliers. Key aspects would include confidence, the safety of the product, its quality, price and, if relevant, ongoing support. Making supplier comparison decisions is said to bring down costs for businesses by between 7% and 8%. It can be a significantly larger margin for consumers.

Despite worries about online security, instant online sales and ordering facilities are a huge benefit to customers. They can secure a product or a service, having established its availability.

Provided the customer has confidence in the security of the system, they are able to make transactions without having to visit a traditional retail outlet. Even businesses that have always relied on their retail outlets, such as Argos, have turned to online sales as both an alternative and an addition to their overall sales offerings. It is now possible to either:

- Visit the retail store to check availability of products and then make a purchase

- Use an automated reservation system on the telephone and then visit the retail outlet for purchase
- Use the online reservation system and then visit the store to make the purchase
- Use the online reservation system and complete the purchase online

Obviously the only major disadvantage of products compared to services is that buying them from a remote location means that there are delivery costs to be incorporated into the price. Many businesses will either have a small, standardised delivery cost, regardless of the size of the order, or they will have built the delivery cost into the price of the product sold via the website. Many businesses now recognise that adding unreasonably high delivery costs at the online point of sale deters customers from completing the transaction. Rather than lose the sale, the pricing structure is reorganised to incorporate delivery charges. Businesses are able to do this as they are undoubtedly making a larger profit per unit sold, by dealing directly with the customer rather than selling their products to wholesalers and retailers for resale.

128

# Global and international markets

Even the smallest business, if it uses effective Internet marketing activities, can reach a global market place. Not only this, but it can also reach parts of markets that were closed to it through traditional bricks and mortar retail outlets, or the use of sales personnel.

Marketing no longer ends at the borders of a territory or a country. The Internet can allow global initiatives to take place. At a most basic level, a business's website can be mirrored in several different languages and customised to meet country-specific demands.

Businesses will often enter into joint ventures with similar organisations in different parts of the world, collaborating in their email campaigns and the placement of banner advertising. Businesses begin the process by learning about the likes and dislikes of business and consumer populations in each of their target countries. They will also need to understand local languages, legislation and regulations.

Such is the importance of global marketing that there are university degrees in it and many job titles stressing global marketing responsibilities. The Internet is growing even in less-developed countries. This allows marketing communications to take place with an ever-growing worldwide population. The number of computer owners is broadly doubling every three to five years. One of the major areas for growth has been Asia – India and China alone account for a possible 2.1 billion customers.

Businesses can use Internet marketing in order to branch out into new markets and offer their existing products to new customers, either in the country in which they already operate or in new countries, which are experiencing growth in terms of Internet connection.

Some adaptation is necessary in the way that a business operates, designs its products, offers its services or indeed markets them. The use of the Internet makes this far more cost-effective. We can see that the cost savings come when we compare Internet marketing with traditional forms of marketing, including the placement of advertisements, renting billboards and running sales promotions in specific marketplaces.

In developing a new market, the first thing that needs to be done is to understand the market and identify the opportunities. The business then needs to see if there is a fit in terms of its existing products, and whether they are appropriate for the new market, or if a new concept will be required. The product can now be tested and a suitable price is arrived at. It is then introduced into the market.

## QUESTION TIME
### 27 minutes

1 Some potential customers will not order a product through a website because they fear a lack of online security. What does this mean? *(2 marks)*

2 What is an advantage of online shopping for a customer? *(3 marks)*

3 Why can businesses like Amazon and CD-Wow sell their products at cheaper prices through the Internet than those available through book and music shops? *(4 marks)*

4 What advantages does a website provide in dealing with complaints both for the customer and business? *(4 marks)*

5 How does the Internet enable a business to reach an international market? *(6 marks)*

6 Argos customers would originally have bought their products through its retail stores but can now also buy them online. Was Argos right to enter the online market? *(8 marks)*

129

A fully functional website can be designed by website specialists for very little outlay. However it is perfectly possible with a minimum amount of experience for a business to create a basic website, albeit with limited functionality. What does become the more expensive part of developing websites is the addition of secure shopping areas and online transactions. Businesses can purchase off-the-peg website designs with fully functional shopping carts. These can then be customised to incorporate the business's logo, designs, text, and product photographs. Website design software can cost from as little as £50, although businesses recognise that lower-cost software is often not as flexible as the more expensive and better designed software options.

# The purpose of a website (1)

YOU WILL FIND OUT:

- about levels and types of online presence
- about passive brochure-ware
- about complementing offline services
- about mail order
- about online transactions

## Levels and types of online presence

First and foremost, a business needs to define the specifications for its website content. There are two major kinds of content to be considered: static and dynamic.

### STATIC CONTENT

Company identities including logos, slogans, corporate messages, etc.

Company information including history, organisation, company culture, personnel, contact information, etc.

Business information including ordering procedures, shipping, credit terms, etc.

General product information including quality, material, sizing guide, what's new, etc.

### DYNAMIC CONTENT

A database has to be set up. The data will include important information such as product categories, codes, description, sizes, colours, materials, prices, images, etc.

Database design has to coincide with the display format and design of the online storefront.

Consideration also will be given to incorporate ease of updating the data to minimise the cost of ongoing maintenance.

The theme of the website needs to be designed to deliver a most appropriate intended image. Apart from the content, endless possibilities exist to maximise the return on the investment made by the business:

- Increase the exposure of the website by submission to thousands of search engines around the world.
- Registered site viewers can generate a highly accurate and targeted source for online marketing activities.
- An online ordering system, built on the foundation of the online product and customer data infrastructure can effectively transform order processing online.
- A website eliminates issues such as time difference for global enterprises and allows better tracking of ordering and shipping by both customers and administrators.
- The web's advantages of global coverage and timely delivery of important business information are increasing by the minute as its usage grows.
- A business's online presence continues to grow as the media is being fuelled by its increased usage.

## Passive brochure-ware

A website can either be a dynamic tool focused on achieving a specific set of business objectives, or it can be a passive electronic brochure telling visitors what the business is, where it is, what it does and when it is done.

Most shop websites today take the brochure-ware approach. Although generally not very effective, this type of site can help keep the shop's image current and offer some convenience to existing customers.

A dynamic website features helpful, frequently updated content that keeps customers returning to the site. It also offers what are known as 'actionable' tools that allow a business to communicate with its customers.

Independent shops and small chains have always suffered from limited choices for promoting their businesses, providing convenient solutions to customers, and increasing their profit margins. Many argue that a dynamic website can be the most cost-effective solution for achieving these objectives. Most shop websites in use today are only passive brochure-ware types because the cost of creating and maintaining a dynamic site has been prohibitive. Easier and more affordable tools to create dynamic websites are now available and passive brochure-ware websites are becoming a thing of the past. A dynamic website is clearly the best choice for helping independents and small chains maintain a competitive edge.

## Complementing offline services

In the past, if a business wanted to be successful online, it might have also felt that it should have an offline, or conventional presence. This is still the case, though its importance to customers seems to be declining.

Recent research shows that a physical 'bricks and mortar' presence is still important to many consumers in theory – around 50% of all customers rated having a physical offline presence as very or somewhat important, with only 15% per cent stating that it was not important at all. However, offline presence as an influence on the purchase decision appears to be declining. Although 35% of customers stated they would be more likely to make a purchase from a website if the brand had a physical offline presence, 34% said it would not affect their purchase decision.

> **Interactive customisation** – Increasingly, online businesses focus on customer interaction, with an emphasis on organisation and ease of navigation, to make sure they have a pleasant experience with the website. To complement this, businesses also concentrate on the customer's interface. These interfaces allow the customisation of websites to appeal to their customer's needs. Cookies offer an innovative means of collecting data on the demographics and behaviour of Web users, and allow easier estimates of site visits. They also allow the customisation of websites without making the user reset preferences every time the site is revisited.

## QUESTION TIME
*16 marks*

**1** Why might a small business that sells direct to customers face-to-face or on the telephone opt for a static website? *(6 marks)*

**2** If the same business wanted to offer its products and services to a wider range of customers and wanted to sell online, suggest the features necessary for its new website. *(10 marks)*

It was the youngest group (the under-25s) that placed the most importance on a physical presence, with 61% rating it as very or somewhat important. Men and women showed virtually identical attitudes towards online shopping and purchases.

## Mail order

The simple fact that Internet-based businesses are not conventional stores means that they need to deliver the majority of their products and services by mail order. At the top of the list of complaints received by trading standards officers around the UK were non-delivery of Internet goods and other mail-order problems.

In theory, customers are protected by the Sale of Goods Act 1979 and the Consumer Protection (Distance Sales) Regulations 2000. When a customer buys goods over the Internet or by mail order, they enter into an agreement with the seller. These agreements are called 'contracts'. A contract gives details of the main points the customer agreed with the seller (e.g. what they are buying and how much they have to pay). A contract does not have to be written; it may be verbal or partly verbal/partly written.

When a customer buys goods from a mail order or Internet company, delivery should be within a reasonable time. Often, the seller will

specify a certain date. The customer has a right to reject the goods and claim a refund for late delivery, if the seller does not deliver on the promised date, or within 30 days of it. In most cases, buyers are willing to wait a little longer.

The law allows the customer to return goods if for any reason they change their mind about buying them. Normally, they should make the cancellation in writing, within seven days of delivery. 'Goods' include things like cars, toasters, washing machines, food and even animals. Computers, computer discs and computer games are also 'goods'.

## Online transactions

As we will see later in this unit, there are a number of different methods used to enable online financial transactions to take place. Primarily, customers will use a variety of credit and debit cards as well as using direct fund transfers.

Many businesses will use the expertise of professional website designers to find online transaction solutions including online credit card transactions and product cataloguing. These can be incorporated into the web design and development services to produce a fully functional e-commerce site, which is easy to use for both the customer and the supplier.

131

# The purpose of a website (2)

YOU WILL FIND OUT:

- about main features
- about discussion forums
- about polls and voting
- about weblogs and news feeds
- about payment functions
- about feedback forms
- about subscription forms and newsletters
- about password protected areas

## Main features

Websites can provide a vast amount of information as well as products and services. As we have seen, websites can be static or dynamic and can incorporate message boards, discussion forums, news feeds, blogs, downloadable documents and forms and even streaming audio and video. This spread looks at some of the other key options.

Obviously, websites tend to consist of a number of pages that are linked together and provide information for the visitor on the business and its products and services. Businesses will use a mixture of text, photographs and illustrations to make the pages as attractive and user friendly as possible.

## Discussion forums

Discussion forums allow users with similar interests to have conversations with others on the website. Questions are published on the website and others can write their replies. This is a different system to that of emails or chat rooms as the text is available for others to read, and people can join in the conversation when they want to (assuming they have registered with the site).

Discussion forums allow people to learn from each other and useful answers can be read by people who need the same information. They are also valuable as they can make people feel they are part of a community of others who share their interests. It will also mean that more visitors will come to the website. It is, however, important that discussion forums are monitored and managed. This is carried out by an 'administrator' who can remove unwanted content.

## Polls and voting

This is also a popular feature as it allows visitors to the site to vote on different topics. Polls and voting software can also be used by a business to collect feedback on its products and services and to carry out informal surveys.

## Weblogs and news feeds

Personal publishing has become increasingly popular and weblogs (or blogs) are rather like online diaries that can be created either by an individual or a business. They can provide:

- daily news
- articles
- photographs and illustrations
- links to other websites.

The entries on the website are organised by date with the latest entry at the top of the list. Setting up a blog is far easier than in the recent past and a range of ready-designed templates can be used. As far as a business is concerned, other websites can subscribe to the online content. This means that the contents of the blog appear as a 'feed' on another website. Several blogs can therefore be brought together on a single website which makes it attractive for visitors who may be interested in a particular subject, sector or range of products or services. By publishing a blog, the business is able to get its content out to a wider audience as several websites and other blogs may subscribe to the feed.

## Payment functions

Payment is now far easier and safer and more common than before. The table below summarises the key features.

| WEBSITES TAKING PAYMENT FOR | HOW CUSTOMERS CAN PROVIDE PAYMENTS | SOFTWARE THAT CAN PROCESS THE PAYMENTS |
|---|---|---|
| Subscriptions | Simple forms that can be printed out and sent with a cheque. | Shopping cart systems |
| Payment of services or goods | Use of PayPal – or similar specialist payment services. | PayPal payment buttons |
| Donations and gifts | Credit card payment – by linking up with an organisation who can carry out the transaction. | Simple forms linked to payment systems. |

132

QUESTION TIME
*18 minutes*

**1** How might a business benefit from the inclusion of a discussion forum on its website? *(6 marks)*

**2** How might a business use a blog to attract visitors to its website? *(6 marks)*

**3** Why might customers want to use a feedback form instead of another way of contacting a business? *(6 marks)*

133

## Feedback and subscription forms

Feedback forms are rather like survey forms or application forms. The main advantage is that they can be filled in by the user and sent directly to the owner of the website. The business can then process the information instantly, usually by either replying to the sender or adding the sender's name and contact details to the customer or supplier database.

By adding a feedback form to the website, the business is allowing users to get in touch without having to email. Neither do they have to write a letter, make a telephone call, or visit in person. The feedback forms also have the advantage for the website owner that they do not have to put their own email address on the site. This can protect the business from having their email address added to a spam mail database.

A subscription form works in a similar way and can be used to subscribe to a newsletter or receive regular updates from an organisation.

## Password-protected areas

Having a password-protected area on the website can be useful. For example, it could be used for distributing documents that the business does not want to make public, such as minutes of meetings. The business can also use it as a way to provide additional services and content to members of an organisation.

**For updating websites, businesses will often use a content management system rather than a website design package. A content management system is essentially software that enables a number of people to update, delete and add to the content of the website. The software can be set so that it controls what different people are allowed to do and which pages they can change. There can also be a review function which enables the changes to be checked for accuracy and accessibility.**

UNIT 8 ICT SYSTEMS IN BUSINESS

# Business opportunities

## Benefits of online presence

The benefits of web presence for any business are increasing as more and more business communication has made its way online. The Internet has reached its full maturity to become the new medium of choice with huge advantages over conventional media.

The Internet will see its next stage of development as businesses move their commerce activities totally online. Many creative marketing and sales approaches that use the power of online business have been proven in recent years, with great results, translating into increased productivity as well as profitability. The Internet offers great promise for businesses that are determined to be the pioneers in their industries in utilising the Internet as their next platform of conducting their businesses.

A product showroom website is an effective approach for a business to start its web presence; it immediately puts investment to work. The electronic storefront maximises business presence and minimises costs. New product information can be updated in a matter of hours and made available to customers all over the world.

## Global visibility

Around 95% of all web traffic flows through the major search engines, so positioning is the main key to the success of any business online. Standard search engine registry techniques and traditional print ads are often not enough because of the billions of different web pages. Research also shows that only around 1–3% of users view listings beyond the first three result pages.

Acquiring a domain name is a relatively simple and affordable investment for a business, which in turn gives it vast and on-going global exposure on the Internet.

The Internet simplifies internal and external communication through the use of email and of the World Wide Web (instant global mass communication). It allows any business to:

- collaborate with colleagues and customers anywhere in the world
- disseminate information to a global audience
- gather information from global sources
- research competitors from anywhere in the world
- research and gain greater knowledge of potential customers from anywhere in the world
- provide innovative and improved customer service and support 24 hours a day with FAQs (Frequently Asked Questions with answers) and online order taking. This can greatly reduce communication times and improve customer relations.

- sell products and services 24 hours a day, locally, regionally, nationally and globally
- purchase products and services 24 hours a day and enjoy 24-hour technical support from suppliers
- reduce information and distribution costs, as document files can be instantly transmitted around the globe via email and the World Wide Web
- increase market share without increasing advertising budget, by taking advantage of this low-cost, far-reaching, high impact advertising media. The Internet can deliver a real return on investment.

Remember that websites can be fully interactive; visitors read information on products or services and then fill in a form which automatically informs the business of their enquiries. This allows advertising, online order taking, online payments and customer support.

Websites provide a level playing field on which small or medium-size businesses can compete with their larger competitors. This is because for a few hundred pounds, a small business can have the same global exposure on the Internet as a multinational spending tens of thousands of pounds. The Internet is a low-cost advertising medium because Internet websites can contain rich multimedia promotional material, visible all around the world.

134

Although computers are the primary tools used to connect businesses, suppliers and customers, there are increasing moves towards providing other forms of access. Obviously, one of the earlier developments was the laptop computer which can be attached to Internet connections such as those provided in airport lounges and, of course, mobile phones. Mobile communications devices, such as the new generation mobile phones and personal assistants provide businesses with a means by which they can remain in touch with the suppliers and for their own customers to contact them.

## Reduced stockholding and other benefits

Stock levels of products that sell well can be kept under control by using sales analysis and automatic order generation procedures. Sales history can be used to identify products where there are excess stocks to satisfy customer demand. By identifying products that have not sold since a selected date, a business can evaluate its prices and their relation to different manufacturers' products within the same range. The business can then take the necessary action to promote the sale of these products. In addition to ensuring that fast-selling products are automatically re-ordered, an automated system will also ensure that slow-selling items, or items with excess stock, are not unnecessarily ordered.

In theory, many businesses running online operations will not be victims of customers being unable to pay for the products and services supplied to them. This is certainly true of businesses that do not offer credit terms. Offering credit terms means offering the customer a specified period of time to pay for the products and services supplied.

Since many online businesses only deal with consumers rather than business customers, this problem does not emerge as a major concern. Payments are usually made by credit, debit and automated payment systems. This gives the seller a degree of security and assures them of payment provided they have followed the correct procedures. Businesses dealing with other businesses face the same kind of problems with bad debts as conventional bricks and mortar operations. A bad debt is an amount of money owed by a customer that the supplying business (the creditor) has no realistic chance of ever receiving.

Assuming that the business has access to a good Internet connection, the actual physical location of the business does not have to be a great concern. The business also needs to have access to a reasonable supply of skilled employees and not be too distant from major centres of population to make attracting new employees to the business a serious issue.

In addition to the lower-cost location, the business may also be able to claim various incentives from the local government, particularly if the unemployment level is high in the area.

Deliveries to the online business from suppliers does need to be taken into consideration as remote areas are often more difficult to get to and further away, thus increasing the costs to have products delivered to the door. The Scottish islands, for example, suffer from this problem and couriers and delivery services charge an additional fee to cover the extra expense of servicing these areas.

## QUESTION TIME
*16 minutes*

1 Why might a competitor with a fully functional website be considered a major threat by a business that relies on sales from a traditional printed catalogue? *(8 marks)*

2 Why are websites that can handle online transactions less likely to have debtors? *(4 marks)*

3 Why is it likely that a 'virtual shop' with only an online presence will not be located in expensive business offices? *(4 marks)*

135

# Business risks

YOU WILL FIND OUT:
- about potential risks and exposure
- about hostile chat rooms, negative publicity and defamation
- about payment security and unfamiliar trading conditions
- about dealing with increased market interest
- about vulnerability to hostile attack
- about denial of service

## Potential risks

As with any business, the establishing of a website and an online business has its disadvantages. For every advantage mentioned already, there is a downside. As the website is accessible by anyone with an Internet connection around the world, the chances of difficulties, either with attacks on the website, fraud or bad publicity are magnified. The potential dangers of online business for a small company are great, when compared to a small business based in a high street.

## Exposure

Web defacement is just one of the many perils facing websites. It is carried out by hackers who manage to gain access and change the contents of a website. The messages these hackers leave behind vary from merely placing their alias or logo to replacing the original contents with whatever content they wish, in a similar way to that in which traditional graffiti are written.

Recent research has revealed that 85% of organisations (primarily large corporations and government agencies) detected computer security breaches within the last twelve months and that 90% of those attacked reported [website] vandalism up from 64% last year.

## Hostile chat rooms, negative publicity and defamation

Businesses may often find themselves victims of a very different form of attack, that from hostile former customers, employees or activists who have a problem with either the products or services offered by the business or the way in which it does business.

Hostility and negative publicity can be very damaging to a business and even if the root cause of the problem was based on facts, a business can find it very difficult to prevent rumours from circulating. The Internet has thousands of chat rooms and a poor opinion of a business or a website can do immense damage. Worst of all, it is very difficult to stop the rumours from spreading. In a crisis, a business needs to put the Internet to work to help protect its reputation and in the end try to build better relationships with customers and other important groups.

## Payment security and unfamiliar trading conditions

Almost 90% of Internet fraudsters are getting away with their crimes. Around 57% of companies have reported frauds to the police, but 53% encountered a lack of interest. Only 9% of frauds reported by online retailers to the police resulted in prosecution.

Research has shown that around 70% of companies thought that the Internet was more risky than other marketing routes, with the majority of respondents experiencing an increase in fraud on the Internet over the last year. 52% of online traders claimed that Internet fraud was a problem for their organisation and 55% said it was a growing problem.

Retailers seem to become aware far too late when they have been victims of fraud. Almost half (48%) of the companies who reported being victims of card fraud said that it had been more than a month before they were aware of it. A further 18% said it took up to seven weeks.

Fraudsters have realised that methods of prevention are so inadequate they need spend little time or effort covering their tracks. Less than 10% of fraudsters bother with a redirection service at the goods delivery address, and only 10% make the effort to set up a false telephone account. In 58% of cases, businesses thought that the fear of fraud was a significant barrier to successful trading on the Internet.

## Dealing with increased market interest

Flexibility is the key to dealing with increased market demand. Stepping up operations to cope with increased demand can be a challenge, but a worthwhile one. Businesses tend to try to match any increased demand by either installing new systems or employing more staff. A business needs to be sure that while having to cope with increased demand it is certain that this new level of demand will continue into the future. A company does not want the expense of purchasing new equipment and taking on more employees only to discover that the increased demand is temporary and that it falls back to the old levels of demand.

A business which has either already established itself as an online operation, or one that is expanding, faces financial uncertainties at every turn. A huge amount of new businesses fail in their first year simply due to the fact that they over-estimate their income compared to their actual spending.

## Vulnerability to hostile attack

Contrary to what might be assumed, hostile attacks are currently the least significant cause of system crashes and problems. Environmental disruption and operator-error are the biggest sources of problems, followed by software problems and only then hostile attacks. On the other hand, the occurrence of hostile attacks is increasing, roughly doubling each year. Occurrences of operator errors and design and implementation errors are increasing at a slower rate, while the occurrence of problems due to environmental disruption remains constant.

## Denial of service

In a denial-of-service (DoS) attack, an attacker attempts to prevent legitimate users from accessing information or services. By targeting its computers and network connections, an attacker may be able to prevent a business from accessing email, websites, online accounts, or other services that rely on the affected computer. One type of denial of service attack occurs when an attacker 'floods' a network with information. Typing a URL for a particular website into a browser sends a request to that site's computer server to view the page. An attacker might overload the server with requests, so it can't process the request. This is a denial of service because the user cannot access the site.

An attacker can use spam email messages to launch a similar attack on the business's email account. Whether the user has an email account supplied by their employer or one available through a free service such as Yahoo or Hotmail, each user is assigned a specific quota, which limits the amount of data they can have in their account at any given time. By sending many, or large email messages to the account, an attacker can use up the quota, preventing the user from receiving legitimate messages.

The cost of a fully integrated system using the latest technology is still a considerable investment. Computer hardware platforms are increasingly powerful, roughly doubling in capability every 12 to 18 months, while the hardware manufacturers are seeking to maintain or expand their turnover at a time of falling hardware costs. Businesses may need as many as five applications open simultaneously, meaning that the need for ever more powerful machines continues.

Businesses also use terminals – basically a network of computers rather than 'stand-alone' machines. These too have distinct cost-saving and efficiency benefits including:

- lower hardware costs – users can share printers and other office hardware equipment
- the business can be more efficient, as a network allows information to be shared by all employees
- communication between employees is much easier with the use of applications such as email
- a centralised security system that makes it almost impossible for outsiders to break into the system
- users can access their files from a remote location
- improved, more cost-effective and secure Internet access.

## QUESTION TIME
*20 minutes*

Good practice in business to ensure that the computer network remains safe is to install and maintain anti-virus software; install a firewall and configure it to restrict traffic coming into and leaving the computer; and follow good security practices for distributing email addresses. It is also a good idea to apply email filters to manage unwanted traffic.

**1** What is an email filter? *(2 marks)*

**2** Explain how these measures might help prevent a DoS. *(10 marks)*

**3** How might a business reassure customers that payment transactions are safe? *(8 marks)*

137

# What have you learnt?

This section explored how important communication is in businesses and how it is vital as a link to all stakeholders. Communication systems are key in ensuring that a business meets its aims and objectives.

This section leads on to Unit 9, where you will see how businesses use ICT, not only to capture, process, store, retrieve and analyse data, but also as a key communication tool.

We looked at the purpose of communication, examining why it is important and considering some of the key benefits of effective communication systems.

We also considered the communication systems themselves, identifying both the process of communication and the likely channels of communication. And we looked at different methods of communication and why it is important for businesses to choose the most appropriate communication medium in order to convey the message or content of a communication to a particular audience. Potential barriers to effective communication were also considered, as well as how businesses can overcome these barriers.

Linking directly with Unit 9, we looked briefly at the importance of ICT in business communications, providing a basic introduction to the characteristics and uses of application software. We also looked at local and wide area networks and, more broadly, at intranets and the Internet.

In the final part of this unit, we examined the Internet and e-commerce, looking at why businesses use the Internet and also why it is becoming increasingly important. The Internet gives businesses the key advantage of being able to market their products to, and reach, the widest range of potential customers. Creating a website and becoming involved in e-commerce is not without risk: it opens businesses to greater competition, there are set-up and maintenance costs, and customer support needs to be available every hour of every day. In addition, there are other risks that come from hackers, unauthorised access, systems failures, and the protection of customer data.

If you have tried all the *QUESTION TIMES* in this section, you should have a good idea about the speed at which you need to work and the level of detail you will need to provide in the examination. Your teacher or tutor will also be able to give you a copy of the 'Unit Revision Pack' from the *Teacher Support Pack*. It will help you identify all of the key areas to revise.

It is important to remember that good communication is at the heart of a successful business. A business needs to be able to communicate internally, and communicate with its various stakeholders in an efficient, accurate and prompt manner.

## Integrated questions from Section 3

Try these exam-style questions. They bring together topics from the four parts of the Communication section. Remember the mark-a-minute approach, as it will help you to plan your time.

138

# POOR COMMUNICATOR

**N**eil Gunn is the chief executive of Toncaster Football Club. Although only a small club, they are relatively successful on the pitch. They have just three shareholders and a small, full-time, non-playing staff of eight. They regularly attract 1,100 people to their home games, although the stadium could take as many as 2,500. One of their biggest problems is that the local population knows very little about the team. There is rarely any news, the club never seems to have a local presence, it does not have a website, and it offers only a basic range of merchandise in its tiny shop, which is open for only three hours on a Saturday. Neil wants to improve all of this but does not know how to start.

## QUESTIONS
### 28 minutes

**1** Briefly explain the process of communication. *(4 marks)*

**2** Suggest TWO typical types of business information that the club should communicate, and TWO that it should NOT communicate. *(4 marks)*

**3** The club owns two desktop computers. Explain why a relatively small investment in a broader network could help the business. *(6 marks)*

**4** Neil needs advice on appropriate ways in which he could communicate with different stakeholders. Suggest how he might communicate with the local media, local businesses and fans. *(6 marks)*

**5** Rick Moss, one of the major shareholders, is convinced that the club needs a website and a simple e-commerce facility. Explain the key advantages and disadvantages to a business such as the football club in pursuing this option. *(8 marks)*

# Written paper

**Time allowed: 1 hour**

The marks for each question are shown in brackets. The maximum mark for the paper is 60. You need to use good, clear English. Quality of written communication will be assessed in questions 2(c), 2(e) (ii), 3(e), 4(b) and 4(c).

## QUESTION 1

Read the scenario, then answer the questions that follow. Total for this question: *9 marks*

## Scenario

Handy Rides is a charity. It provides free transport to the elderly and to disabled people. The charity has three mini-buses, six volunteer drivers, three full-time members of staff and five part-time members. It relies on donations from fundraising, a small grant from the local authority and irregular contributions from local businesses and wealthy residents.

**1** Handy Rides has been given £1,500 to invest in a better computer system. It wants to spend the money on some better data-output devices. Name each of the output devices shown below. Explain the benefits of each device to Handy Rides. *(9 marks)*

## QUESTION 2

Read Item A, then answer the questions that follow. Total marks for this question: *19 marks*

## Item A

Handy Rides operates out of a small industrial and garage unit. It has a large office area above the garage. The team of full-timers and part-timers works well.

The full-timers concentrate on administration and fundraising, and the part-timers handle the minibus bookings and the rotas for the drivers. They also organise the servicing and repair of the vehicles.

**2 (a)** State one objective that Handy Rides may have identified. *(1 mark)*

**(b)** State one group of stakeholders that Handy Rides will have. *(1 mark)*

**(c)** Georgina, the manager of Handy Rides is keen to reorganise the office space and go for an open-plan office. Do you think that Handy Rides would benefit from this? Explain your answer. *(5 marks)*

**(d)** The full-time staff are involved in external communication. Using an example from Handy Rides, explain what is meant by external communication. *(2 marks)*

**(e)** Each month Georgina gets all the staff together to discuss fundraising targets and Handy Rides expenditure in the previous month.

**(i)** Why might discussing these figures with all the staff not be the best idea and use of time? *(4 marks)*

**(ii)** Suggest how Georgina should organise each of these discussions. Explain your answers. *(6 marks)*

## QUESTION 3

**Read Item B, then answer the questions that follow.**
**Total marks for this question:** *15 marks*

## Item B

Handy Rides has a basic website. It provides information and contact details. A local website developer has offered to improve the website at a reduced cost. Neither Georgina nor the other staff have any real idea about what they would like the website to look like or do.

**3 (a)** Explain two advantages of adding content and features to the website. *(4 marks)*

**(b)** Gavin, one of the drivers, suggested that they have a blog on the site. Georgina has no idea what this is. Explain what is meant by a blog. *(2 marks)*

**Read Item C, then answer the questions that follow.**
**Total for this question:** *17 marks*

## Item C

Handy Rides uses paper-based filing to store its records. Georgina is sure that everything would be far more efficient if the charity were to switch across to computerised records. It would take some time to do this, but she believes that it would be beneficial in the long term.

**3 (c)** Give one reason why it might be more efficient to switch over to computerised record-keeping. *(2 marks)*

**(d)** Georgina thinks that a relational database would be very useful for the fundraising effort. What is meant by the term relational database? *(2 marks)*

**(e)** How might the other records kept by the charity, such as rotas and routes of the minibuses be stored and accessed electronically rather than on paper? *(5 marks)*

## QUESTION 4

**Read Item D, then answer the questions that follow.**
**Total marks for this question:** *17 marks*

## Item D

At a recent meeting with the directors of the charity it was decided that Handy Rides should advertise for a marketing manager. It is hoped that this would raise the profile of the charity and bring in more donations so that Handy Rides could expand and offer a broader range of services to its clients. Creating the post would mean writing advertisements, taking responsibility for the new improved website, organising fundraising events and talking to the media. The charity intends to advertise the post in the local and regional newspapers.

**4 (a)** Gavin, one of the volunteer drivers, wants the job. If he was to get the post, what kind of recruitment would this be and why? *(2 marks)*

**(b)** Using the information from Item D and your knowledge of recruitment procedures, explain the stages necessary in recruitment to ensure that the best possible candidates are attracted, shortlisted and interviewed. *(10 marks)*

**(c)** Gavin worked as a sales manager in the past and has some experience of marketing. Should Georgina offer the job to Gavin and save on the recruitment expenses? Explain your answer. *(5 marks)*

141

# Introduction: Studying and the exam

### What is the unit about?

This unit introduces a range of different software applications, all of which are routinely used by businesses to support their functions or operations. It aims to help you understand how businesses use software to capture, store, retrieve and analyse data.

The unit is split into seven parts, each of which focuses either on different aspects of software or on the specific uses of software:

- The selection and use of appropriate software
- Using word processing software
- Using spreadsheet software
- Using database software
- Creating and using graphics
- Using presentation software
- Web authoring.

The unit headings and amplification (additional information and the required coverage) exactly match the exam specification. Throughout the unit, there are technical terms that you will need to remember and be able to apply where necessary.

Unit 9 provides much of the knowledge and skills that you will need for this unit and also for Unit 10.

### Why is it important?

All businesses use a range of software applications to support their functions and operations. From the one-person sole trader, to the multinational employing tens of thousands of people, computer-based applications have become essential.

Unit 9 explores the ways in which businesses select and use appropriate software, looking at types of data, the uses of data and the presentation of data. The manipulation of data can be undertaken using different types of software, each of which is appropriate for particular uses. Financial data, for example, can be manipulated and analysed using spreadsheet software, such as Microsoft Excel.

It is important to remember that this unit is not only information-based, but it is also a practical one. Much of what you will learn, and the skills that you will acquire, will be used for the controlled assessment of Unit 10.

This unit is worth 35% of the overall GCSE mark but it will also help you achieve the 25% that is allocated to Unit 10.

### What is the assessment like?

Unit 9 is assessed by a computer-based examination, taking the form of a series of tasks, rather than questions. The examiner will have prepared a number of basic documents, files and templates for you to use.

The examination lasts 1 hour and 30 minutes, and there will be 60 marks available – equivalent to 1½ marks per minute. So if a task has a total of 20 marks available, this tells you that you should spend no more than 30 minutes on it. Each of the tasks is broken down so you can see which parts are most important.

| ASSESSMENT OBJECTIVE | WHAT IT SAYS | HOW IMPORTANT IS IT? |
|---|---|---|
| A01 | Recall, select and communicate knowledge and understanding of concepts, issues and terminology. | 10.5% of the marks for this unit and 30% of the overall GCSE. |
| A02 | Apply skills, knowledge and understanding in a variety of contexts and in planning and carrying out investigations and tasks. | 12.25% of the marks for this unit and 35% of the overall GCSE. |
| A03 | Analyse and evaluate evidence, make reasoned judgements and make appropriate conclusions. | 12.25% of the marks for this unit and 35% of the overall GCSE. |

## How do I get a good grade?

Examiners use a uniform marking system, which means that you need 36 marks out of 60 (60%) to achieve a Grade C, or 54 marks (90%) to achieve an A*. However, it is important to remember that whatever your mark for this paper, your final GCSE mark is gained across the three units.

Examiners are particularly interested in the *quality* of your answer. They have set three assessment objectives, as shown in the table above.

So we can see that Unit 9 is worth 35% of the GCSE. The examiners will also be interested in ensuring that you produce good-quality written English.

They will identify which of the tasks includes an assessment of your communication skills. Unlike in Unit 8, you will not see many references to assessment objective AO3, but this does not mean that you should ignore this aspect of the assessment.

Each of the double-page spreads has an activity or a series of activities on the right-hand side. Some of these carry on from one spread to another, requiring you to manipulate the same basic data, adding to it and adapting it for different uses. In some cases there are questions rather than activities and these are designed to help ensure that you

understand basic concepts and ideas.

At the end of the unit there is a revision guide and integrated question section, along with a checklist to make sure that you have acquired all the necessary skills that you will need. There is also a full mock examination paper for you to try out, which follows exactly the format and style of a real examination paper.

# Selecting appropriate software

YOU WILL FIND OUT:

- about capturing and storing data
- about the retrieval of data
- about ease of analysis
- about dissemination and appropriate formats

## Capturing and storing data

There are few aspects of businesses today that do not rely on some form of data in order to successfully carry out their daily operations. This means that businesses establish data policies to ensure that they can rely on the data they capture and use, and do not base their decisions on incomplete or incorrect data.

The capture stage involves collecting data that aims to meet the needs of the business's functions. They need to set up flexible systems for the capture, storage and processing of information.

A database is a series of records. Each record consists of a set of **fields** containing information about a person, a product or other information relevant to the business.

A field is a cell that holds a specific part of the record such as a person's name, part of their address or date of birth). The database is designed so that:

- the user can design the overall structure of the database
- each field can be created to contain specific information
- the number of fields is the choice of the user
- fields can be amended or deleted as required.

Specialist computer software is available to create these databases:

- Microsoft Access allows a business to set up data capture forms to ensure that all records are formatted in exactly the same way. It also allows the business to store that data so that it can later be retrieved and used.

- Microsoft Excel is widely used for the capture and storage of financial data. Financial data is usually stored in a document called a spreadsheet. A spreadsheet is a specialised data record that is also able to make calculations. Again, purpose-built spreadsheets are created, and allow members of staff to simply key the figures into the appropriate boxes. From this basic form the figures can be analysed, and then a number of different types of report or calculations can be made.

Businesses use standardised hardware and software to ensure the efficient capture and storage of data. Ultimately this means that data can be shared across the business and manipulated for specific purposes. In the past, much of the data was captured and stored on paper-based systems, but electronic capture and storage of data allows real-time capture and storage, and instant access by managers and employees across the business.

## Data retrieval

When a business uses a database it may not necessarily want to retrieve all the records that are stored on it. It may only be interested in certain aspects of the database. The user enters what is known as a query. A query would look at particular characteristics in the data, such as customers living within a 50-mile radius of the business, or customers who have not ordered within the last three months. The user can then retrieve the data that they need from the database without having to look through all the data, and identify the characteristics they are looking for themselves.

Data retrieval from a database is rather like typing a search into an Internet search engine. The software looks for any data records that are relevant to the query. We look at searching database records in much more detail in section 1.4: Using Appropriate Software: Databases.

144

**For example** Discovering a fault

A business discovers that there is a fault with one of the products it has been selling to customers. It needs to contact each customer who has bought one of these products. When searching a database to find the relevant customers, one of the fields searched might be the product code that the business uses to identify that product. The result should be a list of customers who have purchased the relevant product. These can then be contacted by the business.

## Ease of analysis

Collecting and storing data and then being able to retrieve it is only part of the process. The business needs to be able to retrieve it and then analyse it in order to use it or act upon it. This means that the software needs to be able to present the data to the user in a way that can be easily analysed.

The data records themselves are often referred to as raw data. They contain all the information, but before it has been sorted or categorised. When the business retrieves some of that data it has already narrowed down particular parts of the data that it is interested in looking at. To make the analysis even easier it now needs to be presented in the most appropriate way for the job at hand. As we will see, this might be a chart, a table or a graph, or it may simply be a list of names and addresses or telephone numbers.

The data needs to be user friendly. It should also suggest conclusions and support decision-making. The data analysis should identify patterns in the information gathered. If the data can be looked at in an understandable format then the analysis of the data will be a much easier process.

## Dissemination and appropriate formats

Dissemination is the process of communicating the data to those who need to see it or to use it. As we have seen, data can be retrieved and formatted in a variety of different ways, including charts, tables and graphs or in a specific business format, such as a report. Businesses will also use spreadsheets as a way to disseminate financial information.

The exact way in which the data is disseminated and the format chosen will depend on the type of data, as we will see on the next spread. It is not always possible to strip down data in the form of text to a very short and understandable format, but it can be summarised as a number of bullet points, or perhaps presented as slides as part of a PowerPoint presentation. Numerical data is often much better displayed in a table, chart or graph.

Businesses will have preferred formats and this will help them to analyse the data over a period of time, perhaps comparing last month's set of sales figures with this month's.

## QUESTION TIME
*14 minutes*

**1** Suggest SIX fields in a database that would be useful for storing data regarding suppliers. *(6 marks)*

**2** Which functional areas of the business might be interested in retrieving data to identify their fifty top business customers? Explain your answer. *(8 marks)*

**145**

— **K E Y   T E R M** —

**Field ▶** a line or a row in a data record. Each field will be of a particular format, e.g. numbers, text and numbers, text only or date.

# Types of data

## Qualitative data

Qualitative data is extremely varied. It is essentially any information that can be captured that is not in numerical form. It can include: documents, newspapers, magazines, books, websites, memoranda, annual reports and questionnaires.

Qualitative data presents businesses with particular problems because it comes in so many different forms. Collecting it can be a problem, sorting it can be a major issue, and then deciding which parts of the qualitative material are relevant is also difficult. Businesses will routinely

| INTERNAL SOURCE | CHARACTERISTICS |
|---|---|
| Data records | These are customer records, containing information regarding the customer such as name, address, purchasing habits and credit ratings. They can be used as the basis for marketing and advertising by matching the customers' purchasing habits and preferences with new products and services as they become available. |
| Loyalty schemes | Supermarkets run extensive loyalty schemes and programmes. They are able to match customers' purchasing habits with targeted offers to encourage them to buy more of the same product or similar products. Loyalty schemes encourage regular purchases, repeat purchases and volume sales. |
| EPOS | Electronic Point of Sale was originally envisaged to link the sale of a product to the stock control system. EPOS would enable the business to automatically generate a stock re-order once the stock of a particular product had dropped to a minimum level. Increasingly, however, EPOS is used in conjunction with loyalty cards to monitor customer purchases and to generate sales offers linked to their popular brands. In its basic form EPOS can indicate to a business when particular products are more or less likely to sell on a particular day or in a particular month. The business can then organise its sales displays or even its website to highlight popular sales items when they are most likely to be required by their customers. |
| Website monitoring | Website monitoring is a form of observation. It involves monitoring the number of clicks made by customers on an organisation's website, noting how long they have been on the website and which pages they have visited. It is also possible to judge the activities on the website and the pages visited compared to the purchases made by the visitor. Businesses often encourage customers to register on the website, and by doing this they can customise the way in which the page appears to match the preferences of that customer. |
| E-transactions | E-transactions include all forms of monetary transaction on a website. This includes the use of credit cards, debit cards and electronic payments, such as PayPal. Increasingly, by linking up with specialised finance companies and banks, businesses, regardless of their size, can offer secure online payment systems. In monitoring e-transactions the business is able to ascertain which is the most popular form of payment, whether customers are hesitant about entering their credit card details and indeed, which form of payment and customer provides the biggest share of sales and which region of the world they come from. |
| Accounting records | Accounting records can be differentiated from sales in that they detail when and how customers made actual payments. It is not always the case that customers pay on order for their products or services. They may pay in instalments or they may pay on delivery or after the production of an invoice. By monitoring the accounting records a business is able to see how long, on average, it takes a customer to pay an invoice and which payment method they have chosen. |
| Production information | Many manufacturers only have a relatively small stock of products and do not over-produce and store huge levels of stock in anticipation of sales. Therefore production is very much reliant on accurate sales data or at least accurate orders. |
| Sales figures | Sales figures should show the accurate level of sales, as well as highs and lows in demand. Sales figures should be the most accurate way of showing when, where and how much each product was sold for over a given period of time. By looking at trends in the sales figures, businesses can more confidently predict the level of sales in a similar future period, assuming the same conditions apply. |
| Sales personnel | Many businesses recognise that professional sales personnel, while they have experience and knowledge of products and services, are not necessarily the best people to ask about future sales trends, product development or marketing. Many sales personnel are over-optimistic about new products and the impact of new advertising. |

collect a wide variety of different pieces of qualitative data. There may be a relevant newspaper article, a report on a new market, or some information received from suppliers.

Computers can be used to manipulate text, so if all the text material is digitised then it can be searched via keywords, phrases or even dates. Computers are able to do this very quickly and can identify relevant qualitative text.

## Quantitative data

Quantitative data is numerical data, which is often displayed in tables, charts or graphs. Another term used to describe this is statistics. It therefore includes any information that can be counted or expressed as a number. This is ideal for computer storage and manipulation.

## Internal and external sources of data

An internal source of information is data held by the business itself. Other areas of the business may have collected it and it may not be routinely shared. The table on the left-hand page shows the kind of data that could be available internally.

External sources of data can come from a wide variety of different places. Some of it is free, while other data must be paid for. The table below outlines some of the key sources of external data.

## QUESTION TIME
### 10 minutes

**1** Would a business's sales figures be qualitative or quantitative? *(2 marks)*

**2** Suggest the type of data that a business could capture using customer loyalty cards and identify whether they are qualitative or quantitative data. *(8 marks)*

| EXTERNAL SOURCE | CHARACTERISTICS |
|---|---|
| Internet | Many businesses will use the Internet to trawl for information, reactions and opinions, either about themselves or their competitors. This information can be valuable, as can constant monitoring of competitor's websites, which can reveal information about future direction, strategy, tactics and advertising. |
| Government statistics | The government produces an enormous array of statistics, from the census, different industries, the Department of Trade and Industry, marketing initiatives, trade initiatives and a host of other topics. Much of the data is well researched and has been collated from wide sources. In addition to UK government statistics there is European-wide information compiled by the European Union. |
| Libraries | Businesses will not routinely use local libraries as centres of information gathering, despite the fact that they may have access to online databases. Businesses tend to use dedicated business libraries, which compile data from industries by trawling magazines and newspapers, as well as the Internet, for clippings and references to specific businesses. |
| Universities | A major part of universities' work, beyond teaching, is research. They will routinely carry out their own research and may well cooperate with businesses or industry to collect and collate data. |
| Company reports | The structure of a company report is determined by law, and requires a business to outline its profit and loss, balance sheet and use of funds. It is also a means by which the business highlights its key personnel, notes its major successes and failures and perhaps announces new initiatives. |
| Specialist agencies | There are a number of specialist agencies that operate both nationally and internationally, routinely collecting their own data, which they then compile into reports for sale to businesses. Examples include Mintel, Datastream and Dun and Bradstreet. |
| Trade journals | These are magazines or newspapers whose readership is restricted primarily to those in the industry. They feature articles and information about the trade, as well as advertisements, information about special events and advance information about new legislation that may have an impact on the industry. |

# Use of data

## How data will be used

The primary reasons for the capture, storage, retrieval and dissemination of data are:

- to allow the business to make informed judgements and decisions
- to ensure that the business has fully up-to-date information
- to ensure that the business has information that will be legally required (for accounts purposes, tax and other reasons)
- to allow the business to communicate information to its stakeholders (such as shareholders, customers or suppliers).

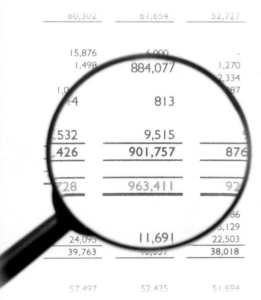

## The capabilities of different software

### Microsoft Word

Microsoft Word is the industry standard word-processing software. See page 120 for more information.

### Microsoft PowerPoint

Microsoft PowerPoint is the industry standard for presentation software. It is easy to use and can produce some very professional-looking results.

The application offers users a number of different templates (colour and layout) that can be chosen or amended. The user can also design their own layouts for each of the slides. The slides are single-screen or page designs, with areas for text and graphics.

Typically, users will have both text areas and graphics areas on the slide. They can also have bullet points, different fonts and sizes and the ability to insert business names and logos.

PowerPoint presentations are often displayed either on laptops or using projectors. The key advantages of PowerPoint are:

- It is easy to customise the slides
- It is easy to update the slides
- Customised graphics, images and sounds can be used
- The presentation does not need to be printed out

### Microsoft Excel

All businesses need a simple way to keep track of their spending and their income. Spreadsheets are designed to do this. They are most commonly used to list and order data (usually numerical data). The software can also add, divide, subtract and multiply.

It is possible to create spreadsheets that can add all the figures in one column and then take the total away from the total of another column, to give a final figure.

Microsoft Excel has become the industry standard spreadsheet application software. Some businesses will have their own, or non-specialised spreadsheet software. This will be particularly true of businesses that use other non-Microsoft software to keep track of their **stock levels** and other activities.

For the most part nearly all businesses will opt for Excel as it offers huge advantages if used with other parts of the Microsoft Office suite. For example, spreadsheets and tables created in Excel can be **imported** into Microsoft Word very simply.

Excel is a powerful tool for businesses. It tends to be used by those who deal with the financial side of the operation, such as accountants.

Spreadsheets have many capabilities, the key ones are:

- They have a grid of 'cells' into which numbers, text and formulae can be typed.
- The cells can be formatted, so the spreadsheet knows if you are inputting text, numbers, dates or currencies.
- The width of the cells can be changed to fit in longer data.
- The spreadsheet can order the columns in alphabetical order for text or value or numbers.
- By re-ordering the columns all data related to that column (in the lines) is also moved.

149

Businesses will use spreadsheets to help them predict changes that could happen and their effect on the business. This is called modelling. It is achieved by simply changing the data that has been put into the cells of a spreadsheet.

The uses of modelling are:

- Predicting sales if prices increase or decrease
- Predicting changes if the **interest rate** changes
- Predicting changes of temperature or other factors relevant to the product

### Microsoft Access

In effect, a database is an electronic filing system. Microsoft Access is the dedicated database, but Excel could also be used for the same purpose, although it does not have all the features of Access.

Businesses can use a database for many different reasons, including:

- Collecting and storing information about customers and suppliers
- As a product or service listing, with all of the features and prices included
- As an internal database containing information about each employee (human resources records)

Microsoft Access comes with several different database templates. These can be amended to suit the needs of the user. Alternatively, the user can create their own personalised database and set it up so that it contains a number of fields for each of the records.

Specialist databases can also be designed by database professionals. They can be custom-made to match the specifications and needs of a business.

The main advantages of a database are that:

- all information can be instantly accessed
- all information can be tracked
- it is easy to update or delete records
- it is not paper-based, so less storage is needed
- it is safe (assuming it is backed up on a regular basis)
- it can be used with other systems, such as stock control.

Databases can also be locked to prevent access. This means that only authorised people can view, update or delete records from the database.

--- **KEY TERMS** ---

**Stock levels** ▶ the amount of products stored by a business before being sold.

**Imported** ▶ data transferred from one application to another.

**Interest rate** ▶ the cost of borrowing set by the Bank of England each month.

## QUESTION TIME
*14 minutes*

**1** **What type of data would a business NOT wish to communicate to its customers and why?** *(6 marks)*

**2** **What are the key differences between Microsoft Access and Microsoft Excel? Give examples where possible.** *(8 marks)*

# Presentation of data

## Word-processed documents

Even the simplest memo or letter must follow a particular format and set of conventions. These are rules which require the person who is creating the business document to follow particular steps in terms of the way in which the document will look. Each different type of business communication, or document, has a different set of formats and conventions. By following these the person or people who receive or see the communication will have a much better chance of understanding the information contained in it.

### For example

When a business wishes to disseminate information to a large number of employees, it may choose to do so by placing a notice on one of the staff noticeboards. The notice can be formal or informal and could tell the employees about a change to usual procedures or perhaps inform them of a forthcoming social event that is being arranged. Notices have the advantage of being quick and easy to produce, and transmit information to a large number of different individuals.

Individuals can also use a noticeboard to inform other employees about things, such as items they may have for sale or events they have planned or are involved in.

Whatever type of notice you are involved in preparing, the following guidelines should help:

- Remember that most noticeboards are not very large, so don't use large paper which will take up all the space and might hide other notices.
- Make the notice bold enough to get noticed.
- Don't use too much text, but state clearly and concisely what it is you want noticed.
- Make sure the reader of the notice knows what they have to do – if they have to contact someone, then make sure that person's name and contact address or number is clear.
- Put a date on the notice so that the reader can tell when it was first placed on the noticeboard and also so that the reader will know if the notice is still current or if it is out-of-date.

Good design of a notice is important too. You want the notice to have impact and attract attention. You could include any of the following:

- bullet points (••○□♦ or ●)
- different fonts to make words more or less obvious
- different font sizes to make important words stand out
- the use of CAPITAL letters or bold or underline and italics to make text stand out
- the use of sub-headings to break up the text
- pictures or graphics for emphasis.

## Spreadsheets and databases

Spreadsheets and databases can both be used to capture data and perform calculations. A spreadsheet, for example, could be used to record payments and expenses. A database could be used to record market research information. Information printed off from spreadsheet or database sources can also be incorporated into a word-processed document. It is possible to use Word to tabulate information, or to import graphics, both of which can come from spreadsheets and databases.

## Desktop publishing and graphics

Desktop publishing software and graphics software make the job of creating eye-catching and interesting leaflets and advertisements comparatively easy. You can use standardised templates, or create your own designs from scratch.

Leaflets are often produced in large quantities and can be delivered to customers, or potential customers, by a variety of means, including being hand-delivered through letterboxes, or inserted into newspapers and magazines, or distributed in the street by representatives of the business. Leaflets can be a form of advertisement, but usually when we refer to advertisements we think of those that appear in newspapers, magazines, on TV and on radio.

There are some guidelines to producing leaflets and advertisements if we consider a technique known as 'AIDA'. This stands for:

**A** TTENTION – *do something in the leaflet or advertisement to gain the attention of the reader*

**I** NTEREST – *tell the reader something that specifically appeals to them to get their interest*

**D** ESIRE – *make the reader either want to buy what you are offering or get in touch*

**A** CTION – *encourage the reader to act on their desire, get in touch and buy*

### For example

Although notices are often only seen inside the business, leaflets and advertisements are aimed at customers, or those the business hopes will become customers in the future.

If you think of the leaflets or advertisements you see each week, you will realise how important it is to make your own stand out.

It is very important to try to get the readers' attention. The following list could help you do this:

- *Use a headline* to catch the readers' attention and make them want to read on.
- *Offer a benefit* – promise the reader something, for example a solution to a problem or another kind of benefit they would receive from reading further.
- *Appeal* to the reader personally.
- *Say it with pictures* – use images that help to reduce the amount of text (words) you use to provide an alternative means of capturing attention, and make the overall appearance attractive.
- *Use sub-headings* to reduce the amount of words involved.
- *Explain* – be careful what you say and how you say it so that the reader does not misunderstand your message.
- *Help the reader* by giving them all the information they need to do what it is you want them to do, for example include any contact names, addresses and telephone/fax numbers, e-mail and website addresses.

## ACTIVITY

**Create a suitable one-page job advertisement using the following information:**

- **Job title – Full-time Administrative Assistant**
- **Duties – Reporting to the Assistant Manager, this position will be responsible for providing a variety of administrative/clerical and reception support duties.**
- **Qualifications required – OCR Level 2 in Administration. Proficiency in the use of word processing and spreadsheet applications is also required.**
- **Competitive salary**
- **Closing date – 24 March**
- **Application process – submit CV and details of experience to: Assistant Manager, Walpole Marine, PO Box 1838, Walpole, Suffolk. Telephone/ Fax: 0207 425-0045. Email: Walpolemarine@bt.com**
- **Instructions – Your covering letter and CV should clearly demonstrate related qualifications and experience since selection will be based on the information provided.**
- **Job code – 102 WM 07.**

151

# Importing and inserting data

## Documents – importing and exporting data

You can, of course, move text from one document to another. This can be done by highlighting the text you wish to move, right-clicking on it and selecting 'Copy', then opening the document you wish to move it to. You then find the right place, right-click again and select 'Paste'. This simple series of steps is pretty much what is required for everything else.

There may be occasions when you will wish to put a graphic or a chart or table into a Word document.

In this case, select 'Insert' from the drop-down menu at the top of the screen. Select and click on 'Picture' and click on 'From file'. The **directory** will then appear. What happens next confirms that you need to name things properly. You will see all the items that you could insert into the document, and you will need to select the right one. By choosing it and clicking on 'Insert', the picture will appear in your Word document. It may be the wrong size, but we can deal with that later.

Create a Word document and click on the 'Insert' menu at the top of the screen. Click on 'Picture' then click on 'Clipart'. Choose a suitable piece of Clipart, featuring a computer. Click once on your chosen picture. A new box will appear and you should select 'Insert Clipart'. The Clipart will now appear in your word document. Select 'Save as' and call this file 'First exercise v3'.

## Exporting database files into spreadsheets

It is sometimes necessary to move data that is stored in an Access database into an Excel worksheet. This will allow the user to analyse the data using Excel. The conversion is fairly straightforward:

- The database is opened
- Switch to 'Table view'
- Double-click on the data in the database window to open the appropriate table
- From the file menu choose 'Export'

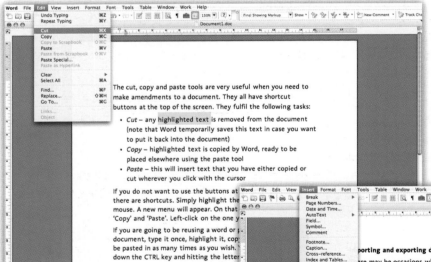

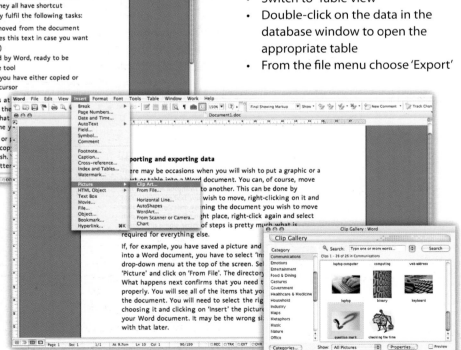

--- K E Y   T E R M S ---

**Directory** ▶ a complete list of all files and folders that have been saved on the drive.

**Salutation** ▶ this is how you address an individual in a letter, for example 'Dear Sir' or 'Dear Mrs Jones'.

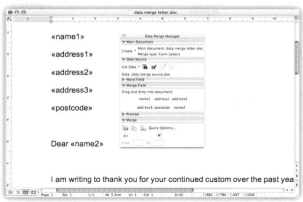

- You will now see a box that asks where you want to export the data – choose Excel from the 'Save as' type menu
- Choose a file name
- Click 'Export all' and the process is completed
- Make sure you open the spreadsheet to see that all of the data has been exported

## Creating a mail merge letter

It is relatively easy to bring information from one Word document into another. Information on a data source can be imported into another Word document. The data source is a list of names and addresses of customers.

The information on the data source can be imported into a standard letter and mail-merged to different customers. The letters will have the appearance of being personalised.

### The merge

You need two things to accomplish a mail merge. These are:

- A standard letter, created in Word. We will call this the main document. It will contain all of the information that will be sent out to each person
- A data source, with a list of names and addresses of people who will receive a copy of the main document. This is also created in Word

By clicking on 'Tools' and selecting 'Mail merge' a new menu will appear. It will give you the option to create

a 'Form letter', which is your main document. It will also give you the opportunity to create a data source. By clicking on this you can choose which 'fields' you think you will need for the data. Delete the ones you don't think you will need. Once this is completed a new box will appear for you to type in the names and addresses of each of the people the letter needs to be sent to.

Now the merge fields need to be inserted into the main document. These are the places where names, addresses and **salutations** will go in that letter. This is achieved by having the cursor in the right place and clicking on 'Insert merge field'.

In effect, the mail merge removes the need to type separate names, addresses and salutations into each letter.

### Alternative mail merges

This is a mail merge operation just within Word. When we look at Access we will see that the mail merge is a lot more flexible and can insert all sorts of data into a letter or document. You can also use Access to create mailing labels, lists and forms.

If you are using a 'Dear Sir' or 'Dear Madam' or 'Dear Sir or Madam' salutation, you should end the letter with 'Yours faithfully'. If you know the person's actual name and are using it with 'Dear', then you should end the letter 'Yours sincerely'.

**ACTIVITY**

**Y**our teacher or tutor will give you a basic letter and instructions to create a simple data source. You will be expected to merge the two to create four personalised letters. You should save your letter as 'Main document' and your data source file as 'List'.

153

# Word processing

## Word processing

Word-processing software is probably the most commonly used application in businesses and at home. Using software such as Microsoft Word, it is easy to make professional-looking documents. The key features of word-processing software are:

- It is easy to enter and edit text
- Errors can easily be corrected
- Changes to the size of the text or the font are straightforward
- Margins, **page breaks**, **headers** and **footers** can be added or changed
- The software has a spelling and grammar checker
- Indexes and contents pages can be made
- Specific words can be found and replaced
- Single or multiple copies can be made
- Letters can be mail-merged with databases to produce personalised documents
- Labels and envelopes can be printed

Typically a business will use word-processing software to create its letters, reports and memoranda. With a little practice most people can produce a professional-looking document.

## Accurate copy

It is vital that documents created by word-processing software are not littered with spelling mistakes and grammatical errors. Microsoft Word does help to some extent in dealing with this:

- Incorrectly spelled words are underlined in red
- Sentences that do not make grammatical sense are underlined in green
- Additional spaces between words are underlined in green
- Errors in punctuation are underlined in green

It is very important to make sure that the spelling and grammar checker is set for UK English. You can do this by clicking on 'Tools' and selecting 'Language'. When you click on 'Language' the option is 'Set language'. When choosing this option you can find 'English (UK)'.

As you are typing a document, Word will automatically highlight any spelling or grammar mistakes. You can either ignore these, deal with them when you have finished typing, or handle them as they appear. Even if there are not any highlighted errors, always run the spellchecker after you have completed the document.

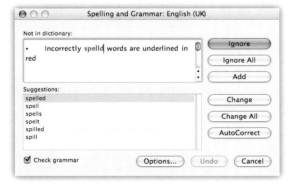

--- **K E Y   T E R M S** ---

**Page breaks** ▶ when a certain number of lines have been typed on a page, Word will automatically start a new page – this is called a page break.

**Header** ▶ a name, title, date, or other information that can be set to appear at the top of every page of a document.

**Footer** ▶ similar to a header except that it appears at the bottom of every page and is usually a page number.

There may be something that has been missed. The spellchecker will highlight the word or phrase and then offer a suggestion. You can simply choose from a list and click 'Change'.

## Correcting errors

It is important to remember that the spellchecker and the grammar checker will not pick up every single mistake. If the wrong word is typed in, but it is still a proper word, the spellchecker will ignore it. It is therefore important to check every word and sentence yourself and not to rely on the spellchecker and grammar tools to do the job for you.

### *Line-spacing*

This is the gap between each line of text. Single line-spacing is quite close; double line-spacing is far easier to read because the lines are further apart. To change the line-spacing in Word, select 'Format' then 'Paragraph' and a new box will appear. On the bottom right of the box will be a line that tells you what line-spacing is being used in the document. To change the line-spacing, use the pull-down menu. The most common ones to use are single, 1.5 and double.

It is important to remember that changing the line-spacing will not affect the text already typed into the document. To change the line-spacing on text already typed, you must highlight the text and then click on 'Format' and follow the same procedure.

A shortcut is to highlight the text then hold down the CTRL key and press '2' for double line-spacing or '1' for single line-spacing.

## Text features

In Word you can decide how your text lines will appear by choosing either left-aligned, right-aligned or centred text. You can also break up your text by putting in numbered or bulleted lists. To do this, start a new line and click on either the bullet point icon or the numbered list icon. Both of these can be found in the top right-hand corner of the screen. You can type normally, but when you press 'Return', a new bullet, or the next number in sequence will appear. When you have finished, either simply hit 'Return' twice or hit it once and click off the relevant icon.

### *Other text features*

To make your text look even better you can always use:

- Capitals – this can be achieved by using the 'Caps lock'. This capitalises every letter until you take the 'Caps lock' off.
- You can also make text appear in bold or italics. There are two ways of doing this. The first is to click on the B or I icon in the top right-hand corner. As a shortcut you can hold down the CTRL key and press B or I. To come off either, you repeat the process.

## ACTIVITIES

**1** You will be expected to produce accurate copy, identify and check errors, and use line-spacing, centring, justification, numbered points and bulleted points. Your teacher or tutor will give you a copy of The Spelling Mistake worksheet. Read the document and underline any errors you have found.

**2** Your teacher or tutor will give you a copy of the Text Features Worksheet. Follow the instructions to find out more about fonts (type styles) and point sizes.

155

# Creating a document for business purposes

## Agendas

Meetings are held in all businesses. They can be formal or informal, depending on the type of business and the type of meeting, and tend to be held for the following reasons:

- to share information
- to discuss new ideas or proposals
- to maintain interest
- to ask for assistance
- to report back on an activity
- to report on progress
- to discuss problems.

Most meetings lead to the generation of various documents.

An agenda is the document used to inform individuals about a forthcoming meeting, listing points to be discussed at that meeting. The following basic information is given at the top of an agenda:

- The date of the meeting
- The time of the meeting
- The venue (location) of the meeting.

Other items that commonly appear on an agenda are:

1 *Apologies for absence* – a list of those not able to attend the meeting. Apologies are sent in advance to the chairperson (sometimes called the 'chair').
2 *Minutes of the last meeting* – checking the accuracy of the minutes (the written record) of the previous meeting held (if any). If the minutes are approved, the chairperson will sign them as being a true and accurate record of what took place
3 *Matters arising* – discussion of any matters arising from the minutes of the last meeting.

Following these first three agenda items, the chair will list those issues that are to be discussed specifically at this meeting. There could be any number of these items and it could be that certain individual employees are given the task of presenting information to the meeting on any number of agenda items.

- *AOB (any other business)* – provides the opportunity for members of the meeting to introduce any matters they wish to discuss that have not been included on the agenda
- *Date of next meeting* – the final item on the agenda that allows members of the meeting to decide the date on which they will meet again.

The chair will call the meeting and is the person in control once the meeting gets underway. He or she will control the order of the discussion, aiming to make sure everyone has a chance to speak. The chair will also ensure that items on the agenda are discussed in the correct order.

---

**SAFETY REPRESENTATIVES' MEETING**

A meeting of Safety Representatives will be held in the business suite on

**Friday 25 January 2009 at 11.00 am**

### Agenda

1 Apologies for absence
2 Minutes of the last meeting
3 Matters arising from the minutes
4 Report on research into safety issues on the factory production line
5 Report on financial cost implications of the proposed extension to the production line
6 Any other business
7 Date of next meeting

---

## Minutes

The minutes of the meeting should be an accurate, written record of the meeting and are provided for all those who attended, as well as those who offered their apologies and could not attend. The minutes are distributed after the meeting and appear in the same order as the items on the agenda. Minutes include the following information:

- an account of those present at the meeting
- an account of the discussions that took place during the meeting
- any specific jobs given to individuals during the meeting
- any reports received from individuals during the meeting
- any specific actions that have to be taken before the next meeting
- any specific decisions made or votes taken during the meeting.

Minutes do not have to be a word-for-word account of what was said, and should be brief and to the point, but they must be accurate.

## Business letters

Business letters are usually sent to individuals outside the organisation itself. Letters may be written for a number of different purposes, including:

- to contact potential customers (people who are either buying or may buy the organisation's products or services)
- to commmunicate with suppliers (other businesses that may provide items such as products, photocopy paper or office equipment to the organisation)

**Streamline Plumbing**

814 Pipe Lane, Olivebrook OL9 8JB
telephone 01234 567890 fax 01234 567891
enquiries@streamline-plumbing.net

01 September 2009

Dear Sir

Thank you for your enquiry. I am enclosing a copy of our latest catalogue and complete price list, which provide details of all our current products and services.

If you have any further queries, or wish to place an order, please telephone our office and one of our assistants will be happy to help you.

Yours faithfully

pp *[signature]*

Mr J Simons
Head of Marketing

Encs: brochure, price list

- to answer a customer complaint
- to tell existing customers about a new product
- to contact job applicants.

Business letters need to be neat, accurate and well-presented in order to give a good impression of the business's professionalism. Businesses tend to use headed paper, so the same details do not have to be re-typed every time a letter is sent.

Headed paper will usually contain the following business details:

- name, postal address, telephone number and fax number
- e-mail address
- website address
- registered address (this could be different to the normal postal address of the business)
- registration number (a number given by Companies House, where most businesses have to register when they are created)
- names of owners or directors
- names of other associated businesses, such as professional organisations.

The letter itself might then include some or all of the following:

- the name and address of the recipient
- the date the letter is being prepared or sent
- a reference – this can be the initials of the writer or a set of numbers and helps with filing
- the word 'Urgent' or 'Confidential', to help the recipient recognise how important the letter is
- a salutation – for example: 'Dear Mr Smith' or 'Dear Sir'. If the name of the recipient is known, then it is usual to use it. If the name of the recipient is not known, then it is more appropriate to use 'Dear Sir' or 'Dear Madam'.
- a subject heading – to help the recipient see immediately what the letter is about.
- the main text of the letter, arranged in paragraphs
- the complimentary close – this is the way the letter ends. If 'Dear Sir or 'Dear Madam' has been used in the salutation, then the letter ends with 'Yours faithfully'; if a name has been used, for example 'Dear Mr Smith', then 'Yours sincerely' is used.
- The printed name of the person sending the letter (and their job title) will come after the complimentary close, leaving enough room for their signature
- If the letter includes any additional items, this is indicated at the end of the letter by 'Enc.' (or 'Encs.' for more than one enclosure).

The most common way to display a business letter is the fully blocked (left-aligned) method of display. This means that each part of the letter starts at the left-hand margin (see the example above). An alternative is to indent, which means leaving a space at the beginning of each paragraph so that the first line starts a few spaces away from the left-hand margin.

# ACTIVITY

You work in the human resources department of a business, and you have received a letter from someone who has applied for a job with you and has been invited to come in for interview. They cannot make the time set for the interview as they have to go to hospital for a routine appointment, but have told you they could make the same day and time the following week. Your business is very keen that the interview should take place. Write a letter to Mrs Susan Dodd, 75 Chancery Lane, West Bromwich, WB41 5DT, dated today, informing her that you would still like to interview her, but can only make next Friday at 11.30, in your office. You can design your company headed paper.

157

# Using fonts and page layouts (1)

## Using a range of formats

Businesses will have particular house styles, where they prefer the use of particular fonts, colours and styles. Fonts can be easily changed by clicking on the font window in the menu box, or by using Control, Shift and F. Alongside the font type is the font size. For normal business, font size 11 or 12 will be appropriate

It is also easy to change the font colour, as this is also on the toolbar at the top of Word. By clicking on the font colour you can choose theme colours or standard colours. If you wish to change the colour of existing text simply highlight it and then click the font colour you require.

## Paragraph formats

If you want to change the format of a paragraph you can highlight it and right-click. From here you select 'Paragraph' and you can change the indent (where the first letter of each new paragraph starts) and the spacing before and after the paragraph. You can also change the margins using this facility.

### Line spacing

This is the gap between each line of text. Single line-spacing is quite close; double line-spacing is far easier to read because the lines are further apart. To change the line-spacing in Word, select 'Format' then 'Paragraph' and a new box will appear. On the

bottom right of the box will be a line that tells you what line-spacing is being used in the document. To change the line-spacing, use the pull-down menu. The most common ones to use are single, 1.5 and double.

It is important to remember that changing the line-spacing will not affect the text already typed into the document. To change the line-spacing on text already typed, you must highlight the text and then click on 'Format' and follow the same procedure.

A shortcut is to highlight the text then hold down the CTRL key and press '2' for double line-spacing or '1' for single line-spacing.

### Indentation

There are two ways of achieving this. In the tool bar there is a decrease and increase indent. This sets how far across the page your paragraph will begin. The other way of doing it is to set it in centimetres by opening the paragraph dialogue box. You can change the indentation to the left and to the right.

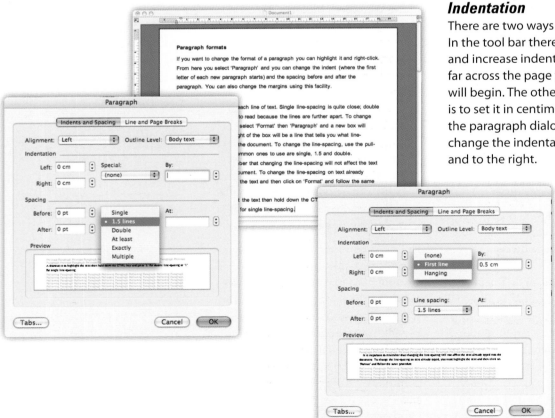

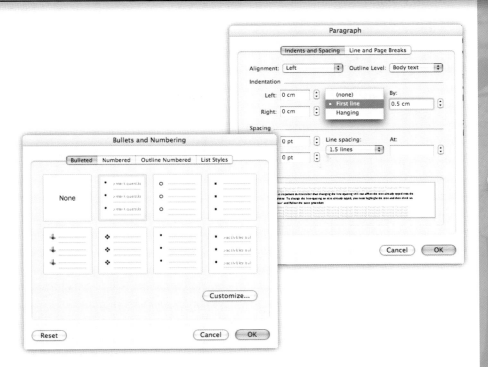

# Bullet points and paragraph numbering

Bullet points are ideal for listing points or breaking up text so it is easier to understand. Bullets and lists come in a number of different formats. The easiest way to create a bullet or numbered list is to click on the icon in the tool bar. In Word, once you have created a bullet point you can right-click to bring up a dialogue box. Select 'Bulleting' from the dialogue box and then choose the bullet format or style you prefer.

The process of using numbers is exactly the same. In Word, numbers also includes letters and Roman numerals. Again click on the numbering icon in the tool bar to start numbering. Once you have done this you can then right-click and select 'Numbering' from the dialogue box and choose your preferred number format.

The third option is multi-level lists. These can either be bullets, letters, numbers or even headings. Each one will be indented according to the way in which you want the multi-level list to be formatted. They can either be in a straight line or will indent each time.

# Alignment

There are four basic types of alignment:

- **Left-aligned (flush left)** – means the text is aligned along the left-hand margin – this is sometimes referred to as ragged right.
- **Right-aligned (flush right)** – the text is aligned along the right-hand margin and is also called ragged left.
- **Centred** – the text is not aligned with either the left- or the right-hand margins, which means that both left and right margins are ragged. Each line is centred across the page.
- **Justified** – the text is aligned along the left-hand margin and Word spaces the letters and the words so that the text is also aligned along the right-hand margin.

In order to access these options, the four variations are usually in the formatting tool bar at the top of the page. The default is left-aligned. You can also change the alignment by right-clicking, choosing 'Paragraph' and then changing to left, right, centred or justified in the dialogue box.

## ACTIVITY

**T**ry creating your own bulleted and numbered lists:

1. Open a new Word document.
2. Click on the bullet icon.
3. Type in the word 'Spaniel' following the first bullet.
4. Hit the enter key.
5. Type in 'Labrador' after the next bullet.
6. Follow this procedure, adding Yorkshire Terrier, Beagle, Retriever and Poodle.
7. Highlight your bulleted list and change the bullet format to a tick.
8. Now convert your bulleted list to a numbered list. Use the number format A, B, C for your list.
9. Now change the colouring of your list by alternating red and blue for each item.

159

# Using fonts and page layouts (2)

YOU WILL FIND OUT:

● about columns

● about tables

● about text boxes

● about headers and footers

## Columns

By highlighting text and then clicking on the 'Columns' icon at the top of the page, you have the option to create up to four columns of text across the page. Four columns look much better if you change the page layout to **landscape**, rather than **portrait**.

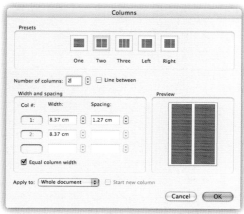

## Tables

Tables are a great way to organise and present data in an easy-to-understand format. All the tables are made up of rows and columns. Where a row intersects a column this is a cell. Into the cell you can type text and/or numbers. Creating a basic table is very straightforward. The simplest way of achieving this with Word 2007 is to select the 'Insert' tab at the top of the tool bar and click on the table icon. A dialogue box will appear, allowing you to create up to a 10 x 8 table. This is 10 cells across and 8 cells deep. Simply highlight the size of table you require and it will be inserted into your document. Make sure your cursor is in the right place within your document before doing this.

There are dozens of different table styles to choose from, in a variety of colours, and you can even shade individual cells if you wish them to look more prominent. You can type into each cell, making the text or numbers bold, in italics, justified or aligned as you wish and you can even put bulleted lists or numbered lists into each of the cells.

If you want your table to be larger than 10 x 8

you can click on the last cell in your table and hit the tab key. This will automatically give you a new row of cells. To make other amendments to your table go to 'Layout' in the table tool bar. Here you can merge cells, split cells, insert columns and rows and also change the direction of the text within a cell.

If you are struggling to fit your table onto the page you can highlight the table and right-click. This allows you to 'auto-fit' the table, or even to distribute the rows and columns more evenly. You can also use this to insert a caption for your table, or change the table's properties (the rows and columns) or each cell.

## Text boxes

Text boxes can be added to a Word document by clicking on the 'Insert' tab on the tool bar. There are many different styles of text box, but they all have the same properties. When you choose a text box it will appear over any other text or graphics in your Word document. You can type into the text box. You can change the shape of the text box by left-clicking on any of the corner or mid-line points and stretching in the direction you wish to change the shape. You will also see that a new format tool bar has appeared, that allows you to change the colour of the box itself, the colour of the text, the outline, the shadows, and provide 3-D effects.

Once you are happy with your text box you can then move it around. Put the cursor over the textbox and wait for a cross to appear, then left-click and move the text box to your desired position. You can also align the text box, rotate it or set it so that it appears in front of or behind other text or graphics.

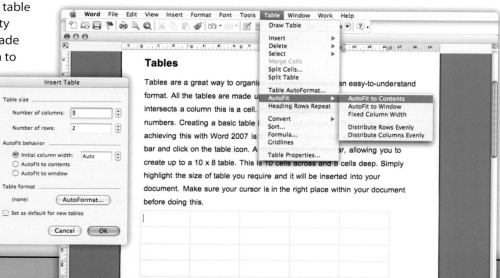

You do not have to insert a new text box every time if you are using more than one in a document. Right-click on the outline of the textbox and select 'Copy'. Then select 'Paste' and an exact copy of your original text box will appear. Hover over the text box with your cursor until the cross appears and move it to your required position within the document.

## Headers and footers

Headers, footers and page numbers can add much to the look and user-friendliness of a document. If you choose to use these, they will appear on every page of a document.

Clicking on 'Insert' and selecting 'Header or footer' can access them. You will automatically be looking at the header, and you can type in the title of the document or choose to put a page number in here. What you use as a header is your choice.

An icon on the header box will also take you down to the footer which will appear at the bottom of each page in your document. Again you can put the document's title or your name, page number and date. Headers and footers can be left-aligned, centred or right-aligned. You are given those options in the pop-up box. To exit from the header or footer you can shortcut by double-clicking on the centre or main part of the document itself.

--- **KEY TERMS** ---

**Portrait** ▶ the standard way of printing, with the short side of A4 to the top.

**Landscape** ▶ an alternative page layout that switches the long side of a sheet of A4 to the top.

## ACTIVITY

**O**pen a Word document and insert a header. Type into the header the words 'header practice', which should be centred. Now insert a footer and type in 'practice document', which should be left-aligned. Save your document as 'headers and footers'. You can click on the headers and footers and change their format or style via the library.

161

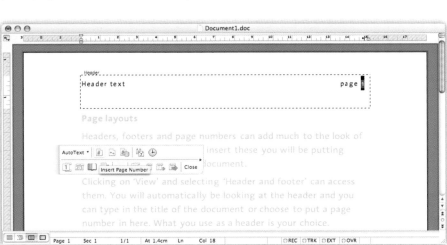

# Using graphics

YOU WILL FIND OUT:

● about callouts

● about WordArt

● about pictures, drawings and diagrams

● about borders

## Callouts

Callouts are like speech bubbles and can be used to feature quotes or phrases in a document. You can access the callouts from the 'Insert' tab on the menu bar at the top of the screen. Select 'Shapes' and then click on the 'Callout' that you prefer from the available designs.

The image will not immediately appear on your screen. Your cursor will have changed to a cross. Click and hold down the left mouse button and then move your mouse until you have a callout approximately the size you need. You will now see your callout inside a blue-outlined box. You can type straight into the box but you can also use the 'New format' menu that has appeared at the top of the screen to change the style and look of your callout. This includes the fill, the shape outline, shadow effects, 3-D effects and the position of the callout.

Once you have typed into the callout box you can resize it, rather like changing the size of any other graphic. You can also move the

callout around and position it exactly where you want it. The other great feature is that you can move or change the direction of the callout by left-clicking on the yellow box and pulling it in the direction required. You can also copy and paste your callout once you have the format and style that you prefer.

## WordArt

WordArt is also accessible using the 'Insert' menu tab. Choose a WordArt style and a new dialogue box will appear. Type in your text and you can change the font and its size, as well as making it bold or italic. Once you are happy with this click 'OK'. The WordArt box will now appear on your document. You can click on it and resize it. If you wish to reformat the WordArt, right-click on it and select 'Format WordArt' from the dialogue box. This gives you an opportunity to change colours, style of line, its size and its layout. You can also copy WordArt and paste it elsewhere in your document.

## Pictures, drawings and diagrams

Pictures, including ClipArt, Shapes, SmartArt and Charts, are all available via the 'Insert' menu tab. By selecting 'Picture' a new dialogue box will open. The software will automatically find where pictures are stored on your computer and you can choose any of these by clicking on them and then clicking on 'Insert'. The picture will appear in your Word document in its full size. You can of course resize as you wish.

Clipart will open up a new search dialogue box. Type in a keyword and it will search through the available Clipart on the computer or network. If you are connected to the Internet it will also search for other appropriate Clipart images.

We have already seen that the Shapes option includes Callouts: it also has lines, basic shapes, arrows, flow charts and stars and banners. All of these can be inserted into a Word document and resized, moved or manipulated as you wish.

SmartArt is another option. These are very professional-looking, basic diagrams. Choose one that would suit your purpose from lists, processes, cycles, hierarchies,

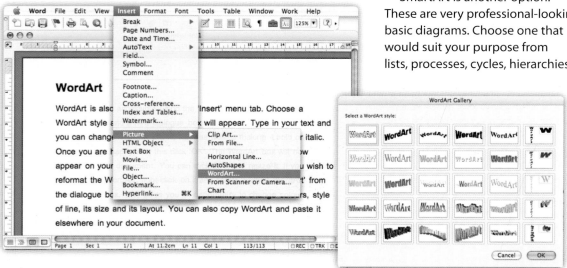

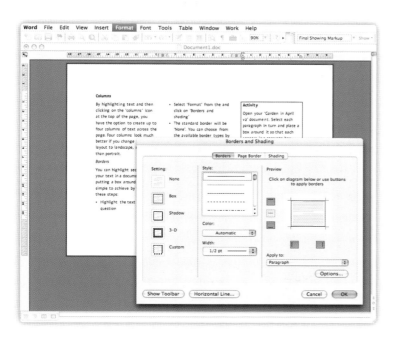

Create a new Word document. Using WordArt, position the word 'newsletter' at the top of the page in any style you prefer. Now create a Callout and type into it 'We need your help'. Copy this Callout box and then paste in a second one. In this Callout box type in 'Volunteers needed'. Now insert a piece of Clipart. Find a picture that features two people talking. Now reposition your Callouts so that each appears to be coming from the mouth of one of the two people.

relationships, matrixes and pyramids. The hierarchies, for example, would be ideal for showing an organisation's chart. Select the one you wish to use by clicking on it and then clicking 'OK'. This will now appear in your Word document and you can type straight onto the piece of SmartArt. A new menu bar will have appeared at the top of the page for you to change colours, styles and layout.

The final option is to insert charts. These are a selection of different types of graph, including columns, pies and bar charts. As usual, select the type that you prefer by clicking on it. Click 'OK' to confirm and a new dialogue box will appear. It looks very much like an Excel spreadsheet. Type in the data that will allow you to change the names of the axes and other features, as well as the figures included on the chart. When you have finished, simply close that dialogue box and your amended version of that chart will appear in your Word document. As usual you can resize it, and by right-clicking you can change the chart type, edit the data, insert a caption, or format the whole box.

## Borders

Instead of selecting 'Insert' from the tabs at the top of the screen, to access page borders use 'Page layout' tab. Click on the 'Page border' menu and a new dialogue box will appear. You have various options, including box, shadow or 3-D. You can also specify the line style, colour and its width. Most importantly, you can also apply the border to the entire document or just to a highlighted paragraph.

Once you have chosen your border, click 'OK' and it will now appear on the screen. If you change your mind about including a border just highlight the area, go back to the 'Page border' and simply amend from the menu in the dialogue box.

# Combining text and graphics

YOU WILL FIND OUT:

- about combining text and graphics
- about wraparound
- about overlapping text on a graphic

## Combining text and graphics

To give a document a really professional look, you can always combine text and graphics to highlight key points, facts and figures, as well as illustrating particular points. By graphics we mean pictures, Clipart, shapes, SmartArt, charts, Callout boxes, text boxes or WordArt. They can also include tables and diagrams.

It is important to make sure that the page does not look too cluttered, but it is equally important not to waste any valuable space. This means that some practice is required to make things look just right. Word is able to help you combine text and graphics to make a document professional-looking and effective.

Businesses would combine text and graphics by using their logo, symbol or name, rather like a watermark, which would appear underneath the text. This would mean that they would not have to use ready-printed business stationery, and that all their template documents are set up so that the graphic or logo will always appear underneath the text of a letter, newsletter or any communication with customers, suppliers or other stakeholders.

It is important to realise that multicoloured graphics underneath the text can make it difficult to read. Be particularly careful if you are using a black-and-white graphic underneath black text, as it will be impossible to read some of the text. Always choose a graphic that has fairly solid lines and shapes. This will make it easier for the reader to distinguish between the text and the graphic. If you are ever in any doubt about the graphic under the text, reduce it to a single, pastel colour. This will make it far easier to read the text over the top of it. The other option, of course, is to change the colour of the text itself. However, do not choose too bright a colour as again this is difficult to read and is tiring on the eyes and will put the reader off.

It is also important to bear in mind that Word is not necessarily the best piece of applications software with which to combine text and graphics. More specialist software has more features to offer. Microsoft Publisher is designed specifically to create professional-looking business documents that readily combine text and graphics. This application software has a number of ready-made templates and is very user-friendly once some basics have been understood. Essentially it works very much the same as Word, but is more flexible. It is therefore ideal for creating more sophisticated combinations of text and graphics that might be used in newsletters, business fliers, leaflets and brochures, as well as information sheets, guides and other documents that could be used for internal communication in a business organisation.

## Wraparound or text wrapping

Once you have inserted a graphic, click on it, then right-click your mouse button. A new dialogue box will appear. One of the options is text wrapping. Move your cursor to this option and a second dialogue box will appear. The following options offer you a variety of text-wrapping styles:

• In line with text
• Square
• Tight
• Behind text
• In front of text

You also have the opportunity to determine precisely where the picture is positioned. This can be important, because graphics have the habit of moving around and getting in the wrong place. This option allows you to lock a graphic in position, or even to move it along with the text around it.

## Overlapping text on a graphic

There are two ways of achieving this. The simplest is to click on the graphic then right-click and choose 'Through' from the 'Text wrapping' options. This will allow you to type across and over the graphic.

Alternatively, once your graphic is in your Word document, click on the 'Insert' menu at the top of the page.

Select 'Text box' and choose a text box, as you have done previously. Type your words into the text box and then reposition your text box over the top of your graphic. Click on the text box and choose the 'Format' menu button. You now need to access the 'Advanced tools', so click on the small icon to the right of 'Text box styles'. A new dialogue box will appear. Choose the 'Colours and lines' tab. You will see that the first option is 'Fill'. Using the arrow keys, slide the transparency to 100% and then click 'OK'. Your text will now appear over the top of the graphic, allowing you to see the graphic beneath it.

Make sure that you have also chosen a text box style that does not have a visible line around it. To change this again go to 'Format', and select 'Shape outline' from the options. A new drop-down menu will appear and you should select 'No outline' by clicking on it. Now your text box will have no visible outline, either on the screen or when it is printed out.

**O**pen a new Word document. From your Clipart gallery select a single, pastel-coloured piece of Clipart. Insert it into the page. Now resize the piece of Clipart so that it completely covers a portrait-shaped page. Note that the image itself may not cover the whole page, but the box in which it is contained will cover the whole page by resizing. Now insert a simple text box. Make sure that you click off the Clipart before you do this, otherwise the text box will simply replace the Clipart on your page. Type in a caption of your choice and then reformat the text box so that it is transparent and has no visible border.

# Using spreadsheets

## Purpose of spreadsheets

The main purpose of a spreadsheet is to process numbers. Word can be used to process text, but it does far more than that. In the same way, Excel does more than simply process numbers. It can do many things that are beyond what you will need to do for this course. Excel will allow plotting graphs, ranking data, and even performing some of the functions of a database. Even if you are just doing basic mathematics, Excel has a number of advantages. Sometimes you might be required to describe these in your work to justify using a spreadsheet application.

A spreadsheet is an application program commonly used for budgets, forecasting, and other finance-related tasks. In a spreadsheet program, data and **formulae** to calculate the data are entered into tables or worksheets for analysis and planning.

With a spreadsheet, once you have entered the appropriate data and formulae, it will automatically recalculate and update the calculations as the data is changed. It also has many powerful tools for simplifying even the most complex of calculations. A spreadsheet provides powerful, but easy-to-use, graphing capabilities and a variety of formatting options for printing text and numeric data.

### KEY TERM

**Formula** ▶ this is a sum. It may be a simple addition (+), multiplication (*), subtraction (-) or division (/). Formulae affect all the cells and the figures in them.

## Structure of a spreadsheet

It is important that you understand the basic structure of a spreadsheet before you start to use one. Although the structure of a spreadsheet may vary depending upon the program that you are using, most spreadsheets are set up in a similar way.

Each document or file that you create is known as a workbook. The workbook actually consists of a number of worksheets. A workbook can have as many worksheets as you need.

Each of the worksheets are like pages in document. Just as each page in a document will have different information, so too will each of the worksheets in your workbook. There are sheet tabs that can help you to move back and forth from one worksheet to another, just by clicking on the tab. You can rename the tabs to make it easier to remember what is on each of the worksheets.

Each of the worksheets has a grid network of columns and rows. Each of the columns are labelled A,B, C etc and each of the rows 1,2,3 etc. Where a column and row meets, this is called a cell. So a cell that is in column C and row 27 is called C27.

You can enter data into any cell. This could be text, numbers, or a combination of the two. Just how you organise your worksheet is entirely up to you and it will depend on what you intend to use it to do for you. You will always need to carefully plan what you want the worksheet to do for you before you start putting data into the worksheet.

## Using a spreadsheet

A business might use spreadsheet software, such as Microsoft Excel, for:

- Keeping a list of sales it has made
- Calculating its costs
- Calculating its profit
- Working out pay for employees

Excel allows users to make calculations and save data that can be then amended. Spreadsheets are very flexible tools. They can:

- allow numbers, text or formulae to be entered into a cell
- use the formulae to make calculations (such as adding up all the numbers in a column or a row)
- copy formulae into other groups of cells
- save time, because once a word or phrase has been entered into the spreadsheet, the software will predict it and offer the opportunity of pasting it in the next and subsequent times.

When you want to put data into a spreadsheet, it is useful to have all the information readily at hand. You should ask yourself a few questions before you begin putting the data into the spreadsheet:

- How should the information be laid out?
- Do I have all the data needed or are there gaps?
- What do I want the spreadsheet to do for me?
- How do I want the spreadsheet to present the information to me once the data has been inputted?

One great bonus with Excel is that many of the icons along the top of the screen are exactly the same as those in Word.

## ACTIVITY

**K**aty was just getting to grips with her new job. She was an assistant manager in a shop. One of the tasks she had to complete each week was to send a spreadsheet attached to an email to head office. The spreadsheet needed to tell accounts how many hours the staff had worked that week. Katy had to send them on a Monday, covering the seven days before, running up to Sunday.

The first thing Katy needs to do is to work out how many hours people have worked in the week, and put that figure in the total column.

Katy has been told that all she has to do is to go to the first cell in the Total column and press AutoSum, then she'll see a formula. This will add up cells B2 through to H2. Then she needs to copy the formula and paste it into each of the other Total cells. The spreadsheet will automatically slightly change the formula so it will add up all the figures in that row.

Create a new spreadsheet and key in the data from the table. Follow the instructions that Katy was given and total the work hours for each employee. Save your work as 'Katy spreadsheet'.

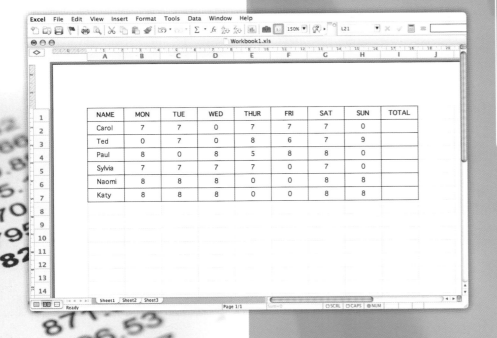

| NAME | MON | TUE | WED | THUR | FRI | SAT | SUN | TOTAL |
|------|-----|-----|-----|------|-----|-----|-----|-------|
| Carol | 7 | 7 | 0 | 7 | 7 | 7 | 0 | |
| Ted | 0 | 7 | 0 | 8 | 6 | 7 | 9 | |
| Paul | 8 | 0 | 8 | 5 | 8 | 8 | 0 | |
| Sylvia | 7 | 7 | 7 | 7 | 0 | 7 | 0 | |
| Naomi | 8 | 8 | 8 | 0 | 0 | 8 | 8 | |
| Katy | 8 | 8 | 8 | 0 | 0 | 8 | 8 | |

# Creating a spreadsheet

## YOU WILL FIND OUT:

- about inputting data and headings and titles
- about headers and footers
- about font formatting

## Inputting data and heading and titles

To enter something into a cell, you will need to do the following:

- Click on cell A1 with your left-hand mouse button
- Type the text 'Numbers' (without the quotation marks)
- Press the keyboard Return key
- The darker border will jump down one cell to A2
- Type a 3 and then press the Return Key on your keyboard
- The darker border will jump down one cell to A3
- Enter a 6 and a 9 in exactly the same way

When you have done this, the spreadsheet will look like this:

We used 'Numbers' as our column header, but this can be changed too. When you need to enter data into a cell, you simply click on the individual cell and type in the data. However, you cannot edit the data in a cell in the same way if there is something already in that cell. If you used the normal technique, you would erase the original data. This is how it works:

- Click on the cell A1
- Type the letter 'A' of 'Add'
- The word 'Numbers' is erased
- Click on Edit from the menu bar
- From the menu that drops down, click on 'Undo typing'
- The word 'Numbers' will be restored

In order to edit the data in a cell, you need to work from the Formula bar. This is the text area that runs across the top of the spreadsheet.

To edit the cell data you need to:

- Click on the cell 'A1'
- Click inside the 'Formula' bar
- The cursor will flash.

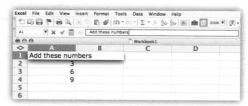

See how the formula bar is now showing the contents of cell A1. In order to edit the contents of the cell you can use the backspace key on the keyboard to erase any of the data that needs to change. When you are ready to make the data change all you need to do is to just type and it will appear in the formula bar. When you have finished, hit the 'Return' key on the keyboard.

We have changed 'Numbers' to 'Add these numbers'.

This has caused a problem, notice how the words go across columns A and B. To sort this out, you will need to either widen the A column or format cell A1. Also, you will notice that the formula bar is showing the contents of cell A2.

## Headers and footers

It is quite straightforward to add a header, footer or page number to your spreadsheet. It is very much like adding to a Word document. You need to:

- Select 'Insert' from the Excel menu at the top of the screen
- Scroll across the tool bar and select 'Header and footer', which is located next to the 'Text box' icon
- Now you are in the header and footer menu bar. You will see that there is a wide selection of options. You can insert the header on every page, on just the first page, or on alternating pages. The footer can be dealt with in the same way.
- You can also switch from header to footer on this tool bar, as well as inserting the date, time, total number of pages and pictures from this menu. If you are unsure at this stage where you are, click on the 'Header and footer design' tab and see what you have done already.

# Font formatting

It is easy to change the font you use for text and numbers, or to embolden the cell data. It is also possible to change the size of the font and the colour.

To format the text in the cell A1, you will need to:

- Click on cell A1 with the left mouse button
- Click on 'Format' from the menu bar
- From the menu that drops down, click the word 'Cells' with the left mouse button
- The Format dialogue box should appear
- Click on the word 'Font'

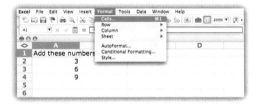

You can now change the type of font, the font style and its size. The cells do not have to be white – you can change their colour. To do this you need to:

- click on 'Format' from the menu bar  (having highlighted the cells you want to change colour).
- click on 'Cells', from the drop-down menu.
- The format dialogue box should now appear.
- Click on 'Patterns'.

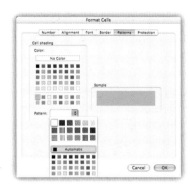

Choose a colour by clicking on it. If you want a pattern, then click on the down arrow and the pattern options will appear. When you have chosen the colour or pattern, just click 'OK'. When you have done this, the cells you have highlighted will change to that colour or pattern. If you do not like what you have done, then select 'Undo format cell' from the 'Edit' menu. Alternatively, you could just highlight the cells again and pick another colour or pattern.

You may have come up with something like this with contrasting colours for the cell header and another for the cells.

169

Notice that we have also widened the column 'A' so that the words 'Add these numbers only' appear over it.

# Keying in labels, values and formulae

YOU WILL FIND OUT:
- about inserting and deleting
- about labels
- about values and formulae
- about formatting

## Inserting, amending and deleting

Additional information or changes in information may be required, which means that the spreadsheet has to be amended. Additional information may require extra rows or columns. Changes to data on a spreadsheet may require clicking on each cell and manually changing the values. Additional formulae may have to be added.

## Labels

If a column or row does not have a title then it is relatively straightforward to add a new one. Click on the grey area and choose the 'Insert' row option. To add a column you will have to decide whether you wish the new column to go to the left or the right of the one you've clicked on.

Deleting works in exactly the same way. Simply highlight the row or column in question and select 'Edit' then 'Delete' to remove the whole row or column. If you just want to remove the label, highlight the text in that cell and hit the space bar. In other words hitting the space bar empties the information out of a cell.

Amending a label is achieved by highlighting the cell and typing to replace the existing label, or by double-clicking on the cell. You can then change the label in the same way as you would change text in word processing.

## Values

New values or numbers on a spreadsheet may first mean adding new rows or columns. Sometimes you may need to add numbers to a spreadsheet and put them into cells that were blank. Any empty cell can be typed straight into by simply clicking on it. But you must remember that if you do this in a full cell, then it will remove the existing number as you type the new one in. To avoid this, when amending numbers, you should double-click on the cell and change the values just as you would in Word. Simply clicking on the cell and hitting the space bar can instantly delete values.

When you type a number into a cell it will automatically be **right-aligned**. When you type in text it will automatically be **left-aligned**. A formula always starts with the = sign.

## Formulae

If you wanted to add the figures in two cells, and the cells were A2 and A3, you should simply click on A4 and type in '=A2+A3'. Other formulae are just as easy. 'A*' would multiply the two figures, 'a/' would divide them, and if you wanted to find out the percentage of a figure, you would just type in, for example, '20/100*A2'. This would give you 20% of the number in cell A2.

To amend a formula it is usually better to start from scratch. Simply go to the cell, hit the space bar and retype the formula, so that it takes into account any additional rows or columns you may have added. Obviously if you were just deleting the formula you would click on the cell and hit the space bar.

### KEY TERMS

**Right-aligned** ▶ on the right-hand edge of the cell.

**Left-aligned** ▶ on the left-hand edge of the cell.

## Formatting cells

As we have seen, the format of a cell depends on whether you are typing in numbers or text. You can change the way the cell looks. It would be laborious to change each cell one at a time. So the best way of formatting cells is to highlight all the cells that you wish to change.

## Formatting options

There are many things you can do to format a cell to fit the purpose of the job. Sometimes it is simply a case of making the spreadsheet look clearer when it is printed out. All options appear by clicking on 'Format' and selecting 'Cells'. Options include:

- Number – by scrolling down the list you can tell the spreadsheet whether you are inputting dates, currencies, ordinary numbers or numbers with decimal points.
- Alignment – you can click on left-aligned, right-aligned, centred or justified. You can also set the text to appear at the top or the bottom of the cell and, particularly importantly for text, you can click on 'Wrap around'. This automatically creates a text column rather than just a line.
- Font – just as in Word, you can change the font in a cell, all cells or some cells. You can also change the size of the font.
- Borders, patterns and shading – these can be used to highlight or draw attention to some or all of the spreadsheet

 **ACTIVITIES**

1 Retrieve your file 'Katy spreadsheet' and make the following changes:
- Amend the names to read:
    Carol Smith
    Ted Barrett
    Paul Trigg
    Sylvia Simms
    Naomi Watts
    Katy Northover
- Add in a new employee, 'Frank Spencer' – M5, T6, W-, T8, F7, S8, S2.
- Place this new employee between Ted and Paul in the list and AutoSum his total hours.
- Save your amended file as 'Katy spreadsheet v2'.

2 Next, your teacher or tutor will give you a copy of the amendments to be made to your spreadsheet.

3 Retrieve your 'Katy spreadsheet v3' and immediately save it as 'Katy spreadsheet v4'. Change the label font to Bell MT 9 point. Show the numbers to two decimal points in the 'Overtime' column and embolden the names of the employees.

171

# Manipulating data

YOU WILL FIND OUT:
● about working with rows and columns
● about displaying and printing formulae
● about sorting rows
● about formatting cells
● about column widths and rows

## Inserting, deleting and resizing rows and columns

Sometimes the labels for columns or rows and the text and numbers that need to be put into cells just won't fit. The easiest thing to do is to resize them. This is achieved in the following way:

- Your cursor appears on a spreadsheet as a fat, white cross.
- Move the cursor to the grey column headings or row headings – it changes into a thin, black cross.
- Click on the line between the columns or rows, and move your cursor to the left or right. This increases or decreases the size.

Keep an eye on the dotted line on the right-hand side because this shows you how much of the spreadsheet can be printed onto one page of A4 paper.

Inserting or deleting rows and columns could not be simpler. To delete a row or column simply highlight it by clicking on the column letter or the row number. Then select 'Edit', and choose 'Delete' from the drop-down men.

To insert a row or column, highlight the row or column in question and click on 'Insert', selecting the row or column option.

## Displaying and printing formulae

Sometimes when you print out an Excel spreadsheet, it is useful to see the formulae that have been used, so that these can be checked. Normally when a spreadsheet is printed it will show the results of the calculations and not the formulae.

When we set up 'Katy's spreadsheet' we entered data and used the AutoSum button on the toolbar to give us a total number of hours worked. In order to see the AutoSum formulae, all we need to do is to click on 'Tools', scroll down to 'Options', and a box will appear. From the tabs at the top of the box, select 'View' and click to tick the 'Formulae' box. See below for how the formula cells on 'Katy's spreadsheet v4' will look.

Now that the formulae are visible on the spreadsheet, you can print the spreadsheet. Beware! The length of the calculation in any of the columns or rows may have changed the width or length of your spreadsheet. It may not now fit on an A4 sheet. You may have to change the widths of the columns or rows or reduce the point size of the font that you have used. The other alternative is to change the page layout from **portrait** to **landscape**.

If you wish to check whether a formula is correct, then click on the cell it is contained in and look at the formula bar (the long, thin bar at the top of the spreadsheet).

## Sorting rows

Depending on the type of information included on a spreadsheet, it may be valuable to sort the rows of data or information into a particular order. Perhaps the information has been added to the spreadsheet as and when it was discovered, or as it has occurred. There may be no particular order to the data in the spreadsheet. There are three basic options. These are:

- Numerical ordering
- Alphabetical ordering
- **Chronological** ordering

### *Sorting rows in numerical order*

Highlight the column that you wish to sort into numerical order. Remember that you will be given a choice about whether you want the numbers to be ascending (smallest first) or descending (largest first). When you highlight the column you should click on 'Data' then select 'Sort'. A box will then tell you that you can either just re-order the column or expand the sort to include all the data.

If you don't choose the 'Expand' option then it will simply move the figures in the column that you have selected, leaving the rest of the spreadsheet unchanged. This would not be very useful. At this point you can also choose ascending or descending order.

172

| NAME | MON | TUE | WED | THUR | FRI | SAT | SUN | TOTAL | STANDARD WEEK | OVERTI |
|------|-----|-----|-----|------|-----|-----|-----|-------|---------------|--------|
| Carol Smith | 7 | 7 | 0 | 7 | 7 | 2 | 0 | =SUM(B2:H2) | 30 | =(I2-J2) |
| Ted Barrett | 0 | 7 | 0 | 8 | 6 | 7 | 9 | =SUM(B3:H3) | 30 | =(I3-J3) |
| Frank Spencer | 6 | 6 | 0 | 8 | 7 | 8 | 2 | =SUM(B4:H4) | 30 | =(I4-J4) |
| Paul Trigg | 8 | 0 | 8 | 5 | 8 | 4 | 2 | =SUM(B5:H5) | 30 | =(I5-J5) |
| Sylvia Simms | 7 | 7 | 7 | 7 | 0 | 6 | 0 | =SUM(B6:H6) | 30 | =(I6-J6) |
| Naomi Watts | 8 | 8 | 8 | 8 | 4 | 0 | 0 | =SUM(B7:H7) | 30 | =(I7-J7) |
| Katy Northover | 8 | 8 | 8 | 0 | 8 | 8 | 6 | =SUM(B8:H8) | 30 | =(I8-J8) |

| TOTAL | STANDARD WEEK | OVERTIME |
|-------|---------------|----------|
| =SUM(B2:H2) | 30 | =(I2-J2) |
| =SUM(B3:H3) | 30 | =(I3-J3) |
| =SUM(B4:H4) | 30 | =(I4-J4) |
| =SUM(B5:H5) | 30 | =(I5-J5) |
| =SUM(B6:H6) | 30 | =(I6-J6) |
| =SUM(B7:H7) | 30 | =(I7-J7) |
| =SUM(B8:H8) | 30 | =(I8-J8) |

## KEY TERMS

**Portrait** ▶ the standard way of printing, with the short side of A4 to the top.

**Landscape** ▶ an alternative page layout that switches the long side of a sheet of A4 to the top.

**Chronological** ▶ in date order.

## Sorting alphabetically

It is possible to sort A–Z or Z–A. Highlight the cells involved, then click on the A–Z icon at the top of the screen to sort the data in ascending order. If you want to sort in descending order choose the Z-A icon.

## Sorting chronologically

Using the same principles as numerical or alphabetical sorting: if you have a column containing dates, you can sort either from the earliest date to the latest, or in reverse.

## Formatting cells

Before you can format any cell data, you have to highlight the cells. To highlight cells, do the following:

- Position your mouse pointer over cell A1
- Make sure the pointer is in the shape of a thick white cross
- Hold down your left mouse button
- Keep the left mouse button held and drag downwards
- Release the left mouse button when all four cells are highlighted.

The cells A1, A2, A3, and A4 are a different colour to the other cells, which are white. The four cells also have the darker border around them. This is because they are highlighted. Once cells have been highlighted, you can do something with them.

To centre the data in your four highlighted cells, do the following:

- Click on 'Format' in the menu bar
- A menu drops down
- Click on the word 'Cells' with your left mouse button

When you click on cells from the menu bar, a dialogue box pops up.

Number, Alignment, Font, etc are the headings for Tab Strips. Click on 'Alignment' and the dialogue box will change. You can now position your text as you please. Use the other tabs to change the font, border or pattern.

## Column widths and rows

To widen a column you will need to:

- Move your mouse pointer up to the letter A
- The pointer will be in the shape of a white cross
- Now move the mouse pointer – the white cross – to the line in between the A and the B.
- The mouse pointer will change shape again to become a black cross with arrowheads.
- When the mouse pointer changes shape, hold down the left mouse button
- Keep it held down and drag your mouse to the right
- Release the mouse button when you are satisfied with the width of your column

You can widen a row in the same way.

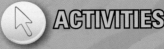

## ACTIVITIES

**1** Open your 'Katy spreadsheet v4'. Print your 'Total', 'Standard Hours' and 'Overtime' columns with the formulae showing. Check your formulae with those in our illustration (opposite).

**2** Order your spreadsheet alphabetically by surname of employee. Amend the 'Name' column so that the surnames appear first, followed by a comma and then the forename.

**3** Now sort the names of the employees into alphabetical order, but make sure you keep all the relevant information in the same row as the employee's name. Save your work as 'Katy spreadsheet v5'.

173

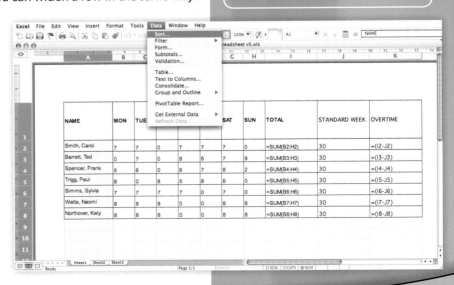

| NAME | MON | TUE | | | | SAT | SUN | TOTAL | STANDARD WEEK | OVERTIME |
|------|-----|-----|---|---|---|-----|-----|-------|---------------|----------|
| Smith, Carol | 7 | 7 | 0 | 7 | 7 | 7 | 0 | =SUM(B2:H2) | 30 | =(I2-J2) |
| Barrett, Ted | 0 | 7 | 0 | 8 | 6 | 7 | 9 | =SUM(B3:H3) | 30 | =(I3-J3) |
| Spencer, Frank | 5 | 6 | 0 | 8 | 7 | 8 | 2 | =SUM(B4:H4) | 30 | =(I4-J4) |
| Trigg, Paul | 8 | 0 | 8 | 5 | 8 | 8 | 0 | =SUM(B5:H5) | 30 | =(I5-J5) |
| Simms, Sylvia | 7 | 7 | 7 | 7 | 0 | 7 | 0 | =SUM(B6:H6) | 30 | =(I6-J6) |
| Watts, Naomi | 8 | 8 | 8 | 0 | 0 | 8 | 0 | =SUM(B7:H7) | 30 | =(I7-J7) |
| Northover, Katy | 8 | 8 | 8 | 0 | 0 | 8 | 0 | =SUM(B8:H8) | 30 | =(I8-J8) |

# Creating tables using single and multiple (linked) sheets

**YOU WILL FIND OUT:**

- what consolidation is
- about consolidating by position
- about consolidating by category
- about consolidating by formula

## What is consolidation?

As we know, each workbook can have a number of worksheets. You can bring together, or consolidate, the information from each of the separate worksheets into a master worksheet. This allows Excel to do all the hard work of assembling the data for you.

### For example

On each worksheet you might have the income and expenditure for different retail outlets. A business would use consolidation to bring these figures together so that total income and expenditure could be shown on a master worksheet.

174

In Excel 2007 the 'Consolidate' command is on the 'Data' tab. This will allow you to arrange the data in your worksheets in identical order and location (known as consolidate by position). You can organise the data differently on the worksheets, but using the same row and column labels, so that the master worksheet can still match the data (consolidate by category). Alternatively, you can use formulae with cell references to other worksheets so you don't have to use 'Position' or 'Category' to consolidate (consolidate by formula).

## Consolidating by position

In order to consolidate by position you need to set up the data properly. Here are some key points to remember:

- Each range of data has to be in list format, so each column has to have a label in the first row and have similar facts. There must not be any blank rows or columns in the list.
- Each range can be on a separate worksheet. You should not put any of the ranges on your master worksheet.
- Each range must have the same layout.
- Make sure you name each range. To do this, select the range, then use the 'Formulas' tab and select 'Define name'. Give a name for the range in the 'Name box'.

The next thing you need to do is to click on the upper left cell of the area where you want the consolidated data to appear on your master worksheet. Then using the 'Data' tab, go to the 'Data tools' group and click on 'Consolidate'. A new dialogue box will appear. In the 'Function' box, choose what you want Excel to do with the consolidated data. If the data is in another workbook, you can use the 'Browse' option to find the file. Click 'OK' when you have found it. You then need to type in the name that you gave that range and click 'Add'. Repeat this for every range.

You now need to decide how you wish to update the consolidation. You can update manually by changing the cells and ranges, or you can set it up so that it automatically updates when the source data is changed.

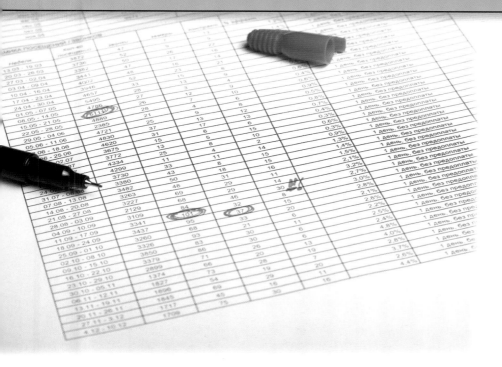

## Consolidating by formula

In order to consolidate by formula you need to include the cell references to source cells on each worksheet that contains the data you wish to consolidate. You need to enter a formula with the cells references to the other worksheets. You need to do one for each separate worksheet.

### For example

If you wanted to consolidate data from a worksheet named 'Norwich' in cell B6, Ipswich in cell B8 and Colchester in cell B9, in the cell of your master worksheet you would enter:

=sum(Norwich!B6,Ipswich!B8, Colchester!B9)

You can set your workbook to automatically update these formulae when you update data on one of the worksheets.

If you wanted to add another worksheet to the 'Consolidate by formula' then you would have to add the new worksheet cell number to the formula on your master workbook.

### For example

If you now wanted to add the data from Chelmsford cell B10, your new formula would be:

=sum(Norwich!B6,Ipswich!B8, Colchester!B9,Chelmsford!B10)

## Consolidating by category

This will allow you to consolidate data on separate worksheets. Once again you need to make sure that each range of data is in list format. Each column needs to have its own label in the first row and have similar facts. Each range should be on a separate worksheet and do not put any of the ranges on your master worksheet.

Make sure that your labels for the columns or rows that you wish to consolidate have identical spelling, and if you use capitals make sure they are consistent.

### For example

'Sales Figures' should not be 'sales figures' or 'Sales figures'.

You need to name each range. Select the whole range, then using the 'Formula' tab, click on the arrow next to 'Define name' and type a name for the range in the name box. Once again click on the upper left cell of the area in which you want the consolidated data to appear in your master worksheet. Now click on the 'Data' tab and from the 'Data tools' group click on 'Consolidate'. As with 'Consolidate by position', you need to tell Excel what you want it to do in the function box. Again you can bring in information from another workbook. Use the 'Browse' button to find this workbook and click 'OK' when you have found it. Type the name that you gave the range into the 'Reference' box, then click 'Add'. Repeat this for each range. Once again you have the option of telling Excel to automatically update by putting a tick into the 'Create links to source data' box. If you want to do this manually then do not click on the 'Create links to source data' check box.

If there are labels that do not match up with labels in source areas then separate rows or columns might be generated in the consolidation, so make sure that anything you do not wish to consolidate has different labels.

# Creating and applying validation rules

## Inputting data using data validation

Inputting data onto an Excel spreadsheet can be time-consuming and quite boring. As we will see, this does not have to be the case, as, instead of having to type the same data into spreadsheet cells each time, you can use data validation. This means turning the cells into drop-down lists, from which you select the item you wish to use.

### For example

A marketing department could keep a spreadsheet relating to telephone interviews with potential customers. If they had a column heading called 'Rep to call' and there were only two replies possible, it could become laborious having to type either 'Yes' or 'No' in each column.

Data validation helps to eliminate spelling mistakes because boredom can cause lack of concentration.

## Using data validation

Data validation is not complicated once you have done it a few times. We will work through the steps for constructing a spreadsheet with drop-down lists.

Open a new spreadsheet worksheet, and key in the headings:

- Name – cell A1
- Department – cell B1
- Pay grade – cell C1
- Comments – cell E1

Now you need to key in some data to go in the lists. Starting at cell F2, add the following to your spreadsheet:

It is the information contained in columns F, G and H that will go into our drop-down lists, and we will be able to hide this data so that it is not filling up our spreadsheet and making it difficult to see on the screen without scrolling. But before we do this we also need to turn the information in Columns A, B and C into lists.

To turn the cells contained within a column into a list, you need to:

1 Highlight the whole column by clicking on the letter at the top of it.
2 With the whole of the column highlighted, click on 'Data' from the Excel menu bar at the top of the screen.
3 From the data menu bar, click on 'Data Validation'.
4 The following dialogue box appears:

- Select the 'Settings' tab
- In the 'Allow' window, click on the arrow at the side of 'Any value'.
- A new dialogue box will appear and you should choose the 'List' option.
- A new dialogue box will appear and this one will include a 'Source' window.

The term 'source' relates to the data that will be included in your list. Select the names of the cells that contain the names of the employees on your spreadsheet. To do this you need to:

- Click on the icon to the right of the Source text box and the dialogue box shrinks in size, leaving you to view your spreadsheet
- Click inside cell F2 on your spreadsheet.
- Hold your finger down on the left of the mouse button, and drag your cursor to cell F9.
- Then click on the icon again. This will return the dialogue box to its original size.
- Your dialogue box should look like the one below.

Your source information should read '$F$2:$F$9'. If you have achieved this you can click 'OK'.

The cells in your column will now be drop down lists. This means that each of the cells in your column will have a black arrow to the right of them. When you click on this arrow you will see a list appear of the members of staff for your organisation.

You can click on any of the names in the list. However, because we initially highlighted the whole column, the list also applies to the heading cell. You would not want this to be included on a heading cell, so to turn off the list in cells A1, B1, C1 and E1 you should:

- Click inside cell A1.
- From the Excel menu bar at the top of the worksheet, click on 'Data'.
- From the drop-down menu, click 'Data validation'.
- Using the Settings tab of the dialogue box, change 'Allow list' to 'Allow any value' by clicking on the arrow at the side of this window.
- Click 'OK'.

177

# Using conditional formatting

## What is conditional formatting?

Sometimes, when you analyse data, you might want to highlight the most important cells or ranges, particularly outstanding or important figures. You might, for example, want to find out which department of a business is either spending the most or generating the most money. You might want to highlight the names of all employees who have worked for the business for more than five years.

### For example

Schools and colleges may want to highlight their star students, or subjects in which students have achieved higher than national average grades in examinations.

## Formatting cells (two colour)

The easiest way to achieve this is to select a range of cells and then click on the 'Home' tab. Go to the 'Styles' group and then click on the arrow next to 'Conditional formatting'. From the new menu select 'Colour scales'. There are four different two-colour scales available:

- yellow/red
- red/yellow
- green/yellow
- yellow/green.

You can see what the effect will look like as you put your pointer over each of the colour scales. Simply choose the one that you prefer.

### For example

If you were choosing Green/Yellow then green would represent the higher values and yellow would represent the lower values. Those values in between can be more or less yellow, depending on whether they are at the higher or lower end of the scale.

## Formatting cells (three colour)

Three colour scales give you slightly more visual impact. In effect you can now show a high value, a middle value and a low value. Your options are:

- Green/Yellow/Red
- Red/Yellow/Green
- Blue/Yellow/Red
- Red/Yellow/Blue

Once again you will need to highlight the cells in which you wish to use the conditional formatting. Click on the 'Home' tab, then click on the arrow beside 'Conditional formatting'. Move your pointer down to 'Colour scales' and now select from the three-colour scales at the top of the new pop-out. You can see what the figures will look like by hovering over each of the four main options.

## Formatting cells that contain text, numbers, dates or times

This is a way of formatting cells so that you can automatically identify specific cells within a range of cells.

### For example

A business might want to highlight product stock levels lower than 100, and show these in yellow. Alternatively, it might want to show all its retail stores that have achieved an increase of more than 10% in turnover in the last month.

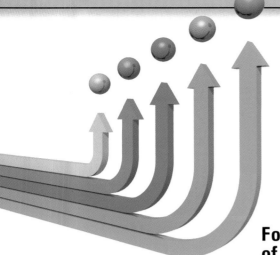

Again there is a quick way of doing this. Select your range of cells. Go to the 'Home' tab and to the 'Style group'. Click on the arrow beside 'Conditional formatting' and this time choose 'Highlight cells rules'. You are given a number of options:

- Greater than – this will highlight any values that are greater than a figure that you define.
- Less than – this will highlight any values that are less than a figure that you define.
- Between – this will highlight any values in a range that you have defined.
- Equal to – this will highlight any values that are exact matches for a figure that you have defined.
- Text that contains – this could highlight a keyword, such as 'sales' or 'profit'.
- A date occurring – this would highlight only a specific date that you have chosen.
- Duplicate values – this will highlight figures in the range of cells that are the same.

All you need to do is to click on your format choice and then enter the amount, number, text or date into the dialogue box. You can then define what colour you wish those entries to appear in, such as light red fill with dark red text.

## Formatting top or bottom of ranked values

This kind of conditional formatting allows you to highlight either the best or the worst values, according to your own criteria.

**For example**

A business might wish to identify its top five best-selling products, or its top five best-performing sales representatives. Or it may wish to identify the five products that produce the least amount of profit.

In order to use top-ranked or bottom-ranked conditional formatting, select the range of cells and then click on the 'Home' tab. Go to the 'Styles group' and click on the arrow beside 'Conditional formatting'. This time select 'Top bottom rules'. You will be given a number of alternatives:

- Top 10 items
- Top 10 per cent
- Bottom 10 items
- Bottom 10 per cent
- Above average
- Below average

Once you have chosen your top/bottom rules you can then change the new dialogue box.

**For example**

When you choose 'Top 10 per cent' a new dialogue box will appear. On the left it states 'Top 10 per cent'. You can adjust this by using the up and down arrow keys to make it the top 20 per cent or 5 per cent, or any range between 1 and 100. You can also select how these figures will appear in terms of fill and colour of text.

## Formatting unique or duplicate values

You may wish to highlight only unique values (those that appear once) or duplicate values (those that appear on more than one occasion). To do this, highlight your range of cells and click on the 'Home' tab then go to the 'Styles group' and click on the arrow alongside 'Conditional formatting'. Choose the 'Highlight cells rules'. Scroll down to the bottom of the new pop-up and click on 'Duplicate values'. A new dialogue box will appear. It will have 'Duplicate' in the left-hand box. If this is the one that you wish to highlight, then once you have chosen your fill and text colours, simply click 'OK'. If you want to switch it to 'unique' just click on the down arrow, select 'Unique', amend your fill and text colour and then click 'OK'.

179

# Creating charts (1)

YOU WILL FIND OUT:

● about charts

● about chart formats

## Charts

Charts and graphs are very useful in helping to understand numerical data. A graph, bar chart or pie chart can make data much easier to understand and far easier to compare.

Excel offers a considerable selection of different chart types. Some of these are standard and accessed through the Chart Wizard. You can even create your own type of chart using the 'Custom' function.

### The spreadsheet

To create the data required for a chart you must first begin by creating an Excel spreadsheet, showing the data in numerical form. By choosing the right type of chart you will be able to look for trends and patterns in the figures.

Let's begin with an example. We have collected the following data and put it into a simple table, which we will then input into a new Excel spreadsheet.

| PREMIERSHIP GOALS AND RED CARDS | | |
|---|---|---|
| MONTH | GOALS | RED CARDS |
| August | 55 | 5 |
| September | 62 | 6 |
| October | 65 | 6 |
| November | 69 | 7 |
| December | 73 | 8 |
| January | 59 | 6 |

It is important to make sure that any of the data inputted into the spreadsheet is correct. The next stage is extremely straightforward. Excel will do much of the work when we want to create a chart.

### The chart

Going back to the spreadsheet, we highlight all the data and labels that we have just input into the sheet. We then click on 'Insert' and from the menu choose 'Chart'. A new menu will appear. On this occasion we are going to choose a line graph. There are several different **sub-types** of chart to choose, but we are happy with the first option. By simply highlighting this and clicking 'Next', the Chart Wizard will create a graph using our data. The illustration above shows how the graph will look.

The Chart Wizard will then ask you to give the chart a title, which we have already done in the version shown below. You can also label the **X and Y axes**. Once you have done this, click 'Next' and then 'Finish'. The chart will appear on your spreadsheet worksheet. You can change the size of it and you can right-click on it to copy and paste into a Word document.

Many of the tabs, shortcut keys, icons and facilities of Excel are just the same as Word.

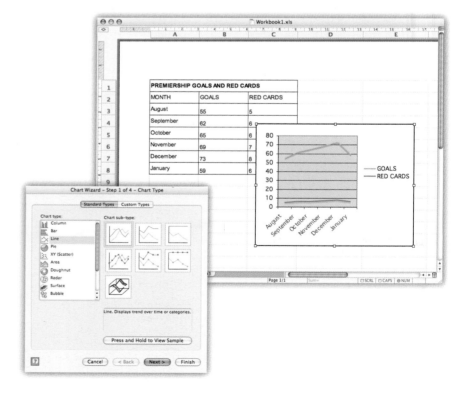

## Chart format

Choosing the right kind of chart format is very important. You will have seen in the last activity that there is a huge range of standard types of chart available. All of them, in the right circumstances, have their place.

Some of the formats, however, particularly if the data is complicated, can actually confuse more than simply displaying the data as a simple line graph or bar chart.

Businesses will routinely use charts to illustrate financial and other information. The purpose of these charts is to serve as an instant visual reference for the data.

As you will have seen in the activity, the relationship between the two sets of temperature showed that on average there was a difference of around 8 or 9°C. This is far easier to visualise as a chart than it is as a series of words.

—— K E Y  T E R M S ——

Sub-types ▶ variations or versions of a particular type of chart, such as a line graph.

X and Y axes ▶ the X axis is the horizontal axis and the Y axis is the vertical one.

## ACTIVITY
### Halesworth twinning

**H**alesworth has recently been twinned with Malia on the Greek island of Crete. Both the British and the Greeks know that the average temperatures of the two towns are very different. To show how different it is they have compiled a table in °C, identifying the main holiday months:

| MONTH | HALESWORTH | MALIA |
|---|---|---|
| May | 19 | 24 |
| June | 20 | 28 |
| July | 21 | 30 |
| August | 21 | 30 |
| September | 16 | 27 |
| October | 15 | 25 |

The towns want to put a helpful bar chart or line graph on their websites. They would like to see several different chart options before they decide which one to use. You have the task of putting the data into a spreadsheet and then making it look as attractive as possible. You must not forget to label your chart and also to label both axes. You will not have to input the data more than once because you can experiment with different chart types, providing you save each version by copying and pasting it into a Word document.

> Input the data in the table into an Excel spreadsheet. Then, using the Chart Wizard, select at least FOUR different chart types, to include line graphs and bar charts only.

## QUESTIONS
### 6 minutes

**1** Can you see a relationship between the number of red cards and goals now that you can see the data as a line graph? If you can, what is it? *(2 marks)*

**2** A line chart is just one option. Suggest another type of chart that might show this data more clearly. *(4 marks)*

181

# Creating charts (2)

## Line diagrams

Line diagrams basically come in two different variations:

- A straightforward, unbroken line
- An unbroken line with **data points** shown on it, as either squares or dots

Line graphs are more popular than other graphs because they are easy to create and their visual appearance reveals data trends clearly. They are especially useful in showing **statistics** and are probably the most common tools used to present scientific data.

## Bar charts

Excel actually offers two different types of bar chart. The first type is the column bar chart with columns running vertically. These are useful when you are comparing parts of a whole number. So, for example, if you interviewed 100 customers and 62 of them said they were satisfied, 20 said they had no opinion and the remaining 18 said they were dissatisfied, different colours on the column could help a business compare the figures.

A bar chart, as it is called in the Chart Wizard, is just like a column chart. The major difference is that the coloured lines run horizontally, rather than vertically. In all other respects a bar chart does exactly the same as a column chart.

Another variation of the bar chart or column chart is that you can select a version that separates out the parts of a whole figure into separate little bars or columns. This is actually more visually revealing, as the differences in height or length show the key differences within a set of figures.

## Pie charts

Pie charts are another visually appealing and useful way to present data. In effect, a pie chart is a circle, and the total of all of the data is represented by the whole pie or circle.

Parts of the total figure are represented by slices of the pie. The larger the figure within the total amount, the larger the slice. It is possible in Excel to make all the different slices a different colour, so that it is far easier to pick each one out. In other words, you can see how much each slice represents as a percentage of the whole.

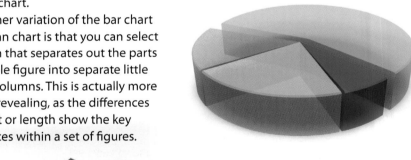

## Inserting titles and data legends

As a part of the Chart Wizard, Excel will prompt you to give your chart or graph a title. It will also ask you whether you wish to give the X and Y axes their own titles. These are called data legends.

As you go through the Chart Wizard, having selected your type of chart, you will arrive at Step 3, which gives you Chart Options. A number of tabs will appear at the top of the box, but it is the first tab that is of particular interest. By typing into the box 'Chart title' you can give your graph a title. Usually Excel will place the title above the graph or chart.

Underneath 'Chart title' are your 'X axis' and 'Y axis' legends. Try to remember which axis is which. It is not always easy, as some of the graphs and charts will be on a reverse side. Type into the X and the Y boxes and you will see the labels for those axes appear on your graph.

Now click on the tab 'Data labels'. There will probably be only two options here: 'Show values' or 'Show labels'. This option allows you to show the precise information from your spreadsheet, actually on the graph or chart.

## More on labels

By clicking 'Finish' in the Chart Wizard the graph will appear on your worksheet. When you paste this into a Word document you may find that the graph has been squashed, either horizontally or vertically, to take your axis labels into account. Simply stretch the graph until you can read the graph and the labelling clearly.

There is one other part during the Chart Wizard that can be changed. In Step 3, when you insert the chart title and label the axes there is also a tab labelled as 'Legend'. Excel will have automatically taken your description of a column of figures when you originally labelled the spreadsheet. This gives you an opportunity to amend the position of the legend. To do this, simply click on 'Legend' and choose the position on the page where you would like your legend to appear.

--- **KEY TERMS** ---

**Data point** ▶ this is a numerical figure that you will have inputted into the spreadsheet.

**Statistics** ▶ facts and figures, e.g. Government statistics.

## QUESTION TIME
*10 minutes*

**1** Which of the types of chart mentioned on this spread is similar to another Excel chart option – the Doughnut? *(2 marks)*

**2** How many Bubble chart options are there and how might this be useful? *(4 marks)*

**3** What might be the problems if you were to give your chart an extremely long title? *(2 marks)*

**4** What part of a chart do you think is called the 'legend'? *(2 marks)*

183

## ACTIVITY

Your teacher or tutor will provide you with a copy of the 'Making a chart' worksheet. Follow the instructions and print a copy of your completed chart, which you should save as 'Chart activity'.

# Using databases

## Databases

The old-fashioned way of keeping records was to put them into some kind of paper-based filing system. For centuries this has worked fairly well and still does. However, with the development of databases as software applications, people have realised that there is an alternative. Instead of searching through a card-based index then finding the right filing cabinet and hoping that the file is there, computerised files are taking over. Nonetheless, many businesses still cling on to the old ways of doing things.

## Microsoft Access

This is the leading software application used by businesses around the world. It has some powerful features, including:

- The ability to store data in the form of records
- The creation of a specific database with categories of information called **fields**, so the user actually defines what the database holds in terms of information
- The ability to enter information onto the database and sort it in a variety of different ways
- The ability to take information from the database as individual records, lists or groups of records
- The ability to combine the data into a report so that it can be included in other documents

Microsoft Access offers a flexible data management system. It aims to provide the software to organise data with the ability to add, modify or delete data from the databases. It allows the user to ask questions about the data that is stored in the database. It can also allow the user to produce reports, which summarise a selection of the content of the data.

Although Microsoft Access may not be the best data management system and there are other competitors, many businesses will use it because of its familiarity with other Microsoft products. It is also bundled together with Word and Excel, for example, into the Microsoft Office package.

Access provides user-friendly ways to enter data, and for businesses the use of Wizards allows the users to create highly attractive summaries of data, or reports, in minutes.

### For example

A business could easily create a catalogue of its products, which it could send out to customers. The relevant information could be retrieved from their database and presented in the form of tables, graphs or charts. It could identify product numbers, names, key features and the unit price.

Microsoft Access 2007 was a significant upgrade on previous versions. An enormous number of developments were made, with plenty of new database **templates**, new layout views, better ways of searching and filtering data and easier ways to import and export data from other sources. We look in more detail at these Access options over the next few spreads.

## Business use of databases

Because Access can be used to collect and sort enormous amounts of information, a business could use it for the following purposes:

- Details about customers
- Information about stock in a warehouse
- Membership of a club or society
- Patient details at a dentist or a surgery
- Student or pupil records at a college or school
- Job vacancies at an employment agency
- Lists of suppliers used by a business
- Properties for sale or rent by an estate agent
- A collection of books in a library

184

## For example

If we were to think about the data that you would find in a telephone directory, the following information would be included:

- A person's name
- A person's address
- Their dialling code
- Their telephone number

If we were putting this information into Access then each of the four categories of information would be called a field. This would allow us to search the database by name, by address, by area from the dialling code and by telephone number.

### KEY TERMS

**Field** ▶ in Access this is a category of information, such as first name, last name, address or postcode.

**Template** ▶ this is a ready-made database format, which can be automatically used or adjusted and saves a great deal of time in creating your own database format.

 ## ACTIVITIES

**1** The examiners may expect you to design and create a database with the right fields and then be able to search it for particular features of the records you have inputted into the database.

**a** Open Access and find out the maximum amount of characters you can use as a field name.
**b** What is a character?

**2** There are 43 police forces in England and Wales. Every week the police forces receive thousands of non-emergency calls. These take up the time and effort of the police and the same questions are asked hundreds of times. In order to sort out this problem the Police National Legal Database team used data capture to identify the 500 most frequently asked questions.

They covered aspects of everyday life, including personal safety, road traffic accidents and anti-social behaviour. It now means that when a call is made to a police station the call handlers can use the database to respond immediately to the enquiry. In addition, all the frequently asked questions have been placed on a database that can be accessed at www.askthe.police.uk.

In the first five months of the launch of the website 150,000 questions were answered. The police believe that setting up the database will save them around £2 million per year.

Visit the website mentioned above and then answer the following questions:

**a** What are the THREE initial options offered to you when you open the home page?
**b** How many sub-questions are there for 'abandoned motor vehicles'?

# Designing and creating data capture forms

YOU WILL FIND OUT:

- about designing data capture forms
- about data types
- about creating input masks

## Data capture sheets

A data capture sheet is any type of form, like a **warranty card** or a **guarantee**, an application form or a questionnaire, designed to collect information about an individual or their opinions.

Businesses will routinely collect data about their customers and suppliers. They will also hold data about their employees. A local library would hold records about everyone who borrows books from them. New borrowers will need to complete a form, giving their name, address and telephone number, and will probably have to provide proof of these details. The records become extended, as once an individual starts borrowing from the library, a note is taken of every loaned book, CD or DVD. The database needs to be clever enough to flag up when items borrowed become overdue. It also needs to be able to allow library staff to note that an item has been returned.

## Data types

In theory, databases can take any type of information. But in practice they tend to fall into the following categories:

- Text only – including simple entries such as 'yes' or 'no' and longer entries, such as the person's name.
- Alphanumeric – this denotes a combination of letters and numbers. An example would be a postcode.
- Numeric – such as an individual's age.
- Dates – the ideal date format is --/--/--. This can be useful for searching for diary entries or for birthdays.
- Time – you can also insert times using a 24-hour clock, so an employee starting work at 8 o'clock in the morning would have a data record of 0800.

## Creating input masks

An input mask is designed to control what you can or cannot put into a field. An input mask could require the user to enter a date or a telephone number using specific conventions.

> **For example**
>
> If you wanted a date to be entered with the day, month and year, you would use the following input mask: DD-MM-YYYY

An input mask can also make it necessary to actually fill in a particular field with data and prevent users from inputting invalid data, such as putting the date into the telephone number field. Input masks can also be used whenever you want a user to enter data in a specific way.

You can apply input masks to fields that are already set for text, numbers, currency, dates or times. You can also put input masks to control text boxes. The easiest way to do this is by using the Input Mask Wizard, but you can also manually enter your own masks. Access will allow you to automatically create a form. You can amend the input masks on this form, or simply use those that have already been set by Access.

---

**KEY TERMS**

**Warranty card** ▶ comes with certain products. The customer has to complete it and send it back to the manufacturer to ensure that the product is registered with them for repair or replacement if necessary.

**Guarantee** ▶ many products come with a standard one- to three-year guarantee from the manufacturer, stating that (within reason) they will repair or replace it if it proves faulty.

---

To create an input mask:

- Click on the arrow below 'View' and select 'Design view' from the 'Home' menu
- If your table does not contain a text field you can add one by clicking on the 'Data type' column and then selecting 'Text'
- If you have one, or have already done this, then you need to click on the 'General' tab and select the 'Input mask' property box. This will give you a number of options.
- Select the type that you require from the scroll-down list of options and then click on 'Save'.
- Switch back to the 'Data sheet' view and then go onto your next steps, which will test your input mask.

To test your input mask, put the cursor into the field that contains the input mask. Add numbers and letters to the spaces in the mask. If your mask only accepts numbers, Access will prevent you from adding letters, and vice versa.

## ACTIVITY
### *How to capture data*

**Y**ou will be required to show that you can create a suitable data capture sheet. Each section or question on the sheet will become a field in your database. It is advisable, therefore, to only ask questions that the individual can answer clearly and not provide lengthy answers.

Your teacher or tutor will give you the results of interviews to find out the habits of football supporters. The information is jumbled up and you must design a suitable data capture sheet so that you can organise the information before putting it onto a database.

Complete data records are likely to be a collection of the data types listed on the opposite page. In the football supporters example, we have name, team, whether they own a shirt and whether they play football, all as text entries. As we do not know the addresses of the ten individuals, we will not need an alphanumeric field, but we will need a numeric field for their ages.

187

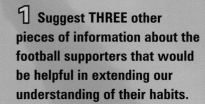

1 Suggest THREE other pieces of information about the football supporters that would be helpful in extending our understanding of their habits.

2 Categorise your three choices as Text, Alphanumeric, Dates or Numeric fields.

3 Using your data capture sheet, enter the 10 sets of records into your new database. Save the database and print a hard copy of it. At this stage you do not need to make any changes to the database.

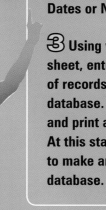

# Designing and creating database tables

**YOU WILL FIND OUT:**

- about designing and creating a database
- about identifying data types
- about inserting, editing and deleting

## Designing and creating a database

We are going to be using the data that you have compiled on your data capture sheets to explain how you can design and create a simple database.

When you open Microsoft Access you will be given a series of options. Unlike Word or Excel you will need to save your Access database before you start working on it. You will be selecting 'Blank database' and then be prompted to say where you wish to save the database and what you want to call it. We will call our new database 'Football supporters'. You should save your database in the sub-folder that you created at the beginning of this section.

Once you have typed in 'Football supporters' as the file name, click the 'Create' button, which is alongside it.

A new menu will appear and you should choose 'Create table in design view'. This will allow you to **customise** the database by deciding what you will call each field.

### ——— K E Y   T E R M S ———

**Customise ▶** to make a standard database fit your own requirements.

## Data types

Once you have settled on your field names you will then be able to start entering data. Each time you create a field you will have to decide what data type is going into that field. Running through the list of information that you have, we can identify the following:

- Name – this is a text field
- Age – this is a number field
- Team supported – this is a text field
- Shirt ownership – this is a text field
- Plays football – this is a text field
- Home games – this is a text field.

Once you have created each field and identified the data type, you can then close the design view by clicking on the red cross in the top right-hand corner of the window. You will be asked if you wish to save the changes, to which you must reply 'Yes'. It will then ask you whether you wish to identify a primary key. For the purposes of this simple database this is not necessary.

When you re-open the database you should now see all of your field names along the top of the columns, in the grey area. You may have to slightly adjust the width of the columns, in much the same way as you did in an Excel spreadsheet.

You can always add in additional fields to your database by clicking on the 'Design' icon.

Using your data capture sheets, enter the ten sets of records into your new database. Save the database and print a hard copy of it. At this stage you do not need to make any other changes to the database.

## More data for your database

Some more information has been collected for the 'Football supporters' database. However, only the day and the month have been collected so far for the dates of birth, and only postcodes for the addresses. You will have to work out the year in which each individual was born.

If you need to make amendments to a database you need to go back into Design View. You can add new fields, and identify the type of data that you will be inputting into that field. You can also decide where exactly you are going to put these new fields. Perhaps the simplest thing would be to put them at the end and make them the last two fields. If you would prefer to put them somewhere else, for example the date of birth next to the age, then you will need to:

- Click on the grey part of the row
- Click on 'Insert' at the top of the screen
- Choose 'Row'.

The new row will appear before the data field that you clicked on. Now you can name your field and identify the data type.

| NAME | DAY/MONTH OF BIRTH | POSTCODE |
|------|--------------------|----------|
| Beth | 2nd February | NB4 4BN |
| Rachel | 3rd August | NB3 3PY |
| Harry | 17th December | IP4 4NZ |
| Nora | 14th February | ST11 6BV |
| Janice | 16th June | ST11 6BZ |
| Hamish | 25th January | PZ7 2NU |
| Robert | 24th April | PZ6 4PQ |
| Bernice | 23rd June | JA1 4PU |
| Bruce | 6th April | EA13 2BU |
| Eli | 17th November | EA13 2BU |

# Inserting, editing and deleting records

You can add new records to your database by simply typing into the blank row at the bottom of the database records. This row is marked with an asterisk (*). The database will automatically create a new blank row as soon as you have finished inserting data into the existing blank row. This works in exactly the same way as Excel, by creating a new row ready for new data.

In order to edit records, the easiest way is to move around the data sheet using the cursor keys (in this case the arrow keys). You can move from section to section using the arrow keys until you locate the data record in a particular field that you wish to amend. In addition to this, you can also use the icons at the bottom left-hand corner of the data sheet. These will allow you to:

- Move to the first record in the data sheet
- Move to the next record in the data sheet
- Move to the last record in the data sheet
- Check the total number of records in the data sheet
- Find where the cursor is currently placed in the set of records, such as 4 of 10.

## *Deleting*

You can also delete records on a data sheet by simply placing the cursor in any field of the record row and then selecting 'Edit', followed by 'Delete record' from the menu bar. This can also be achieved by clicking the 'Delete record' button on the data sheet toolbar. Note that this will delete the entire record.

When you wish to add and delete columns it is better to do this in 'Design view', as it offers you more options. You can add them quickly in 'Data sheet view'. This is achieved by highlighting a column by clicking its label at the top of the data sheet. The new column will appear to the left of the column you have selected. If you are happy with its position then select 'Insert' then 'Column' from the menu bar.

In the same way you can delete an entire column. Click on the column and then select 'Edit' then 'Delete column' from the menu bar. This will remove the entire column or data field, along with all the records contained in that field.

If you have made any changes to your database make sure that you save the new version each time.

# ACTIVITIES

1 Using the table provided above, update your 'Football supporters' database.

2 There is one other thing to do – somehow Bernice's age is wrong and she should be 16, not 14. Make this amendment to your database.

3 Your teacher or tutor will give you a copy of the Database Changes Worksheet. Follow all the instructions and save the amended database.

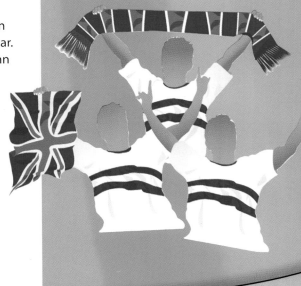

# Sorting records

## Searching, sorting and selecting records

Sorting allows you to rearrange records so that it makes it easier for you to understand your data. Access can display them in the order that you want them. Sometimes you may want your records to be displayed in different ways. In some cases an alphabetical listing might be ideal, but at other times you may want to display the data by date or value. Sometimes you might also want to sort records based on more than one field, such as date and alphabetical order. Sorting records is very straightforward.

One of the great things about Access is that you can re-order your records, so that you can view only the records in the table that match what you are looking for. The most common way of re-ordering records is sorting. This will allow you to sort records by date, number or alphabetical order.

To do this you need to be in 'Table view'. Place the cursor on the column that you want to sort by. You then need to select 'Records' then 'Sort' and then 'Sort ascending' or 'Sort descending'. These are exactly the same kind of options that you had in Excel, so this means that there are buttons to click on instead of using the menus.

Another useful facility is that you can sort by more than one column. To do this, highlight more than one column by clicking and dragging the cursor over the field labels. You can then select the kind of sort method that suits you. This is an ideal way, for example, to sort things alphabetically or by date.

There are other ways to select and sort data, which we will be looking at in the next part and in the activity.

--- **KEY TERMS** ---

**Filter** ▶ this eliminates records that are not relevant to the selection criteria.

## Selecting particular records

Using our database we might want to see how many of the ten football fans support a particular team. In order to select particular records we need to pick the field that we want to **filter** them by. To do this we click on 'Filter by selection' on the toolbar or we could select 'Records' then 'Filter' then 'Filter by selection' from the menu.

If you have made any changes to your database make sure that you save the new version each time.

The other thing to do is to create a query. This means searching for common features of several records. This is the procedure:

- Go to Design View
- Select the queries icon on the left of the box
- Click on 'New query'
- Click on 'Query' in design view
- You'll see your 'Football supporters' table in the box – this will be highlighted
- Click on 'Add' to select that table as being the one you wish to query then close the box
- You'll see the field names from your table in a small box on the left-hand side of the screen
- Double-click on each one to make

190

the fields appear at the top of each of the query columns
- Now close that small box
- Enter your query in the criteria field.

In order to carry out more complicated queries you need to add the criteria to the simple query. In order to do this you will need to:

- Open your query in design view
- Identify the fields about which you want to specify criteria
- If the field is not in your design view you can add it by dragging it from the query design window into the field grid, or by double-clicking on the field
- Now type the query into the criteria row
- You can specify criteria for different fields by using AND.

**For example**

If you wanted to find a particular city and everyone with the name of Jones you would type in:
     City="Norwich" AND
Name="Jones"
     The City field and the Name field are the only ones that contain specific criteria, so anyone with the name of Jones living in Norwich would appear in the results of your query.

You can filter the query results instead of modifying the query criteria if you think that there will be changes to your data. A filter is a temporary criteria that will change the query result without actually altering the query itself.

Alternatively, if the criteria fields will not change but the values that you are interested in might do, you can instead create a parameter query. This will prompt you for field values. Access will then use those values to create new query criteria.

You can use your mouse to select data or records as long as you are in 'Data sheet' view:

- To select particular data in a field you simply click where you want to start selecting and drag across the data.
- If you want to select an entire field then go to the left edge of the field, where your cursor will change into a cross.
- If you want to select a column click on 'Field selector'.
- If you want to select a record click on 'Record selector'.
- If you want to select multiple records then click the 'Record selector' of the first record and then drag to extend your selection.
- You can also select 'All records' by clicking on 'Select all records' in the 'Edit' menu.

# ACTIVITY

**1** Open your Access database 'Football supporters'. You need to do two things. First of all sort your database into alphabetical order, with 'Beth' first, and print a copy. Now sort into reverse alphabetical order, with 'Robert' first.

**2** Create a query to produce a list of just Chelsea supporters. Make sure that all their details appear, and then print a copy.

191

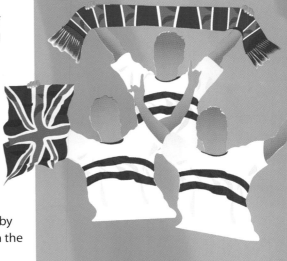

# Searching records

## Searching for records

There are four different ways in which you can find specific records in a database:

- By navigating through each record, one by one, as a table or in view
- By searching, by specifying criteria known as search terms, such as equals or contains and then only looking at those records that match those criteria. Access will highlight those records.
- By filtering – this is similar to searching, but it only brings up the records that match particular criteria, rather than in a search where all of them are brought up but not highlighted.
- Query – this is a question about the data that is stored. It allows you to perform customised searches or filters. These queries can be saved and reused.

### Navigating

There are several different ways in which you can navigate, or browse through, the records in your database. By simply pressing the tab key you can move through each of the records in order, one at a time. If you open a table or go to datasheet view you can use the special record navigation buttons to move through the records. You can go backwards and forwards, you can go to the beginning or the end of the records, you can insert a filter or you can go to the search box.

Access 2007 also has a 'Go to' box. This is in the upper left-hand section of the form. Simply click on the arrow at the edge of the box and select a record from the drop-down list. Access will then automatically take you to that record.

### Searching

You can use the 'Find' tab in the 'Find and replace' dialogue box. This will allow you to search for a specific record. Open the table or view that you want to search, then click on the field that you want to search. You must then go to the 'Home' tab, and select 'Find' from the 'Find group'. You can also press CTRL F as a shortcut.

The 'Find and replace' dialogue box will appear. Type what you want to search for in the 'Find what' box.

### Filtering

You can use a filter to show only records that match your criteria. Open a table or form and then it is best to make sure that there are no filters already set up. Go to the 'Home' tab and look at the 'Sort and filter group'. Click 'Advance' and then click 'Clear all filters'.

Go to the record that contains the value that you want to use as part of your filter and then click on the field. Now go to the 'Home' tab and click on 'Selection' from the 'Sort and filter group'. You can now select 'Equals', 'Not equals', 'Contains', or 'Does not contain'. You can set up multiple filters by filtering other fields based on selections of your choice.

### Queries

Sometimes you might want to do the same search or filter, so rather than set one up each time you can create a query. In order to do this, go to the 'Create' tab and in 'Other group' click on 'Query design'. The 'Show table' dialogue box will now appear. Double-click on the table you require and then click 'Close'. In the query designer double-click on the asterisk: this will make sure that the query will display all the fields from the records it finds.

In the query designer, double-click on the field you wish the query to relate to. If you want to refresh your memory about queries turn back to the last spread.

# Searching using single and multiple criteria

You can use the query wizard to help build a query from one or more tables. Make sure that the tables have a defined relationship in the 'Relationships' window. This is a window that allows you to view, create or modify relationships between tables and queries. It can be found in the 'Database tools' tab. Go to the 'Show/hide group' and click on 'Relationships'. In the 'Design' tab in the 'Relationships group' click 'All relationships'.

To build your query, go to the 'Create' tab and in the 'Other group' click on 'Query wizard'. The 'New query' dialogue box will appear and you should click on 'Simple query wizard' then click 'OK'. In the 'Tables and queries' box, click on the table that includes the information

that you want in your query. In the 'Available fields' list click on the first field that you wish to include and then use the right arrow button to move that field into the 'selected fields' list. You can do this with all the fields from that table that you wish to be included in your query. When you have done this, click 'Next'.

Access will now give you the option of whether you want a detail or a summary query. Choose whichever you prefer and then click 'Finish' to see the results.

You might wish to look at data from two different tables in different databases. In order to do this you need to create a union query. This brings together the results of two or more selected queries. Firstly go to the 'Create' tab and in the 'Other

group' click on 'Query design'. The 'Show table' dialogue box will appear. Click 'Close'.

Now go to the 'Design tab' and in the 'Query type group' click 'Union'. Access will switch to another view. You need to now type in 'Select' followed by a list of fields from the tables that you want to include in your query. When this has been done, hit 'Enter'.

Now type 'from' followed by the name of the first of the tables you want in the query and hit 'Enter' again. You can now type in 'Union' and press 'Enter'. The results will appear in datasheet view.

# Filtering records, data and creating reports

YOU WILL FIND OUT:

● about the report tool and the report wizard

● about the report sections

● about display field headings and titles

## The report tool and the report wizard

A report, as far as Access is concerned, allows you to display information that has come from tables or queries. It also allows you to see labels, headings and graphics. The quickest way to create a report is to use the report tool. It will display all the fields from a table or from a query. It is particularly useful to see the basic data before you move on to create precisely the type of report that you need. You can save this report and modify it later.

In the 'Navigation' plane on the left, click on the table or query that you want to base your report on. Then, on the 'Create' tab in the 'Reports group' click on 'Report'. Access will automatically build your report and display it in layout view. You can now look at it, print it or attach it to an email.

The report wizard allows you to group and sort your information, particularly if you have specified relationships. In the 'Create' tab go to the 'Reports group' and choose 'Report wizard'. Simply follow the report wizard prompts and when you have completed this, click on 'Finish'. You can now look at your report, print it or attach it to an email.

## The report sections

In Access, the reports are divided up into different sections:

* Report header – this is at the beginning of the report and it will usually appear on a cover page. It is usually a title, a date or something similar.
* Page header – this is printed at the top of each page and is often the title of the report.
* Group header – this is printed at the beginning of each new group of records.
* Detail – this is printed for every row in the records.

* Group footer – this is at the end of each group of records.
* Page footer – this is at the end of each page and could just be the page number.
* Report footer – this is at the end of the report and can be used to print report totals or other summaries.

You can view all of these in 'Design view' before you print to make sure that they say exactly what you want them to.

194

## Displaying field headings and titles

In order to insert a title into a form or a report, you need to open the form or report in 'Layout view'. You do this by clicking on the 'Navigation' pane and then right-clicking the 'Formal report' and then clicking to 'Layout view'. Choose the 'Formatting' tab and in the 'Controls group' click on 'Title'. You can now add a new label to the form or report header. When you have created this, the text in the label is automatically selected and you can change this text by keying in the title you want. When you have finished, click on 'Enter'.

You can add titles to existing forms or reports by placing the cursor in the label that contains the title and then double-clicking on the label. Amend the text as you want and hit 'Enter' when you have finished.

You can also insert dates and time of forms or reports by opening the formal report in 'Layout view' via the 'Navigation' pane and going to the 'Formatting' tab. Click on 'Date and time' from the 'Controls group' and the date and time dialogue box will

appear. If you do not want a date, just clear the check box for 'Include date'. If you do want a date, select the date format that you prefer. Similarly, if you do not want the time on your form or report, clear the 'Include time' check box. Again if you do want the time, select the time format that you wish to use, then click 'OK'. The date and time information will now be added to your formal report if that is what you wanted.

You can also add logos to your form or report. Once again use the 'Navigation' pane and click on 'Layout view'. Now go to the 'Formatting' tab and click on 'Logo' from the 'Controls group'. The dialogue box 'Insert picture' will now appear and this allows you to browse your computer or intranet to find a suitable picture or logo. Double-click on the file and the logo will now be added to the form or the report header. You can easily reposition the logo or drag it to a different location, and you can resize it just as you would with any other graphic.

### ACTIVITY

**Try putting your Football Supporters database into a report format. Browse the Clipart available on your computer or intranet, or search the Internet and find a suitable image that you could use as a logo. Practice organising your report by using the report tool and report wizard to see the alternative layouts available. You can also see how use of colour, titles and headings can make the information far more understandable and accessible to the widest possible range of readers. In the examination you may well be asked to create a report to meet specific formats and requirements, so it pays to practice as much as you possibly can.**

195

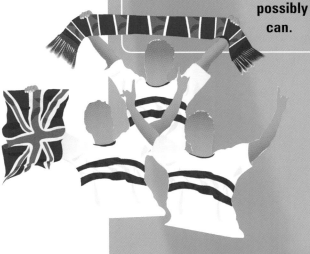

# Using graphics

## Using graphics and Clipart

Using pictures, graphics and Clipart in documents and presentations certainly makes them far more attractive and gives them a greater impact. As we will see in this section, there are plenty of options and there are a large number of sources to find suitable images. You can also do an enormous amount with these images. They can be standalone illustrations, with or without captions. You can wrap text around them or you can use the image almost like a watermark underneath the text. It is also possible to resize and move these images around, so that you can get the presentation of your document just right.

## Vector and Bitmap images

There are two main graphic types; Bitmaps and Vector images. Bitmaps are made up of a number of pixels. Pixels are tiny picture elements, or dots, of an individual colour or shade. The tiny dots make up the image that you see. As a result, the larger you make the image the more likely it is that you will be able to see each

of the tiny dots. This blurs the image and makes it far more difficult to see what the whole image is. The thing to bear in mind is that a Bitmap image may look perfectly fine on a computer screen, but it can look very odd when it has been printed out. This is due to what is known as resolution. This is the number of pixels in each image, usually given as the number of dots per inch (dpi). When you resize an image you are effectively stretching or shrinking the size of the dots that make up the picture. The more you stretch them, the more blurred the image will appear. Common Bitmap formats include:

- BMP
- Gif
- Jpeg or Jpg
- Ping
- Tiff.

Vector images are not as common as Bitmap images, but these are made up of several different objects. The objects can be lines, curves or shapes. You can change the way each of the objects looks without destroying the overall look of the object. You can scale them, which means resizing them, which means you do not need to worry about resolution. You can

increase the size or decrease the size and the image will still look good in print. You can also put these Vector images over other objects. On the down side, however, the images are usually made up of solid colours, so it is hard to shade them. Special software is needed in order to do this.

Vector images are not that commonly used in software applications such as Microsoft Office, but you may find some WMF images, which are Windows Metafile Format. The images do look a little cartoon-like and are not ideal if you want realistic-looking images.

## Formats

If you find images online they will tend to be Jpeg, Ping or Gifs. You can find some very large images in Tiff formats. These will mainly be photographs. Jpegs are good for small pictures but they are not suitable if you want to make them a large feature in a document unless they are very large files. Tiffs are very good but take up a lot of space and may take a relatively long time to print off. Gifs are ideal if your image has limited numbers of colours. They are fast-loading and are great for charts, diagrams and text headings.

196

▲ bitmap image

▲ vector image

## Sources and copyright

There are literally hundreds of thousands of websites with a massive variety of images, including photographs, drawings and Clipart. Many of them are free to use but some are copyrighted. This means that you are not supposed to use them without asking permission from the original source of the picture.

Clipart galleries are another great source of images. They are incredibly easy to find and they are very straightforward to insert into any Microsoft application. Once they are in the application you can resize them, colour them or edit them.

### For example

The best way to find a particular image is to use Google and switch over from web to image search. When we typed in the word 'Business', the Google image results offered us a total of 987 million images. This means that the search is too vague and it would take days to go through every image to try and find the one that we were looking for. By putting 'Business' in quotation marks and adding the word 'Communication' the result dropped to 353,000: still too many. Adding the word 'Systems' to the search brought the total down to slightly more than 2,000 images. This is still a lot of images to search through, but much more manageable.

### For example

On the Microsoft Office website (www.office.microsoft.com) there are over 150,000 free images and sounds that you could use. You can look through all the different types of Clipart as they have been sorted into categories. The business category alone has over 1,200, and the communications category has a similar number. The images are very easy to use; simply click on the box below each image and it will be added to a download. When you have finished selecting your images simply download all the images you want. You can now drop them into your document or presentation.

## ACTIVITY

**Try searching for your own images. Find the following:**

- **A colour photograph of a fruit stall in a Jpeg format.**
- **Go to www.gif.com and find a suitable image that could be used on a newsletter for students about to sit their GCSE examinations.**
- **Use the Google image search to find an ideal image to illustrate Business and Communication Systems.**

197

# Creating graphics

**YOU WILL FIND OUT:**
- about graphics and Clipart
- about creating freehand shapes
- about geometric shapes
- about shading and patterns

## Graphics and Clipart

Pictures, Clipart and graphics can make a document far more interesting. They can also make difficult things easier to understand. Many of these will be in colour, so they will also add interest to the page and attract the eye of the reader.

Graphics refers to any type of photograph or illustration. It can also refer to graphs, charts and tables. Some of these you can make yourself. Photographs, for example, can be taken using a digital camera. You can also find many photographs on the Internet, some of which can be used for free.

Clipart is peculiar to application software and the Internet. It consists of complete, digitally created images. There is a huge variety of Clipart from graphs, charts and tables through cartoons, icons, symbols and drawings. They are designed so that you can easily select them from either a website or a Clipart library and drop them straight into a document.

One of the things that we will be looking at is what to do when graphics and Clipart are the wrong size. They are very simple to resize and you can also move them around, wrap text around them and even give them **captions**.

## Creating freehand shapes

Word has an additional tool, other than word processing. At the bottom of the screen when you open Word there is a tab called AutoShapes. This is part of the 'Draw' set of menus. By clicking on AutoShapes a series of new options will appear. To draw a freehand shape you can either select 'Freeform' or 'Scribble'. Once this option has been chosen, a pencil cursor will now appear on the screen. By holding down the left mouse button you can draw any shape or design. When you release the mouse button the application will assume you have finished your drawing and the newly created image will be contained in its own box. You can resize, move left, right, up or down, or pick up the whole object and move it to another part of the document.

This technique will need practice, as it is not like drawing with a pencil. If you are unhappy with the shape you have created, simply select the object and press delete.

The examiners may ask you to create simple freehand shapes or draw geometric shapes. You may also have to add shading and patterns.

—— **KEY TERMS** ——

**Captions** ▶ brief descriptions of a photograph, graphic or image to explain to the reader what they are about.

**Textbox** ▶ a resizable shape that you can insert onto a Word document. It will allow you to type directly into it and all the text will remain inside that box.

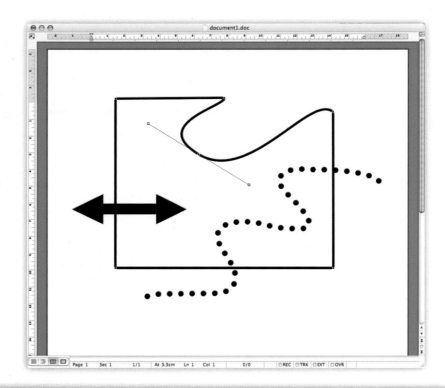

198

## Geometric shapes

The AutoShapes menu in the set of Draw menus offers you many other options to use ready-made shapes and lines in your documents. In each case you can select the shape you require and then move or resize it on the screen. You can also insert inside the shape into a **textbox**. The textbox can be added by using the 'Insert' drop-down menu at the top of the screen. Some way down the menu is the option 'Textbox'. The one irritating feature of the textbox is that it will appear in a random position on your screen and you will have to click on it and move it to your preferred position. You will also have to resize the textbox.

Consider the textbox to be a normal word-processing document, but in miniature, so you can choose the font style and font size. You can also embolden the text, underline, italicise it or centre it within the textbox.

The geometric shapes in the AutoShapes menu include:

- lines
- basic shapes
- block arrows
- flowchart symbols
- stars and banners
- call-outs
- more AutoShapes.

It is worth investigating the choices, as they may save you a great deal of time and effort in creating the shape yourself.

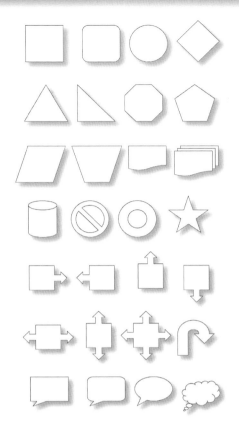

## Shading and patterns

There are many useful things that you can do with a textbox. It does not simply have to be a square or rectangle with a black line around it.

Once you have created a textbox, by right-clicking on it, a new menu will appear. Choose the 'Format textbox' option and a new window will offer you a series of choices. From here you can determine the way the line looks (such as a dotted line), the colour of the line and the thickness of the line. You can then choose to 'Fill' the box with a particular colour. This can either be a solid colour or a colour that gets darker or lighter from top to bottom. You can also choose to change the colour of the text inside the box. It may be useful, for example, having chosen a black background, to change the font colour to white, so that it can be read.

 **ACTIVITIES**

1 Using the 'Draw' tool in Word, select 'Freeform' and try to write your own name in a blank document. You may need several tries at this before you are happy with it.

2 Your teacher or tutor will give you a copy of the 'Autoshapes' worksheet. You will have to identify where to find each of the shapes and suggest a use for each of them.

3 Your teacher or tutor will give you a copy of the 'Customising a textbox' worksheet. Follow the instructions, then save your work as 'Textbox' and print it.

199

# Lines and combining text and graphics

YOU WILL FIND OUT:

- about line styles
- about a second source of lines
- about combining text and graphics

## Line styles

You will have noticed that there are two different opportunities to pick particular styles of line. The first one that you would have encountered is under the AutoShapes menu, where we saw the sub-menu 'Lines'.

Lines can be used to break up text and to provide spaces and shapes and even to set aside a particular part of a document for a different purpose.

Think about a document that tells you about a school trip. It will explain the trip and give a description of the kind of things that you will be doing. At the end of the document there will be a section that either your parents or guardians would have to fill in and sign to inform the school or college that you wish to go on the trip. Obviously you will want to keep the copy of the document, so that you can be reminded of what is in store for you. There are two options: you could photocopy the document and give the whole thing back to your school or college. The simple use of lines, however, gives you the much easier option. A dotted line above the part allowed for parents or guardians to sign shows that you can fold along that line and cut it off. Now you can just send that part back to the school or college. A line can, therefore, have a practical purpose or it can be just there for decoration.

### KEY TERM

Point ▶ a measurement of the size of text or of the thickness of lines in a document.

### Line options

There is no hard and fast rule about which type of line to use in different circumstances. One thing is sure, however, and that is that you shouldn't use too many different styles in the same document. That would just make things too confusing. If you need to use lines, pick one that does the job and stick to that. You may have lines anyway around textboxes.

### The first source of lines

We know that there is a line option in the AutoShapes menu. This offers us straight lines, lines with arrows or lines that we can draw ourselves. This does not even begin to cover the enormous variety of lines that you can pick in Word.

The examiner may expect you to make effective use of different line styles. You may also be expected to combine text and graphics in documents.

## A second source of lines

Along the same menu row as AutoShapes are three icons, all with horizontal lines on them. These are another major source of line options and styles.

The first one has thin to thick black lines. It offers you the following options, which are available to you only after you have drawn a line or selected a line from the line sub-menu of AutoShapes:

- From 1/4 **point** to 6 point
- Solid, black or grey (you will be able to change the colour of these)
- A line that has a thin, black line in the centre, inside a thicker, grey line

The second icon offers you the same kind of options, but this time with dotted or dashed lines. Again you can choose the thickness of the line, you can opt for dots or dashes close together or widely spaced apart. You can even pick alternate dots and dashes, such as stars. Once again,

Please sign and return the form below.

Yours sincerely

*K. Richardson*

Ms K Richardson
Headmistress

- - ✂ - - - - - - - - - - - - - - - - - - - - - - - - - - - - - - - - - - - - - -

I confirm that ................................................. will be able to attend.

signed: ....................................................... date: .....................

after you have created the style of line, you can right-click on it and change its colour.

The final icon has lines with arrows. You can choose the thickness of the line and decide whether you want an arrow at each end or at just one end. The same options apply to change the colour once the line has been created.

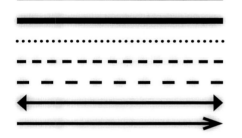

## Combining text and graphics

It is possible to make text flow around graphics that you put into a document. This gives a far more professional look to the document than simply having any images isolated from the text. Just how the text works around the graphics will depend on what you are trying to do and, perhaps, how much space you have on the page.

In order to achieve the perfect balance between graphics and text you need to click on the graphic and select the 'Draw' menu from the bottom of the page. Choose the 'Text wrapping' option. It will offer you several different choices for how the text appears around the graphic. The text can literally follow the shape of the graphic, or it can appear next to it, underneath it, above it or on either side of it.

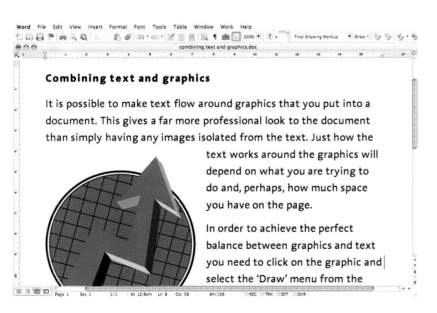

## ACTIVITIES

**1** Open your Textbox document. Right-click on the textbox and select 'Copy'. Then select 'Paste'. You now have two textboxes. Place them at either side of the document, in line with one another. Now connect them with a line with arrows on each end and colour the arrow line the same shade of red as the textbox lines.

**2** You may want to experiment with this function to get the ideal effect in your document.

On the AutoShapes menu, click on the 'More AutoShapes' option and select an illustration of your choice. Place the image on the left-hand margin of a blank Word document. Now write an appropriate caption for the illustration. Experiment with the 'Text wrapping' options that you can find under the 'Draw' menu.

# Editing, moving and alignment

## Editing graphics

Just like sections of text, you can edit graphics in order to delete them, copy them or move them around. The three key options when you right-click on a graphic are:

*   Cut – this deletes or removes the graphic from the document. Remember that Word actually saves the last thing that you cut, so if you have made a mistake you can put it back in by selecting 'Paste', which restores it.
*   Copy – again, by right-clicking you can choose this option. Word will remember this until you choose to cut or copy something else. If you are not ready to paste the graphic that you have just copied, you can finish your other tasks and then paste the graphic in.
*   Paste – this will put either another copy of a graphic onto the page, or restore a graphic that you have cut. You can paste the same graphic as many times as you want, simply by multiple clicks of the paste icon, or by right-clicking and choosing 'Paste' from the menu.

### KEY TERM

**Proportions** ▶ an image's height and width. By stretching or reducing its size from a corner box, the relative sizes of its length and width remain the same.

## Moving graphics

By clicking on a graphic you will see a frame appear around it. The blocks in the corners and halfway along each edge are used to stretch or resize the graphic. However, if you keep your cursor over the graphic you will see your cursor change to a black cross. You can now drag the graphic to a new location in the document. When you have it roughly where you want it to be, take your finger off the mouse button.

## Aligning shapes and text

On the previous pages we looked very briefly at sorting out graphics and shapes with text. It is possible to create attractive designs that use a mixture of graphics and text. This is far more effective than having graphics separate from the text.

The only thing to remember is not to have them too close together, otherwise it will make it difficult to read and understand. Use graphics only when they actually add something to the document. They do not need to be huge, and should certainly not dominate a page, unless they are a graph or a pie chart that actually illustrates something and has information in it.

Although this is the last section on graphics and Clipart, it is by no means the least important. Examiners will expect you to be able to use graphics and text together. They will also expect you to be able to move graphics around and resize them.

## Resizing and moving graphics

When you click on a graphic or a piece of Clipart you will notice that a box appears around it. There are little squares in each corner. There are also squares halfway along each edge of the graphic. These little boxes allow you to manipulate the graphic by stretching it or shrinking it. The options are:

*   Any of the corner squares, if pulled out or pushed in, will resize the graphic in the same **proportions** as it currently appears.
*   By pulling or pushing one of the little boxes halfway along an edge you can stretch or shrink the width or height of the graphic. Obviously the top and bottom squares will let you change the height; the side squares allow you to change the width. Beware, as choosing these options may make your graphic look odd.

A black cross will appear if you do not wish to stretch or shrink the graphic. This is the movement cursor. Left-click on your mouse and drag the graphic to its new position in the document. When you let go or drop it the graphic will appear in your newly chosen position.

## Alignment

Alignment means putting things in the right place and this is necessary when you are using graphics and text together. Neither should crowd the other out, and the shapes should not make it difficult to read the text. The text should not make it impossible to understand why a particular shape has been used.

Let's briefly look at the text and graphic alignment options:

- Square – in effect this creates a new left-hand margin for the text. It will appear in a straight line alongside the graphic until the text becomes longer than the graphic, when the text will run from the document's margin to margin.

- Tight – this is very similar to square, but the text is much closer to the graphic.

- Behind text – this means that the image will appear behind the text. It will look as if you have typed over the graphic.

- In front of text – the graphic appears on top of the text, making it impossible to read all the text underneath the graphic.

- Text top – the text will appear above the graphic and not below it.

- Text below – the reverse of text top, the text will only appear after the graphic.

- Text through image – the reverse of 'In front of text'. The appearance is that the text has been typed over the top of the graphic.

## ACTIVITES

1 **Your teacher or tutor will provide you with a copy of the 'Graphics' worksheet. Follow the instructions and save your final version as 'Graphic 1'.**

2 **Experiment with moving a graphic around a document with text in it. Simply create a graph using the 'Insert' menu or just pick a simple Clipart image from the library. Initially place it at the bottom of the document. Click on it and move it to the top of the document. What happens to the text when this happens?**

3 **There is another option called 'Edit wrap points'. What do you think this means? Experiment with some text and a graphic.**

203

# Presentation

## What is PowerPoint?

PowerPoint is part of the Microsoft Office suite of programs. It is a program that allows you to create presentations. Each of the presentations consists of a number of individual pages, known as slides. The slides can contain graphics, text, objects and even moving pictures.

PowerPoint has a number of ready-to-use themes and slide styles, and also allows you to control the colours, fonts and effects. You can also determine how quickly slides are shown and you can use the software to generate presenter notes and handouts for the audience.

PowerPoint can be displayed on a computer screen or it can be connected via a laptop to a projector so that the whole audience can see the presentation. It is possible to use callouts, speech bubbles and even add speech itself. You can also decide how elements of the slide itself appear through what are known as custom animations. The transitions from one slide to the next can also be animated.

This type of presentation is an ideal visual aid. The software can even suggest the structure of the content of the presentation to match the purpose of the presentation itself. The software has developed over the past 25 years and has been part of Microsoft Office since 1993.

## Why do businesses use PowerPoint?

Microsoft Office is seen as a very powerful tool to create professional-looking presentations. It is relatively easy to make a presentation from scratch, or to use the wizards. It is also straightforward to import graphics and text from other Microsoft Office programs.

PowerPoint is a very simple program to learn how to use and it can produce presentations that give the impression that many hours have been spent structuring them. Businesses are able to incorporate their logos and use their own design templates. It is also possible to use **add-ins** and templates designed by Microsoft or other PowerPoint users.

PowerPoint also has printing options, so the audience can have handouts and note pages.

---

**KEY TERM**

**Add-in** ▶ a mini program that improves the functionality of the main program.

# Business presentations

Although there is no hard and fast rule about how businesses might use PowerPoint presentations, the key point is to keep the audience focused and interested. The following ten points should be borne in mind whenever you begin to design the look and content of your presentation:

- Only feature key phrases – only essential information should be put on the slides. Choose as few key phrases as possible and always limit the number of words that you use on each slide. Never have more than three bullet points per slide. The more clear space on a slide the easier it is to read.

- Slide layout – it is vital that your audience is able to follow the slides as easily as possible. Always have a title at the top of the slide. Phrases should always read from left to right and top to bottom. The most important information needs to be at the top of the slide. It is worth remembering that information crammed into the bottom of a slide might not be able to be read by those at the back of an audience, as other people might be in the way.

- Punctuation and capital letters – although punctuation is important it can clutter the slide, so if it is unnecessary do not use it. Do not use capital letters for whole statements because these are more difficult to read and some people interpret capital letters as 'shouting' to the audience.

- Fancy fonts – stick to the fonts that are easy to read, such as Times New Roman, Arial and Verdana. Avoid fonts that are difficult to read at a distance. Never use more than two fonts on a single slide. Always keep the fonts large enough. If you are giving a presentation to an audience then the font sizes should be at least 24 or, probably better, 30 point. This will ensure that people at the back of the room will be able to read the screen.

- Contrasting colours – putting dark text onto a light background is often the best way to highlight text and make it easier to read. Do not use a white background because it is too harsh on the eyes. Tone down the white with a light colour. If you are using a dark background, use a light-coloured text. Avoid using a patterned or textured background because this makes the text harder to read, and always keep your colour schemes consistent throughout the presentation.

- Slide designs – try to choose a slide design or theme that is appropriate to your audience. Businesses will choose clean, straightforward layouts. For younger audiences, full colour and shapes are best.

- Cut down on the number of slides – keep your presentation down to a minimum number of slides. This will avoid having to change the slides too often and it will also cut down on the overall length of the presentation. Work on the assumption that one slide a minute is about the right speed.

- Photos, charts and graphs – use these, but sparingly. They will add variety and keep the audience interested. If it is possible, avoid having text-only slides.

- Slide transitions and animations – these can be very effective, but if they are too complicated they will distract the audience. The slides are a visual aid and not the presentation itself. If you are using transitions (which we look at later in this section) then use the same type of transition throughout the whole presentation.

- Will your presentation run? – you may have to run your presentation from a CD or a memory stick. Make sure that the computer or laptop you are using can cope with this format. Test it and make sure that the transitions in particular are not jerky due to a problem with the computer being able to read from that storage format. Also be certain that the computer you are using has PowerPoint installed, otherwise this will be a major hurdle.

205

# Creating slides for a business purpose (1)

YOU WILL FIND OUT:

● about using blank slides or templates

● about inserting and formatting text

● about text boxes

● about bullet points and numbering

● about creating a basic presentation

## Creating slides from blank slides or templates

Creating slides is not difficult. When you open PowerPoint, the program will have generated a simple opening slide for your presentation. The first thing to do is to choose your design theme. Click on the 'Design' tab and use the arrow keys to the right of the design themes to view the full selection of available themes. You can (if you are connected to the Internet) look for additional themes on Microsoft's own website.

When you want to add a new slide to your presentation, click on the 'Home' tab and then click on the arrow key beside 'New slide'. You will be offered a number of options:

- Title
- Title and content
- Section header
- Two content
- Comparison
- Title only
- Content with caption
- Picture with caption

The other option is a blank slide. If you choose a blank slide you can then determine its layout. As we will see, you can use this to insert pictures, Clipart, photographs, shapes, SmartArt, charts, text boxes, WordArt, movies or sounds.

## Inserting and formatting text

To insert text you simply click on one of the text box objects and type it in. You can then right-click on the text and a new dialogue box will appear. It will offer you all the fonts that are available on the software. You can also change the point size and the colour of the text. At the same time you can embolden, or italicise the text. Just as in Word, you can also decide how you want to align your text and change its colour.

If you want to insert text from Word, open Word and find the document that contains the text you want to use. Highlight the text, right-click and select 'Copy' from the dialogue box. Go back to PowerPoint, click on the text box where you want the text to appear, right-click again and select 'Paste'. The text from your Word document will now appear in that text box. You may need to resize the text box to ensure that it all fits.

## Text boxes

Although the slides may already have one or more text boxes, they may not be in the ideal position and neither will they be big enough. To insert a new text box, click on the 'Insert' tab and then in the 'Text group' select the option 'Text box'. Click on the icon. Your cursor will not be a thin black line. Position it roughly where you want the text box to start. Press the left mouse key and your cursor will not change to a cross. Stretch the text box to the approximate size and shape you need and then release the left mouse button. Your new text box will now appear.

The corners of the text box allow you to stretch it and reduce it in size. If you want to resize the text box's height or width then use the squares that appear at the mid-point on each axis. You can now simply type straight into the text box or import text from Word.

## Bullet points and numbering

You may want to use bullet points or numbering. Just as in Word, you have different format options. If the text is already in the text box then simply highlight it and click on the bullet point or numbering from the 'Paragraph group'. Alternatively you can highlight the text, right-click, and choose the bullet points or numbering from the new pop-up.

YOU WILL FIND OUT:
- about using blank slides or templates
- about inserting and formatting text
- about text boxes
- about bullet points and numbering
- about creating a basic presentation

## Creating a basic presentation

When you start PowerPoint it will automatically open in 'View' or 'Normal view'. This is where you can create and work on the slides. The larger section is known as the slide pane and the dotted lines identify where you can type text or insert pictures, charts or other objects. The 'Slides tab' on the left shows you a thumbnail of each of the full size slides. As you add slides more thumbnails will appear. By clicking on one of the thumbnails you can go automatically to that slide. You can also use this 'Slides tab' to drag thumbnails to rearrange them or add and delete slides.

At the bottom of the screen is a section called 'Add notes'. You can type straight into this box with notes about the slide that is in view. PowerPoint will always give you a blank presentation slide unless you tell it to do otherwise as you add each new slide.

There are also some other useful icons at the top of the screen:

- The undo icon – which undoes your last action. You can actually tell the program to undo your last typing, bullets or resizing, as it will remember up to your last 20 actions.
- The redo or repeat icon – which repeats or redoes your last change. Again this depends on what you have done.

At the earliest possible opportunity always name and save your presentation. As with Word, you click on the Microsoft icon, which is in the top left-hand corner of the screen. Click on 'Save as' and a new dialogue box will appear. This gives you options relating to where to save the presentation. If you do not type in a name for your presentation, PowerPoint will use the first words that you have used in your presentation.

207

# Creating slides for a business purpose (2)

## Formatting the layout of a slide using text boxes and graphic objects

If you were to start with a blank slide you would see that there are no text boxes or other boxes, and this gives you the option to place whatever you want on that slide, in whatever position you choose. We have already seen how easy it is to insert text boxes. But there are many other things that can be done.

The first option is to insert a picture. To do this go to the 'Insert' tab and in the 'Illustrations group' click on 'Picture' (in exactly the same way as you would for Clipart). A new dialogue box will appear and the program will have identified where you have saved the majority of pictures or pieces of Clipart. If the picture is not there you will need to 'browse' to find it. When you have found it, simply click once and then click 'Insert' to complete the action. By default it will position your picture at the centre of the slide. You can move the picture

by putting your cursor over it and you will see a mouse pointer and black cross. By left-clicking you can now lift the picture and reposition it. Resize it as you would do with a normal graphic.

You can also add in shapes. These will be familiar to you, as we investigated these when we looked at Word. There are flow charts, callouts, stars and banners, as well as lines and other shapes to choose from. Simply click on the one that you wish to use and then position it by depressing the left mouse button, stretching it to size and then releasing the button.

SmartArt can also be inserted. Again, we looked at this when we investigated Word. You can perform exactly the same function by simply clicking on the SmartArt object and it will automatically appear on your slide template.

Charts can also be added. Click on the 'Chart' icon, select the type you prefer by clicking on it and then

click 'OK' to confirm. An Excel style spreadsheet will appear, and you will need to complete this by amending the data in the columns and rows. When you have finished, close that dialogue box.

It is possible also to amend the design of each of the objects that you have inserted. Click on the object itself and PowerPoint will automatically switch to 'Format', where you can change the way in which the object looks from a range of options.

Similarly, you can add WordArt to your presentation. Using the 'Insert' tab go across to the 'Text group' and select 'WordArt'. PowerPoint will by default create a text box that says 'Your text here'. To replace the text, highlight the text in the text box and simply type your own message.

You can also insert headers and footers, dates and times or slide numbers. You can define exactly where any of these will appear on the slide.

# Formatting colours and lines, borders and objects

The simplest way to create a border around a text box is to click on the text box itself and then go to the 'Shape styles' group. On the left you will see a number of options for theme fills. As you move your mouse over each one, the text box will automatically, but temporarily, change to that theme so that you can see what it looks like. When you have found one that you prefer, simply click on it and the text box will transform into that new border shape and colour fill.

Another way of dealing with changes is to click on the 'Format' tab after you have clicked on the text box. In the 'Shape styles' group you can change the colour of the fill, determine the colour of the shape outline, or choose the shape effects (shadow, reflection, glow, soft edges, bevel or 3-D). You can also combine many of these effects.

If you click on an object, the 'Format' tab will reveal a number of options:

- On the left you have the 'Adjust group', which allows you to adjust the brightness, contrast and colour.
- In the centre you have the 'Picture styles', which gives you a number of options to change the shape and the border around your object.
- In addition to these picture styles, which provide you with frame options, there is 'Picture shape', which will adjust the shape of your picture into a rectangle, basic shape or arrow or allow it to become part of a flow chart.
- You can also change the colour of the picture border by clicking on the arrow beside 'Picture border'.
- Finally you can change the picture effect by giving it a shadow, reflection or soft edges, among other options.

If you have inserted a shape it is also possible to amend the colours, the shape's style, fill, outline and effects by using the 'Shape styles' group in the 'Format' tab. This also allows you to highlight the shape. PowerPoint will offer you variations of the same theme, colours and style, with lighter and darker versions to bring your shape box to greater prominence on the slide.

209

# Creating transitions and animations

## Transitions

Slide transitions are animations that take place in your slide show when you move from one slide to the next. PowerPoint allows you to control the speed of those transitions and allows you to add sound. It also allows you to create self-running presentations. These will automatically move from one slide to the next using transitions at a speed that you specify. These self-running presentations will restart when they have finished, or have been idle for more than five minutes. This enables the presentation to be run without a presenter and businesses could send these electronically to a customer.

In PowerPoint, click on the 'Animations' tab and go to the 'Transition to this slide group'. There are a number of options available to you if you click on the arrow button beside the six transitions that are in view. Your options are:

- No transition
- Fades and dissolves
- Wipes

- Push and cover
- Stripes and bars
- Random

Also in this group are the transition sounds. The default is no sound. If your computer has speakers then you could choose from a number of different sounds, including:

- Applause
- Camera
- Hammer
- Laser
- Typewriter
- Wind

These can be accessed by clicking on the arrow beside the 'Transition sound' box.

You can also determine how fast you want the transitions to be. Your options, if you press the arrow key beside 'Transition speed' are slow, medium and fast. The last option is to apply your transition sound, transition type and speed to all the slides in your presentation. By default, PowerPoint will change a slide every time you click on the mouse. If you uncheck this box you can set it to automatically move onto the next slide after a number of seconds or minutes.

## Animations

It is possible to animate text and objects. This means giving them sound effects or movements. You can use the animation to focus on important points, or to control the flow of information on the slide. You can apply built-in animation effects to text or an object. Select the object that you wish to animate, then click on the 'Animations' tab, which is in the 'Animations group'. Select the animation effect that you want from the animate list. Your basic options are fade, wipe and fly in. By selecting one of these, PowerPoint will automatically show you the effect.

You can have even greater control over the animation effects by applying your own custom animation. You can make the text grow or shrink, or you can add applause when a picture or a key set of figures is revealed. In order to do these go to the 'Custom animation' option in the 'Animations group'. A new dialogue box will appear on the right of your screen. The choices are:

- Start on click – the animation will begin when you click on the slide
- Start with previous – the animation will begin at the same time as the previous effect in the list
- Start after previous – the animation will begin after the previous effect

You need to select an item from the list and then click the icon to reveal the menu. The numbers will indicate the order in which the animation effects play. The icons represent the type of animation effect.

In order to apply a custom animation you will need to:

- Select the text or object that you wish to animate.
- Click on 'Custom animation'.
- In the new task pane click 'Add effect'.
- To make the text or object enter, point to the entrance and then click an effect.
- To add an effect to text or objects that are already on the screen point to 'Emphasis' and then click an effect.
- To add an effect that makes text or objects leave the slide, point to exit and then click an effect.
- To add an effect that makes text or objects move in a particular pattern, point to 'Motion path' and then click on a path.

You will now need to right-click the custom animation effect in the 'Custom animation' list and then click 'Effect options'. You can specify the settings but remember that the effects will appear in the order in which you add them.

## The benefits of animations

Animation and slide transitions can provide visual interest to your presentation and keep the attention of the audience, provided you do not overuse them. It is possible to reveal the points on your slides one at a time, so that the audience keeps focused only on the point that you are discussing at any given time.

The other obvious advantage is that you can automate your presentation so that it runs on its own. Other key advantages are:

- It allows you to present ideas in a logical sequence.
- It can ensure that the audience focuses its attention on one point at a time.
- It allows you to build up to a main point and then reveal it.

The truth is that many PowerPoint presentations are unsatisfactory: they are either boring or the designer of the presentation has over-animated, so that the presentation is confusing, too busy and very difficult to follow. Bear in mind that less is definitely more. Using the odd animation here and there on a slide will have far more visual impact than using animations to the extreme. If you think that a single object moving across a slide is confusing, imagine what it is like if you animate everything. It may show your technical expertise, but it will do nothing for the audience apart from annoy them.

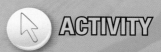

**ACTIVITY**

Create a new PowerPoint presentation and insert a blank slide. Insert a picture or a piece of Clipart of your choice and a text box. Type into the text box the words 'Test slide' using Arial 30 point. Now custom-animate the two objects so that one appears from the left and one appears from the right and position them at the centre of the slide, with the text underneath the picture.

211

# Modifying presentations

## Resizing and cropping

If you right-click on an object a new dialogue box will appear. One of the options is 'Size and position'. Click on this and a new dialogue box will appear. There are three tabs: size, position and alt text (alternative text).

In the 'Size' tab the options are size and rotate, scale, crop, and a section that states the original size of the object. You can adjust the size of the object by using the arrow keys alongside the height and the width, making the object larger or smaller, as you please. Note that as you change the height, the width will automatically readjust, as will the height when you adjust the width.

You can also choose to rotate by pressing the up-arrow key and the object will rotate in a clockwise direction by a degree with each click. By clicking the down-arrow the object will rotate by one degree anti-clockwise per click.

The scale can also change the overall look of the object. It will appear initially as 100% height, 100% width. By default, 'Lock aspect ratio' and 'Relative to original picture size' are checked. This means that as you increase or decrease the height or the width, the other will similarly change by 1%. Note that as you do this, the overall size of the object will also change. By unlocking the 'Aspect ratio' you can effectively stretch or shrink the height or stretch or shrink the width independently of each other.

You can also check the box, 'Best scale for slide show'. This will automatically resize your object to the best size for a presentation.

The crop option allows you to resize the object from the left, right, top or bottom. This allows you a lot more flexibility in being able to resize the object so that it exactly fits into the space that you have allocated for it on the slide.

## Aligning and moving objects

Alignment refers to the position of the text within a text box. Click on your text box and from the 'Paragraph' group you can align to the left or right, centre or justify. You can also decide to have one, two, three or more columns within the text box. It is also possible to align the text within the text box so that it is at the top, middle or bottom by clicking on the down-arrow next to the 'Align text' icon. By clicking on the arrow at the bottom of the 'Paragraph group' you can be even more precise about the alignment, indentation and spacing of characters and words.

The simplest way to move an object is to click on it, and your mouse cursor will turn into a white arrow with a black cross. By depressing the left mouse button you can move the object around the slide. Note that the object will still appear in its original position until you release the mouse button.

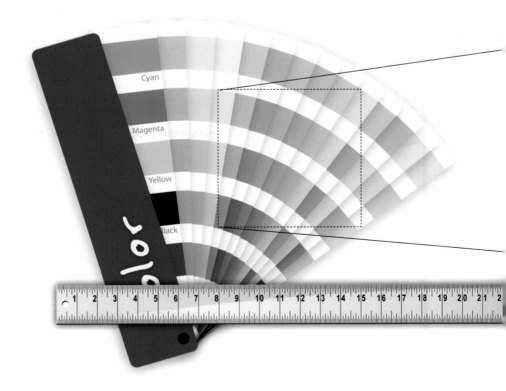

## Changing background colour of slides

In order to change the background colour of a text box you can:

- Right-click on the text box and select 'Format shape'
- From here you can determine the fill, including colour and amount of transparency, the line colour, the line style, the shadow, any 3-D format or rotation and the precise text layout, including the ability to shrink overflowing text so that it fits into the box.
- On a picture, you can also choose 'Format' by right-clicking once you have highlighted the object. You can now re-colour the whole picture from a palette of colours, including dark and light variations.

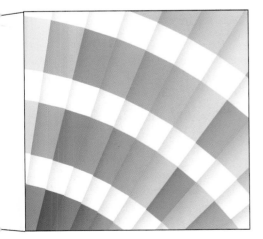

## Adding and inserting slides

The easiest way to insert a slide is to go to the thumbnail pane on the left side of the screen. Right-click and select 'New slide'. PowerPoint will, by default, add a blank slide. If you wish to use one of the ready-made slide templates, go to the 'Slides group' and click on the arrow button beside 'Layout' and choose from the different designs.

The alternative way to add a new slide is to click on the 'New slide' arrow in the 'Slides group'. Here you can select from a range of templates or duplicate slides you have already created, or reuse and modify an existing slide. If you choose this reuse slide option a new dialogue box will appear on the right-hand side of the screen. This allows you to either:

- browse a slide library (your intranet may have a slide library of existing templates)
- browse file – this will bring up 'My documents' and from here you can select an existing PowerPoint presentation and insert those slides from that presentation into your new presentation

**Open a new PowerPoint presentation and create a blank slide. Insert a picture or piece of Clipart onto the slide. Now create a text box and type 'Moving objects' into the text box, in 32 point Verdana. Now move your picture or Clipart to the left-hand side of the slide and resize it so that it occupies half of the slide. Now move your text box to the right-hand side, and resize the text box so that it occupies the remaining right-hand side of the slide. Adjust the size of the font in your text box so that the words are as large as you can possibly get them without them appearing hyphenated. Click on your object and format it so that it now appears only in black-and-white, rather than colour.**

213

# Creating presenter notes and handouts

## Creating and printing presenter notes

You will recall that you are able to insert notes at the bottom of each slide. These are designed to be prompts for the presenter or additional notes for the audience. It is possible for you to print these out and it is also possible to print out copies of the slides in various formats, so that the audience can be given copies to either take away with them or to refer to and make notes on during the presentation.

In order to access both types you need to click on the 'View' tab at the top of the screen. Look at the 'Presentation views group'. From left to right you have:

- Normal – this provides you with a standard view of each slide as you click through them, giving you the ability to add notes at the bottom of the page.
- Slide sorter – by clicking on this you will see all your slides displayed as thumbnails on the screen. By clicking on one of them and then depressing your left mouse button you can re-order your slides.
- Notes page – gives you a snapshot of the slide, along with any notes that you have added beneath it.
- Slide show – simply allows you to view your presentation as you have set it up.

- Slide master – opens your master slide so that you can change the design and layout of it.
- Handout master – allows you to manipulate how your handouts will appear, which we will investigate in the next section on this spread.
- Notes master – shows you the slide itself and then the notes fully formatted underneath, along with header, footer, date and slide number.

In these last two options you are able to change the orientation, the number of slides per page, whether they have headers, footers, dates or page numbers, the colour or theme and the background styles.

Once you have designed your presenter notes and are happy with them, you can then decide to print them. In order to print your presenter

notes you need to click on the Microsoft Office button in the top left-hand corner of the screen. Select 'Print preview'. The tool bar at the top will now change. In the 'Page setup group' you will have the question 'Print what?' Click on the down arrow and here you have the option of printing out the slides themselves, the handouts, the presenter notes or the outline views. The outline views are small icons of each slide in the order in which you have set them, along with the text that appears on that slide.

Choose 'Notes page' and then click 'Print' to get hard copies of your presenter notes. If there appear to be problems with fitting the slide and text onto a printed page, click on 'Print option' and choose 'Scale to fit paper'. The program will now automatically resize your slide and notes so that each one fits onto an A4 sheet.

## Printing slides and handouts

Handouts are incredibly useful for the audience and also provide them with a permanent record of the presentation. Some businesses will print out handouts that incorporate the slides and room for the audience to make notes as the presentation is being made. Obviously it is important that when you are printing out handouts these are the most definitive version of the presentation. There should be no difference in the content of the handouts to the actual presentation that the audience sees, otherwise the audience will be confused.

Rather like the printing of presenter notes, you need to go to the 'View' tab in PowerPoint and then go to the 'Presentation views group'. You will see that there is a handout master. Click on this and a new tool bar will appear at the top of the screen. The key areas are:

- Page setup – which sets the orientation of your handout, either portrait or landscape; the slide orientation so that the slides appear as either portrait or landscape and the number of slides per page (from 1 to 9).

- Place holders – this allows you to add or take away a header, footer, date or page number.
- Edit theme – this allows you to change the theme, colours, fonts and effects of each of the handouts.
- Background – lets you colour the whole of the page on which the slides will appear.

Ideally you should put no more than three or four slides on an A4 sheet. These should appear on the left-hand side of the page, leaving the right-hand side clear for the audience to write their own notes next to each slide.

When you are ready to print your handouts, click on the Microsoft Office button, select 'Print' and from the three options choose 'Print preview'. This gives you the option of printing 1 to 9 slides per page. The program will automatically insert lines for the audience to take notes if you select three slides per page, otherwise it will not.

When you are happy with the overall layout of the handout, select 'Print' and confirm how many copies of the handouts you require, before pressing 'OK'.

215

## ACTIVITY

Create a simple PowerPoint presentation using the information below:

**DOS AND DON'TS OF A POWERPOINT PRESENTATION**

- **Stick to one click per slide**
- **Don't use your mouse as a pointer**
- **Don't use the edges of a slide because some projectors crop the slides**
- **Use large fonts**
- **Don't use dark fonts on dark backgrounds**
- **Don't use annoying, animated or busy backgrounds**
- **Don't use silly animations or Clipart**
- **Don't assume your presentation will work on someone else's computer**

**Once you have done this, add a sentence or two to expand what you might say about each point if giving the presentation, and print yourself off a set of presenter notes. Also print off a suitable set of handouts for your audience.**

# Software for web authoring

## Microsoft Publisher

Although there are software applications dedicated to web authoring, Microsoft Office Publisher is an ideal entry-level application. It is designed to be a desktop publishing application, so it allows you to create letters, brochures, fliers, catalogues and websites. The beauty of using Publisher is that once again it is fully compatible with all the other Microsoft Office applications, making it easy to import text, graphics, charts, tables and diagrams. The latest edition is Publisher 2007. It is designed to be user-friendly and time-efficient, and has an enormous range of templates available.

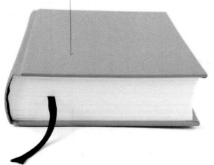

## The key benefits of Microsoft Publisher

The software allows you to create professional design and layout pages for websites even as a beginner. The Help facility, along with the available templates, can take away many of the problems of designing a website.

The other useful thing is that it can allow you to store and reuse items, such as graphics and text, in what is known as the 'Content library'. This allows your website to have a consistent look, once you have designed logos, headings, and graphics features, while also being able to use identical templates.

As far as its website-related benefits are concerned, Publisher offers:

- The ability to send personalised email using email merges
- The ability to add in **hyperlinks**
- The ability to add **bookmarks**
- An enormous number of website and page templates, which are easy to build
- The ability to add **navigation bars**
- Very easy editing

## Why businesses create web pages

Businesses create websites and web pages for a variety of reasons as we will see. It has now become almost essential that a business has some kind of presence on the Internet. The bulk of websites are aimed at the consumer – known as business-to-consumer (b2c) marketing.

Business-to-consumer marketing has two elements, building traffic to the website and then maintaining customer loyalty. Online shoppers are notoriously price-sensitive. They demand high levels of customer service and can be easily lured away from the website, making it difficult for even the largest of brands to remain competitive.

The power of a brand such as Amazon is that for all the thousands of key phrases they use to help them appear as search results through a search engine, the vast majority of their traffic comes from consumers typing the website name directly into the browser. To some extent, the way Amazon has developed shows other businesses how it should be done. They are accessible, they are visible and they have a recognisable brand name. Many websites try to compete for the same money and unfortunately the vast majority of the websites are invisible, never found and never visited by potential customers.

**UNDER WWW CONSTRUCTION**

Sites that require log-ins put people off; others fail because visitors cannot find what they are looking for. Even more fail because high shipping costs are added late on in the transaction. Many online retailers do not have a clear vision of their website, so they never reach the full potential.

For any business seeking to become involved in b2c activities on the Internet, the important consideration is to develop an e-marketing plan. Many of the basics of marketing do remain the same; the difference is that there are other options available. Many businesses will continue to use advertising, public relations and direct mail as a means by which they can inform their target market of the existence of their website and online shopping facility.

The key benefits of e-marketing are:

- The business can achieve global reach
- A properly planned e-marketing campaign can be performed at far lower cost than by using traditional methods.
- If the business is using emails or banner advertising, the effectiveness of each of these can be measured.
- As the website is open all the time, the marketing effort can attract customers at any point during the day or night.
- Personalisation is possible, so targeted offers can be made to particular types of customer.
- One-to-one marketing is possible by sending information directly to mobile phones or PDAs.
- The marketing campaigns themselves can be more interesting, incorporating music, graphics, videos and interactive features.
- Theoretically there should be a better rate of direct conversion to sales. If a customer responds to an email they can click on the link and be taken straight to the online shop.

The most common forms of e-marketing to consumers are:

- Email – but unsolicited email is likely to be sent directly in bulk and may be stopped by a bulk mail or spam filter.
- Short messaging service – allows short messages to be sent to a mobile phone.
- Banner advertising – a hugely flexible method, providing the banner advertisements are placed on websites identified by customer profiling.

Obviously, the main point of these activities is to:

- Attract customers to the website
- Convince them that they need to buy the product or service
- Make the sale
- Support the customer after the sale has been made
- Continually remind the customer of the business and its products and services
- Tell the customers that new versions or additions to the range of products and services are now available

---

## KEY TERMS

**Hyperlink** ▶ an electronic form of cross-referencing that appears in a document or on a web page as text or graphics that can be clicked on by the user to take them directly to another location.

**Bookmark** ▶ A stored web page location that the user can retrieve. Its purpose is to is to allow the user to easily catalogue and access web pages that they have visited before and chosen to save.

**Navigation bar** ▶ also known as a link bar, this is a section of a web page that contains links between the pages of the website. It usually appears on several of the website pages so that users can move from one page to another.

# Creating a business web page (1)

## Starting a web page

When you first open Microsoft Office Publisher you will see that there are a number of different publication types available, from advertisements through to compliments cards. Websites are one of the many options that you can choose.

Click on 'Websites' and you will now be offered a series of designs. They fall into three categories:

- **Classic designs** – these have predominantly white backgrounds with splashes of colour and to many they will appear somewhat dull.
- **Blank sizes** – these too are relatively old-fashioned looking and predominantly white, but bear in mind that the background colours can be changed, as we will see later.
- **Newer designs** – although many of these also have light backgrounds, these are slightly more modern-looking website designs.

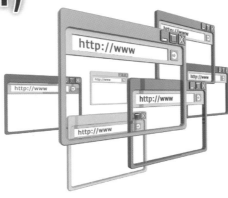

You can also, if you are connected to the Internet, access the latest templates that Microsoft offers.

In this particular set of examples we will choose the simple arrows design. You will notice on the right-hand side of the page there is a thumbnail of the opening page, or home page. By default it uses the existing page colouring. You can choose a colour scheme from a broad range of options. We are going to change it to mulberry.

The other option you have is to specify the font scheme. We are going to choose Comic Sans.

The next customised option is to specify the business information. It

will state as the only option 'Create new'. For the time being this is all we can do with this.

Next is the 'Options' menu. This offers you an opportunity to change where the navigation bar will appear on each of the pages. The default is vertical and bottom, which means that they will appear to the left of the page and at the bottom of the page. This is suitable for our purposes, so we will leave this as it is.

Make sure that the 'Use easy web wizard' box is checked and then click 'Create'. A new dialogue box will appear, which asks you to define the goals of your site. Each time you choose one of these options you will in effect be creating a new page. We will check 'Tell customers about my business', 'Tell customers how to contact us', 'Sell products' and 'Describe services'. Once you have done this, simply hit 'OK'. Microsoft Publisher will now begin creating your website.

## Choosing a consistent format

You may not be entirely happy with the colours on your website. This is very easy to change. You will now be viewing the front page of your website. To the left is a dialogue box, 'Format publication'. Here you can change the colour schemes and the font schemes and you can insert pages or additional functions to your website. Importantly, there is also the 'Preview your website'. It is good to have a look at this on a regular basis because this will help you to see precisely what another person would see if they were visiting your website.

You can easily change the templates from this dialogue box, or even the page size. In the centre of the 'Page view' a dialogue box will have appeared. For now we are concerned with the background, which is at the centre of this tool bar. Clicking on this will change the dialogue box to the left, giving you an enormous number of potential backgrounds for your website. Bear in mind that the more complex the background, the more difficult it is for

people to read your text. Unless you intend to have white text, do not go for anything too dark. We are going to opt for a simple gradient of colour that is darker at the top and lighter at the bottom. Click on this option and you can apply it to the page that is open or you can apply it to all pages. To make the website design consistent you should apply to all pages. Publisher now automatically makes the change for you and we now have a light mulberry background.

Keep returning to the 'Web page preview' option so that you can see precisely how your page would look if users were browsing on the Internet. If there is anything you are unhappy with, then make the necessary changes. You can change the nature of text boxes and illustrations, as well as changing the fonts and repositioning objects on the page.

It is not until we decide to publish the website on the Internet that your opportunities to amend your web page will be over.

**ACTIVITY**

Open Microsoft Publisher and, following the instructions on this spread, create your own website. By choosing the same options that we have chosen you will have created an eleven-page website. Do not be too concerned about the length at this stage because we can easily delete pages later on if this is necessary. The key point is to be able to have sufficient pages in different formats for different purposes, so that we can manipulate text and graphics. You can eventually title your web page and create your own business name and business logo. The important thing at this stage is to investigate all the options that are available to you when using Microsoft Publisher. Just as in Word and PowerPoint, you will be able to insert text boxes, tables, WordArt, pictures, lines, arrows, shapes, forms and design gallery objects.

# Creating a business web page (2)

## Composing and inputting information

Just like a PowerPoint presentation, the template text boxes are of a limited size, so only a limited number of words can be inserted into each of them. If you put too much text into a text box without resizing it, then it will automatically flow into the next text box on the next web page. This may not be desirable, so you always need to carefully plan how much text you are going to put into a text box and adjust it by changing the size of the font.

It is often easier to type out the text that you intend to put into a text box in Word first. Publisher will spell-check for you, but you can see the text more clearly in a straightforward Word document. When you have typed your text, highlight it in Word, right-click, select 'Copy' from the dialogue box and then highlight the text in the text box in Publisher, right-click again and select 'Paste'. It is important to remember that the text will appear in the same font and size as you typed it in Word. If you have forgotten to change this then change the font of your pasted-in text back to Comic Sans.

You can also decide how you want that text to appear. As in Word and PowerPoint, the main options are left-aligned, right-aligned, fully justified or centred. Simply click on the option you prefer.

By typing your text into Word first you can help to ensure that any

text that you put onto your website is correctly spelt and punctuated, and that you have used the correct grammar.

Having imported your first piece of text, you can now highlight it and change the font size, colour, style and type. We are going to opt for Comic Sans 12 point. This can be achieved by highlighting the text and changing the font size from the tool bar. We also want it bold, in italics and centred, and we've decided to change the font colour to a deep red.

You also have the option to change the fill of the text box. This will appear over the top of any existing objects or shapes in the template. The default is 'No fill', so by choosing a colour to go behind the text you will be creating a solid block of that colour. If you do not like the effect that you have chosen then you can undo that action.

## Using a range of formats

One of the purposes of creating the web page is to ensure that you have a consistent page format. Rather like the advice that we gave when we looked at PowerPoint presentations, you should not use too many fonts on the same page. It does not look professional and gives the impression that you have not thought about how the page actually looks. Having said that, there is no reason why you should not use the same font, but switch things around by using bold, italics, centred text or different point sizes.

Do not be tempted to use underlined text, as it would appear that any text that is underlined is in fact a hyperlink when it may not be.

The more consistent your page looks, the better the impression it will give to the user. Remember to keep adjusting the way it looks and checking to see what it looks like by switching to 'Web page preview'. You can do this at any time from the file drop-down menu in the top left-hand corner of the screen. Web-page preview is about halfway down the list of options. It takes Publisher a second or two to produce a sample web page based on the work that you have carried out so far.

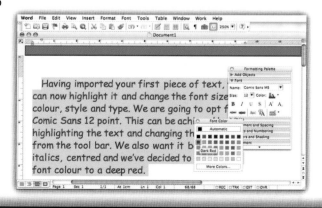

## Paragraph formats

As we have seen, you can do precisely the same with Publisher as you can with other Microsoft applications, such as PowerPoint and Word. We have already dealt with alignment of text. You can also change line-spacing. The easiest way to achieve this is to highlight the text, and from the 'Format' tab at the top of the page select 'Paragraph'. The new dialogue box offers you your alignment options, whether you want the text to be indented, and the line spacing. You can change this by clicking on the arrows next to 'Between lines'. The default is likely to be 1.15. The higher the number, the bigger the space between each of the lines of text. Bear in mind that if this is set at a high number then you will be able to fit far less text into the text box.

It is also possible to use bullet points and numbering. The simplest way is to highlight the text and then click on the bullet point icon or the number icon. Note that Publisher will automatically put a bullet point or number at the beginning of each paragraph (or where you have hit the return key on your keyboard).

You will also notice that next to the number and bullet point icon are two other icons: decrease indent position and increase indent position. This is a way of changing the indentation paragraph by paragraph. Simply highlight a paragraph that you wish to appear further indented than the others, and click on 'Increase indent position'. It will now move the entire paragraph to the right.

Because we are working in a text box, it is not possible to decrease the indent position because the first letter of each line is already positioned at the very left of the text box.

## ACTIVITY

Write two or three short paragraphs in Word and practice importing and reformatting the text onto your home web page. Remember that each time you make a change you can look at a 'Web page preview' to see what it looks like and whether or not it requires further adjustment. Remember also that anything you find that works particularly well needs to be carried over onto other pages so that you can generate a consistent page format to give that professional look to your website.

221

# Animation

YOU WILL FIND OUT:

● about animating

● about changing background colour

● about using borders and lines

● about inserting images

● about using frames

## Animating

In order to insert an animated picture onto the web page you need to go to the 'Insert' menu. Scroll down and go to 'Picture' and then click 'From file' or wherever you have saved the animation. You will need to locate the folder that contains the animated picture that you wish to insert. Then simply click 'Insert'.

It is important to remember that Publisher will not show the animation properly until you preview your web page. If you copy and paste the file it may lose its animated properties, so you must use the 'Insert' routine to do this.

222

## Changing background colour

There are two ways in which you can change the background colour of your web page. You can apply this to either the whole web page or simply to a text box. Go to the 'Format' tab at the top of the page and select 'Format publication'. You can now apply any of the sets of colour schemes or you can devise your own colour scheme. Click on 'Create new colour scheme' at the bottom of the dialogue box. Here you can define the precise colours of your main text, hypertext and other text.

To change the colour of the background this too can be achieved by applying one of the existing colour schemes. The accent colours (1 to 5) allow you to adjust one by one each

of the background colours of your web page. There are an enormous number of variations available to you. In order to ensure that you then use the same formatting for each of your web pages, make sure that you save your custom colour mix once you have adjusted the page. You will be able to see what it looks like from the preview. As soon as you have saved it, the dialogue box will close and the new colour version of your web page will be applied to your website. By default it will change all of your web pages to this new colour format.

## Using borders and lines

Borders and lines can highlight text or images and draw the user's eye to a particular area of a web page. Click on the line and border style icon at the top of your page. The default is 'No line', but you are offered a series of line options of varying thickness. Some options have more than one line incorporated into the design.

You can also determine the colour of the line by clicking on the 'More lines' option at the bottom of the dialogue box. The new box that appears has a number of tabs. Click on the 'Border art' button on the 'Colour and lines' tab to see a number of border art options. Some are black-and-white and others are in colour. You can apply any of these, or you can create customised borders using pictures or Clipart.

It is also worth remembering that you can also add in dashes to text boxes. These will surround the text box rather like a border.

## Inserting images

Using the 'Insert' tab at the top of the page you can insert a number of different picture options. By clicking on the 'Design gallery' object you can insert accent boxes, advertisements, buttons, logos and navigation bars, among others. By clicking on the 'Picture' option from this menu you can insert Clipart images that you have already stored on your computer or are on the Internet or intranet, pictures direct from a scanner or a camera, auto shapes including flow charts, arrows, callouts, stars and banners, or WordArt.

You can also insert objects and this is particularly useful if you wish to import a chart from Excel, a graph, a PowerPoint slide, a whole Word document or a picture that you have created. You can also import video clips and sounds.

## Using frames

A frame is an area on the web page that will allow you to insert a picture at a later date; perhaps you have not found the ideal picture or created it yet, but you know that it needs to be there. Once again you use the 'Insert' menu tab for this. Move your cursor down to 'Picture', and rather than automatically inserting a piece of Clipart or a picture, you can insert an empty picture frame. It will appear as an empty rectangle on your web page, rather like a text box. You can move it around and position it and you can adjust its size and shape, as well as rotating the frame. When you are ready you can then click on the object, then right-click. In the dialogue box that appears you should choose the source of the picture you wish to insert (Clipart, from file, from scanner or camera).

If you wish to insert a piece of Clipart then a new dialogue box will appear on the left-hand side of the screen. This allows you to search for specific Clipart using keywords.

When you have found the piece of Clipart that you wish to use you should click on that Clipart. It will automatically appear and fill your empty picture frame. You can of course adjust the size and position of this frame at any time.

 ACTIVITY

Using the instructions that we have given you on this page, we now want you to change the colours of your web page. We want to create a predominantly green theme for our website. Using the full colour palette, change each of the colours of the elements of the web page. You should retain black or very dark green for the text so that it stands out. All of the other colours should be mid and lighter greens, which complement one another. When you have completed this task, do a web-page preview to see if you need to make any adjustments so that particular features stand out more.

223

# Creating hyperlinks

## Creating hyperlinks

You will recall that hyperlinks can be used in order to help navigation around a website, or to direct the user from the website that they are looking at to another website.

You can insert a hyperlink either into text or into a picture. This means that if the user clicks on a particular word or phrase in the text then they can be directed straight to another page in the website. Equally, you can do this to pictures or graphics.

You will recall that our basic website has hyperlinks built into the navigation bar on the left of the screen and at the bottom of each page. The purpose of these is to aid navigation around the website so that users can quickly find the page that contains the information they need.

Hyperlinks are rather like putting bookmarks onto the website. They help you find a particular part of the website without having to go through each page in turn to find the information required.

The easiest way to create a hyperlink depends on whether you are creating one from text or whether you are creating one from a picture. Although the process is almost exactly the same, the resulting look on the page itself is different.

### *Creating a hyperlink in text*

Suppose you wanted to create a hyperlink to the contact page, and on your first page you had typed in a phrase, such as 'If you require any further information please do not hesitate to contact us'. You might want to create a hyperlink on the words 'Contact us', so that if the customer wanted to do this straight away all they would need to do is click on 'Contact us' to be taken to the contacts page.

To do this, highlight 'Contact us' then right-click. At the bottom of the familiar dialogue box is the hyperlink option. This will give you a number of options:

- Existing file or web page – this will link the web page to another existing document or picture on your computer, an Internet page that you have browsed, or a recent file that you have used on your computer or intranet. For our purposes this is not what we wish to do.
- Place in this document – this is precisely what we need to link to. By selecting this option all of the different pages on your website will now appear, one of which is p3, 'Contact us'. Click on this and to confirm, press 'OK'. The

dialogue box will now close and you will note that the text has changed colour to blue and it is now underlined. This is why we advised not to underline text on a web page.

- Create new document – this would effectively create a new document, but it would be housed on your computer and not be a part of the website, so again this is not a valuable option to us.
- Email address – this is the final alternative. It can be used instead of taking the user to the 'Contact us' page. It takes the user directly to the email address where they can send an email.

### *Creating a hyperlink in a picture*

By right-clicking on a piece of Clipart, a picture or an object you can also create a hyperlink. Right-click and scroll down to hyperlink and exactly the same options will be made available to you as when you created a hyperlink in text. The only difference is that you will not be able to see that there is a hyperlink attached to that picture, so it is necessary for you to alert users to the fact that the hyperlink does exist. This can be achieved by typing 'Click to contact us' or similar in the caption box.

224

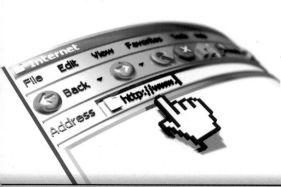

## Moving around the pages and moving to other websites

Any good website should have easy-to-use navigation. Users should be able to move from page to page using a variety of navigation bars, internal hyperlinks on pictures and keywords highlighted with appropriate hyperlinks.

Businesses recognise that if customers have to hunt for information and find it difficult to discover how to contact the business, then the customers will simply take their money elsewhere. This is as important to small businesses as it is to large businesses. Hyperlinks can certainly speed up the search for information and the time it takes for customers to read about the information, make a decision and contact the business.

It is also desirable for businesses to set up hyperlinks with other businesses' websites. There may be reasons why they want to do this, including:

- The business may manufacture a product but may not sell directly to customers, so they may want to direct customers to local stockists.
- They may want to send the customer to an independent website that has a review about their product or service.
- The business may be in partnership with another business offering similar or complementary products and services.
- The business may have multiple websites for other products and services and the customer may have come to the wrong website, or one of the other websites may have more relevant information to their needs.

**ACTIVITY**

Go to page 2 of your web page and highlight 'About us' and create a hyperlink to the 'Contact us' page. You will also see, to the right, a picture that is a Clipart object. Similarly, create a hyperlink to Page 3 and then amend the caption underneath it to tell users that by clicking on the object they will be taken to the 'Contact us' page.

225

### For example Vision Express

Vision Express (www.visionexpress.com) has a comprehensive website where customers can buy their contact lenses and sunglasses online, as well as book their eye examinations. There is also a facility for customers to use hyperlinks to help them find their closest Vision Express retail outlet. In just two clicks a customer can find details of their nearest branch, including its address, contact details, a map and opening times.

# What have you learnt?

This unit has introduced a range of software applications that are used by businesses to support their operations, and has explained how businesses use software to capture, store, retrieve and analyse data. Assessment of this unit is by a 90-minute computer-based examination.

Instead of mark-a-minute style questions, this unit has presented a number of activities, which are exactly the sort of thing that will be expected of you in the examination. You will be expected to select and use appropriate software for a variety of tasks. You also need to be aware that data can be presented in a number of different ways – using text, numbers or graphics – and that data can come from a variety of different sources.

Software can be used to process data and perform calculations, or to present information in a way that is easy to understand. Businesses routinely use software applications to help them record payments and expenses, to set up databases, or to design newsletters or job advertisements. You will also have seen that it is possible – using an integrated set of software applications such as Microsoft Office – to export objects and data from one application and import them to another.

You should expect to be asked to show your ability to use a variety of appropriate software, including: word processing, spreadsheets, databases, graphics, presentation and web-authoring software.

The examiner will have prepared a number of source documents, data and images for you to use in the examination. You will be asked to do various things with this data, such as reformatting, exporting or importing, merging or amending it, or simply presenting it in an appropriate way for a particular purpose.

It is important to get to know all the main functions of the software and to practise as often as you can. In word processing, you need to be able not only to input information accurately, using correct spelling, punctuation and grammar, but also to lay out a document to match particular business formats, such as letters or agendas. You can demonstrate your ability to choose the most appropriate font, colour, style and type; to amend line spacing; to use indents, bullet points or numbered points; and to change the alignment of the text.

## Unit 9 software application checklist

If you can do all the things in the checklist on the opposite page, then you should be ready for the Unit 9 examination. Don't forget that you will also need to use your skills for the Unit 10 controlled assessment, combined with the knowledge that you have gained from Unit 8.

226

# SOFTWARE APPLICATION CHECKLIST

## Word processing

### Can you?

- [ ] Create a document for a particular purpose
- [ ] Use a range of fonts and page layouts
- [ ] Use graphics and combine them with text

## Spreadsheets

### Can you?

- [ ] Create a spreadsheet for a particular purpose
- [ ] Manipulate data
- [ ] Create tables by using single and multiple-linked sheets
- [ ] Key in labels, values, formulae and functions
- [ ] Create and apply validation rules and conditional formatting
- [ ] Create charts

## Databases

### Can you?

- [ ] Design and create data capture forms
- [ ] Design and create database tables
- [ ] Sort records
- [ ] Search records
- [ ] Filter records and create reports

## Graphics

### Can you?

- [ ] Create graphics
- [ ] Edit graphics
- [ ] Combine text and graphics

## Presentation software

### Can you?

- [ ] Create slides for a business presentation
- [ ] Create transitions and animations
- [ ] Modify your presentation
- [ ] Create presenter notes and audience handouts

## Web authoring

### Can you?

- [ ] Create a business web page
- [ ] Animate text
- [ ] Create hyperlinks

227

# Written paper

**You will need:**
- **Appropriate computer hardware and software**
- **A stationery folder**
- **14 sheets of A4 plain paper**

**Time allowed: 1 hour 30 minutes**

**INSTRUCTIONS**

**You are to attempt all THREE tasks. The paper consists of the following tasks:**

- **Task One – Flyer (24 marks)**
- **Task Two – Database (16 marks)**
- **Task Three – Preparing a presentation (20 marks)**

**The maximum mark for this paper is 60.**

**You will be assessed for quality of written communication for your answers in Tasks 1 (b) (i), 1 (c) (iii), 2 (e) (ii) and 3 (f).**

**You cannot use the Internet during this mock examination.**

## SCENARIO: Green Gardener

Green Gardener is a small business that provides natural solutions to common gardening problems. As the name implies, the company does not produce man-made pesticides or fertilisers, and encourages gardeners to make full use of natural remedies and solutions, such as wormeries to deal with their compost. The business is now in its second generation of private ownership and has gradually expanded both its product range and its presence on the Internet. Customers are now able to purchase products from the business either via a traditional printed catalogue, or by direct sales via their website.

The business wants to switch over to a greater reliance on its website as the primary means by which it sells its products and services, but this means updating many of its ICT systems to make the business more efficient. This would be in line with its overall objective to become far more environmentally friendly.

## TASK 1 – FLYER

**Total marks for this task:** *24 marks*

The staff of The Green Gardener are planning to hold their very first open day. They intend to send the flyer as an email attachment to the customers that have ordered from them in the past. They also intend to distribute hard copies of these flyers at local and regional gardening events. The flyer is aimed at encouraging customers to visit during an open weekend, so that they can see many of the products that the Green Gardener sells in position in the business's own gardens.

**(a)** Open the file FLYER, which contains the text and some pieces of Clipart for the flyer.

    **(i)** Select a suitable software application and use a range of tools to create an A4 flyer that will encourage customers to come to the open weekend. You should only use two pieces of the Clipart. Do not change the text. *(6 marks)*

    **(ii)** Save your flyer as FLYER1 and print it out.

**(b)** John and Annie, the owners, would like to know how the flyer was designed.

    **(i)** Using Word, write a brief explanation to John and Annie in the form of an email explaining the reasons for the design of your flyer. *(8 marks)*

    **(ii)** Save the email as email and print it.

**(c)** Re-open your file FLYER1. John and Annie want to use the flyer as the basis for an advertisement. They have had a positive response to the open weekend and want to run another one a month later.

    **(i)** Make three changes to the appearance of the flyer. You should not change most of the text. *(3 marks)*

    **(ii)** Save your file as FLYER2 and print it out.

    **(iii)** Label the flyer using call-out boxes to show the changes you have made and why you have changed the appearance. *(7 marks)*

    **(iv)** Save your flyer as FLYER3 and print it out.

## TASK 2 – DATABASE

**Total marks for this task:** *16 marks*

Green Gardener keeps a database of its customers. This stores information about the products chosen. When an order is made, a new record is created.

**(a)** Open the database file ORDERS. The following field headings have been used:

ID – unique number for each order
Title – customer's title
Initials – customer's initials
Surname – customer's surname
PT – product type

The product type field is coded as follows:
P – pest, F – food, C – compost, O – other

**(b)** A week ago Mrs Farmer made an enquiry (see below). Add her data to the ORDERS file. *(2 marks)*

Mrs H Farmer, 238 Beaconsfield Road, Weymouth, Dorset, PO4 4LP

Mrs Farmer wants some natural weed killer.

**(c)** John and Annie are interested in seeing how the database is being used at the moment.
**(i)** Search the database to find all customers that have ordered compost. *(2 marks)*

**(ii)** Sort these compost entries by the customer's surname in alphabetical order. *(2 marks)*
**(iii)** Print this file in list format.

**(d)** John and Annie are interested to know how the ORDERS database could be used in the future. Addresses could be added to the database to produce address labels using mail merge.
**(i)** Add four fields to the ORDERS database so that a customer's address details could be divided under a number of headings. *(2 marks)*
**(ii)** Save your edited file and print it in list format showing the field headings.

**(e)** Open the word-processing file EMAIL and use it to reply to John and Annie's email below. *(8 marks)*

Thank you for all the work you've done on the database. I want to send all the customers who have bought pest products a special brochure on our compost products. Can you please answer the following questions for me?
- How do I ensure that the brochure is sent to the right people?
- Do you think this is a good way for us to inform them?
- Save and print your file.

## TASK 3 – PREPARING A PRESENTATION

**Total marks for this task:** *20 marks*

Annie is preparing a presentation that she will use when she visits gardeners' groups around the area. She has written notes of what she intends to say but she wants you to prepare the slides.

**(a)** Open the word-processing file NOTES.

**(b)** Select a suitable software application and create the first four slides. Annie wants the slides to have the same layout (but the title page can be different) and for you to use four tools, one of which should be an animation.
Create the four slides and copy and paste the text into the slides.

**(c)** Put the slide show together using a transition.

**(d) (i)** Save your presentation file as GARDENER'S GROUPS.

**(ii)** Print all your slides as a handout on one page.

**(e)** Paste a screen dump from your presentation into a new word-processing document and label it to show where you have used an animation and a transition. Save your screen dump as SCREEN and print it. *(10 marks)*

**(f)** Annie has never used presentation software before. Write her a note to answer each of the following questions:
**(i)** Explain one advantage and one disadvantage of an electronic presentation compared to a paper one. *(4 marks)*
**(ii)** Do you think Annie should go ahead with the electronic presentations? Explain your answer. *(6 marks)*
**(iii)** Save your note as PRESENTATION and print it.

# Introduction to controlled assessments

## What is a controlled assessment unit?

Unit 10: Investigating ICT in Business is a controlled assessment unit. This means that it is an internally assessed unit. However AQA determines the tasks that are set, how you do them (when, where, and how you are supervised) and how the work you produce is marked.

The first bit of good news is that the controlled assessment is rather like coursework. The big difference is that the work you do for this unit is more supervised and that you have a limit on the amount of time you can devote to it. The second piece of good news is that the Unit 10 controlled assessment is completely based on the topics that you covered in Units 8 and 9.

Each year, AQA will release a controlled assessment well ahead of the time that you might be expected to do it, so it will give you plenty of thinking time. You might well do the controlled assessment straight after Unit 8 and 9 so that all the information that provides the background for the tasks will still be fresh in your mind.

Each of the controlled assessments will have a very brief scenario, which sets the scene and gives you a focus for the tasks. There is then a series of research and investigation tasks. Each of them details what is expected of you. You will also have a section that tells you what AQA expect you to include in your final presentation of your work. The important thing to remember is that you will have a limited amount of time to prepare, research, plan and write up your final presentation, which AQA refer to as your findings.

## Dealing with a controlled assessment unit

As we will see later, AO1, AO2 and AO3 marks are all available for the controlled assessment. You will have already covered the relevant sections of Units 8 and 9, which match the tasks in the research and investigation section of the controlled assessment. You will have to carry out an investigation of some sort. There are two key tasks that require you to collect information, sort that information and then use it for your final presentation, as well as using applications software to produce a piece of work. It is very important that you evaluate your findings, but we will look at this a little later.

You will be given between five and eight hours to research and plan your work. Any help that you receive will be recorded. It is perfectly acceptable for you to work with others during the research and investigation stage, but you will not be able to submit group work for your final presentation. The research and investigation stage will probably be split up over several sessions.

When it comes to the final presentation you will be given between three and four hours. Again this might be divided up into more than one session. Your teacher or tutor will collect anything that you have produced in these sessions and you will not be allowed to take it away with you. They will make sure that your work is safe and handed back to you at the beginning of the following session, or stored securely on the intranet. You cannot expect to receive any help from your teacher or tutor during these sessions, as the sessions are under examination conditions. So you will have to work independently, but under supervision.

Once the final presentation sessions are finished and you have handed in your final version of your presentation, your school or college will mark your work according to AQA's marking criteria. Later your work might be re-marked by an AQA examiner, just to make sure that your school or college has followed AQA's marking guidelines.

## Controlled assessment scenario and tasks

The research task sets the scene and explains the focus behind the research and investigation tasks that you will have to carry out. You should also make sure that in your final presentation everything is relevant to the scenario.

Each of the tasks in the research and investigation section tells you precisely what you need to do. This might be carrying out actual research, using application software, producing findings, making screen prints, or writing a report and justifying what you have done.

The investigation section tells you exactly what needs to be included, such as results of any research, your report, any designs that you have made, and most importantly, an evaluation of your work, which highlights the significance of any key findings that you have discovered.

To achieve the best marks, as we will see, you will need to not simply list your findings without comment. You will need to analyse

them and evaluate them in your conclusion. You will also be expected to structure and organise your work so that it is as clear as possible. You will be able to use ICT but you must make sure that your spelling, punctuation and grammar is as accurate as possible. You may also need to produce your own designed work using software applications as part of your final presentation. It is important that you balance your time because content is just as important as design, as are your analysis and your evaluation.

You will have sufficient time to carry out all the research and investigation you need to. Three to four hours should be ample to pull all these pieces of information together, organise them properly, make them look presentable and then write up a good conclusion of your findings, as well as carrying out any designs that you may need to produce.

# Preparation

**YOU WILL FIND OUT:**

- what the skills are that will be assessed
- about the investigation
- about research and investigation

## What will I need to do before the controlled assessment?

AQA will release the controlled assessment towards the beginning of the spring term each year.

You will not be expected to do the Unit 10 controlled assessment until you have finished studying Unit 8 and acquired the necessary skills in Unit 9. Once you have completed Unit 1, you will be in an ideal position to handle the controlled assessment. It really is nothing to panic about – you will be familiar with all the business terms and concepts needed for the controlled assessment.

The idea of the controlled assessment tasks is to make the assessment more valid and reliable than coursework. It actually makes the assessment much more manageable and far less time-consuming and stressful for everyone. It is also clearer that whatever you hand in as your final presentation is all your own work.

The work you will need to do for the controlled assessment means that:

- all the work you do for the controlled assessment will be under direct supervision
- any feedback you receive from your teacher or tutor will have to be noted
- you will have a limited amount of time to complete all your work
- while you can research and plan together, your final presentation has to be your own individual work
- you will have the same access to resources as everyone else in your group, so you will not be disadvantaged if you do not have a computer at home.

By the time you are shown the controlled assessment from AQA, your teacher or tutor will have made sure that you have covered all the content from Units 8 and 9. You will have had an opportunity to practise an investigation into a business, and all of the resources that you will need to be in place, ready for your research and planning and final presentation sessions.

Your teacher or tutor will explain the range of skills required to produce the best possible quality of work for the controlled assessment.

## What skills will be assessed?

The controlled assessment is worth 25% of the overall GCSE, and 40 marks are available for the controlled assessment.

Although 40 marks are available, these marks are broken down and allocated to each assessment objective (AO):

### AO1 (up to 12 marks)

By simply describing and showing your understanding of the information you have collected, you can only expect to receive a maximum of 12 marks. This shows that you can only recall, select and communicate your knowledge. This is AO1.

### AO2 (up to 26 marks)

If you can apply your knowledge and understanding and show that you have been thorough, up to 14 more marks are available. This shows that you can apply your skills, knowledge and understanding in a variety of different ways. It also shows that you can plan and carry out investigations and tasks. This is AO2.

### AO3 (up to 40 marks)

To access the other 14 marks available, you need to be able to produce a good conclusion. It must show analysis and include an evaluation that justifies and highlights the significance of your key findings. This demonstrates that you can analyse and evaluate information, then make reasoned judgements and present appropriate conclusions. This is AO3.

## Sample answers

For example, suppose you are asked to look at a price comparison website and explain why it is an ideal place for customers to look for bargains.

Your answer could be straightforward and without detail, in which case you should not expect a particularly good mark. But if you were to identify the ideal location and explain why you have chosen it, then you are more likely to receive a higher mark.

Below are examples of AO1, AO2 and AO3 answers to this question. As you can see, the AO1 answer is not only brief, but does not have a great deal of detail. It makes no mention of any research that has been done.

The AO2 answer is better, but still not ideal. Very few business terms are used in the response. There are signs that research has been carried out, but the answer does not really make any use of this.

The AO3 answer not only contains business terms, which shows that the person who wrote it understands what they mean, but it also gives a reasoned answer. There is also judgement shown in the answer. The person obviously understands the relevance of what they have discovered.

## About the investigation

In the research and investigation section of the controlled assessment there will be two tasks. They will tell you precisely what you need to do. They will relate directly to the scenario. Key words could include:

- Conduct – carry out some kind of study such as research to identify something about a business or its use of ICT.
- Develop – build onto an idea or a description of, for example, the key advantages of a website.
- Identify – think creatively to suggest a way of doing something such as an ideal way to lay out a flyer or advertisement.
- Calculate – work out a sum, such as the costs of something using Excel.
- Estimate – make a considered guess about facts and figures, perhaps using existing data or using Excel.

Each of the tasks is a discrete part of the controlled assessment. They are practical activities and are directly related to either the subject matter of Unit 8 or the practical side of Unit 9. They will not be beyond your ability and there will be sufficient resources available to you to carry them out. The investigation is the information-gathering phase of the controlled assessment, so it is important that you use whatever time you are given to collect as much relevant information as possible.

### SAMPLE ANSWERS

**AO1**
I think the website is effective because the colours are attractive and it is easy for users to find information.

**AO2**
The website is particularly effective because it enables customers to specify exactly what they are looking for and provides them with relevant alternatives. It ranks the products by price, including delivery, as well as ranking the suppliers by reputation. All of these are important considerations when making a purchase.

**AO3**
The website is particularly effective because it is very user-friendly and easy to navigate. Users are able to specify precisely what they are searching for with a minimum number of mouse-clicks. The website ranks suppliers by price and by reputation. There are also internal hyperlinks to reviews of products and suppliers, all of which can help users to choose the right product. The layout and design of the page adds to the user-friendly nature of the website. All of these features should contribute to the website being a popular resource. Its accuracy and reliability also add to its attractiveness.

## About research and investigation

You will be given between five and eight hours to carry out the necessary research to bring together all the information you will need for the investigation. It is important to use this time wisely and not to collect and hang on to information just for the sake of it. It needs to be relevant to the investigation and it needs to be valuable to you when you produce your final presentation.

Your teacher or tutor can give you feedback, but they will record any assistance that they have given to you. In order to speed up the research and investigation you can work as a member of a group, but you will all need to make sure that you have copies of any information you have collected. When it comes to the final presentation you cannot produce group work – it has to be individual.

The controlled assessment will probably have two parts. The parts will not necessarily take the same length of time and one will rely on information you have collected for the other and will test your understanding of it.

**For example**

Unless you have looked in detail at a business's online advertising and know that they use banner ads and other activities to attract customers to their website, you will not be able to say very much about their marketing. Neither will you be able to work out what kind of marketing messages they might use to attract people to their website.

# The final presentation

## Making the best use of your time

In the research and planning stage of the controlled assessment you will hopefully have collected sufficient information – and understood it – to be able to use the final presentation time wisely. You will already have seen what is required of you in the final presentation, and you may already have had the chance to produce a rough draft.

You will be given up to three hours to write up your findings. If you have special assessment requirements, you will be given extra time. Your school or college will decide whether you will be given a single three-hour period, or whether there will be more than one session.

You will not be allowed to take away with you anything that you produce during the final presentation. Your teacher or tutor will collect it in at the end of each session and look after it for you until the next session. Your teacher or tutor cannot give you any feedback during the final presentation time.

So if there is anything that you do not understand in the research and planning time, ask then – or it will be too late!

You must work independently. If you worked as part of a group during the research and planning stage, you need to make sure that that you have copies of everything that you prepared together.

The final presentation is carried out under exam conditions. You will be supervised all the time, but you will have access to any resources you need, such as a computer.

It is important to remember that the controlled assessment tests your decision-making skills. The examiner wants to see how you use data and information, and how you solve problems. They are also interested in how you analyse and evaluate what you have found out.

## What you need to check before handing in your work

The final presentation section of the controlled assessment paper will tell you exactly what your presentation should contain. You must make absolutely sure that everything you have been asked to do is included in the work that you hand in at the end of the three hours. If anything is missing, you will not have provided sufficient evidence that you have organised your research, planning and presentation properly.

### *Sample contents*

In the box on the right is an example of what might be needed in a final presentation and suggests what needs to be contained in it.

234

## SAMPLE CONTENTS

### Investigation of a website offering a price-comparison service

Your teacher or tutor will probably direct you towards a specific website. Make sure that you thoroughly investigate it and check its functionality, features, use of animation, and where it has used objects and text.

### Identification of the features, content and layout that make it effective in communicating with its customers

Is it user-friendly? How do the colours complement its overall content and layout? How easy is it to find using a search engine? Once you are in the website, how easy is it to navigate around the pages, how many clicks are necessary to find the information that you need? What kind of reputation does it have compared to other similar sites?

### A report identifying those features

Make sure you know what a report looks like. What are the key headings that you will need? What needs to be in each of the sections? Where do graphs, charts and illustrations go in a report and how do you cross-reference information in it?

### A reasoned conclusion about the website

Look at your key findings. What is the significance of them? What makes the website particularly good or bad? How might it be viewed by users in terms of its functionality and value? What are the downsides of the website?

In the second part of the controlled assessment you will be asked to use a specific type of applications software and, perhaps, to design something specific to a scenario. The task does not end with just producing what you have been asked to create. You will need to screenprint your creation and you will also need to justify why you have designed it in this particular way. In order to access the higher-level marks you must sure that you do not spend all your time designing and creating and leaving no time to justify why you have done it that way.

Finally, you will also need to ensure that you include relevant business and ICT concepts, issues and terminology and show that you understand them. Do not fall into the trap of just dropping these terms into a sentence and think that this will do. You should use specialist terms frequently, but effectively.

You will also need to make sure that you have spelt everything in the correct manner. You should check your punctuation and grammar as these need to be as accurate as possible.

Above all, make sure that your work is well structured and organised. Headings are a good idea and so are bullet points and page numbering. Remember that if you are asked to produce something in a specific format, you will be penalised if you do not follow the instructions. This is regardless of the quality of the content of your investigation.

# Evaluating your own findings

## What is evaluation?

Assessment Objective 3 (AO3) requires you to analyse and evaluate evidence. It also requires you to make reasoned judgements and present appropriate conclusions. Overall, the AO3 accounts for 35% of the GCSE and 8.75% of those marks are available in Unit 10, the controlled assessment.

So what is evaluation? It is showing that you understand the relative importance of findings and ideas that you have included in your answer. It involves commenting on your findings, not just listing them. You need to suggest why some of the findings are more important or more fundamental than others. You need to explain how you have drawn conclusions on the basis of the findings. You can only do this by identifying those findings that suggest to you why a particular course of action or a particular set of circumstances, advantages or disadvantages, or even a figure that you have calculated, are of the greatest importance.

Good evaluation begins by making sure that you have all the key findings at your fingertips. You need

to structure your ideas and organise them in a clear and straightforward manner. You then need to look at them carefully, analysing each one and deciding which of them is important and why. Explain why you have identified these as key findings. How have you ranked them? What are their implications?

Do the findings suggest a particular course of action? Why

is that so? What might be the implications if that particular course of action were ignored? Could the business afford to ignore the findings?

Always use business and ICT terms in your evaluation to show that you have understood where the key findings fit into the overall picture, what they refer to, and what they may affect.

### For example

If you were asked to look at a regular newsletter that a business sends out to its customers to update them on new products and services, it would be a good idea to look not only at the purpose of the newsletter, but also at how it has been put together. You might be able to suggest applications software that could have been used to create the newsletter, and where the information might have come from. You might also want to comment on the use of colour, layout, logos and other design features to make the newsletter as attractive as possible and to encourage customers to read it. You could also mention the expectations of the business. What does it hope the newsletter will achieve? Are there clear contact details? Is there an opportunity for customers to make contact with the business so that they can place an order? Where are customers directed? Is there a website, an email address and a telephone number, as well as a postal address? Does the newsletter come with an order form, and is there a prepaid envelope included?

236

## The five levels for Assessment Objective 3

AQA has identified five levels of response in AO3, which focus on the evaluation side of your answers:

### THE FIVE LEVELS FOR AO3

#### Level 0

At Level 0, no marks are given because you have not made any conclusions. You have not analysed, nor have you evaluated.

#### Level 1

At Level 1, you have included some conclusions based on the information that you have collected. You have made some judgements, but have not really explained them. The examiner understands what you have said, but you have not developed your ideas. Also, you have hardly used any business terms. Your spelling, punctuation and grammar are a bit hit and miss, and you have not checked your work. The examiner would give you between 1 and 3 marks only for AO3.

#### Level 2

At Level 2, you have reached some simple conclusions based on the information you have collected. You have also made some judgements based on limited evidence and you have not highlighted the significance of the results of your investigations. Your work is reasonably well organised and structured. Spelling, punctuation and grammar are better, but there are still some mistakes. You have used some business terms but not very often. The examiner is likely to give you between 4 and 6 marks for AO3.

#### Level 3

At Level 3, you have made some appropriate conclusions based on a fair analysis of the information that you have collected. You have made a judgement about your findings and identified the significance of some of them. Your ideas are pretty well organised. Your spelling, punctuation and grammar are quite accurate, and you have used appropriate business terms where necessary. The examiner will probably give you between 7 and 10 marks for AO3.

#### Level 4

At Level 4, you have provided a range of good conclusions based on an analysis of your key findings. You have evaluated the information, and you have given a good justification for its significance. Your work is well structured and organised, clear and appropriate. Your spelling, punctuation and grammar are accurate. You have used business terms quite often and in the right place at the right time. The examiner would be able to give you between 11 and 14 marks for AO3.
Practice really does help. It is important to remember that all three units of this GCSE have AO3 marks available. The controlled assessment itself does not break down the marks available for each part of your presentation, so it is difficult to be precise about where you should evaluate. However, the big clue is in the fact that you will always be expected to present a conclusion. This is where you can make a judgement on the importance of your findings.

# Understanding the marking criteria

**YOU WILL FIND OUT:**

- how the marking works
- about AO1
- about AO2
- about the AQA checklist

## How the marking works

AQA will release a mark scheme that will be used by your teachers or tutors to identify acceptable answers and levels of response to tasks. This will ensure that everyone's work is marked in exactly the same way.

Teachers and tutors are trained by AQA to mark the tasks, but AQA will take a sample of the marking and double-check it. Your teacher or tutor will confirm to AQA that it is your own work. They will also double-mark, to make sure that the grades that you have been given are absolutely fair.

There are 60 marks available for Unit 10:

- By providing just a basic AO1 answer, you will only net a maximum of 30% of the available marks. For an AO1 answer, you are unlikely to get anything more than about an F grade for Unit 10.
- Another 14 marks are available if your answers are of AO2 standard. This now means that you are moving towards a C grade for Unit 10.
- In order to get a better grade than a C, you must include some analysis and evaluation. Another 14 marks are available if your answers are of AO3 standard.

Let's look in a little more detail at what is required for AO1 and AO2. (See page 237 for the five levels for AO3.)

## The five levels for Assessment Objective 1

### THE FIVE LEVELS FOR AO1

**Level 0**

If you have provided very little information and have not shown any understanding of business concepts, issues and terminology, then you will not be awarded any marks at all. This is Level 0.

**Level 1**

You have shown that you have collected some information but it is quite limited, and you have not really made an attempt to organise it. The examiner will not have seen that you really understand business concepts and issues, so the maximum they can award you is **3 marks**.

**Level 2**

Your information collection is fairly limited, but you have made an attempt to organise your work. The examiner will be able to credit you for a limited understanding of business concepts, issues and terminology, so you can expect to get **4–6 marks**. At this point you are still only halfway towards getting the 12 marks available for AO1, so more effort is necessary.

**Level 3**

You have used a range of different sources and your information is relevant. Your work is far more organised, and the examiner can see that you have a good knowledge and understanding of business concepts, issues and terminology. As a result, you could get **7–9 marks**.

**Level 4**

Your work is much more relevant and detailed. You have used a wide range of sources. Your work is well organised and understandable. Above all, you have shown that you really do understand business concepts, issues and terminology. The examiner is likely to award you **10–12 marks**.

At AO1, you have simply shown that you can recall, select and communicate your knowledge and understanding. But you have not really applied anything yet, or shown that you understand the relevance of what you are saying in relation to the scenario of the controlled assessment. To do this, you need to be working at AO2 standard at least.

## The five levels for Assessment Objective 2

AO2 is all about being able to apply your skills, knowledge and understanding. It also means showing that you can plan and carry out investigations and tasks.

Remember there are up to 14 marks available for AO2, in addition to the 12 marks that will automatically be awarded to you at AO1 Level 4, because by providing at AO2 level, the assumption is that you have already recalled, selected and communicated your knowledge and understanding.

> ## THE FIVE LEVELS FOR AO2
>
> ### Level 0
> You have not applied your knowledge and understanding to your investigation, so you will not receive any additional AO2 marks.
>
> ### Level 1
> If you have made some attempt to apply your knowledge and understanding to your investigation, so you can receive up to another **3 marks**.
>
> ### Level 2
> You have really got to show that you can apply your skills, knowledge and understanding when you carry out the investigation and bring all of your pieces of work together. This can give you an extra **4–6 marks**.
>
> ### Level 3
> Plenty of marks are available at Level 3. You will have to show that you can really apply your skills, knowledge and understanding in your planning and the completion of the tasks. The examiner can then award you an extra **7–10 marks**.
>
> ### Level 4
> At Level 4 – the top end of AO2 – there are **11–14 marks** available. You will have to have effectively applied your skills, knowledge and understanding across all of the work you have handed in.

So you may have secured the 26 available marks for AO1 and AO2, but you really need to produce a decent conclusion, which includes analysis and evaluation, to get you those valuable AO3 marks (see page 235).

## The AQA checklist

The guidelines above are general. For each of the controlled assessments, AQA will produce a checklist of everything they expect to see in your final presentation.

The checklist will include:

- key business terms that AQA will expect you to use
- acceptable and unacceptable ways of carrying out research
- correct ways to calculate business figures, such as income, expenditure or profit
- the kind of issues that AQA will expect you to highlight in your analysis and evaluation in the conclusion.

Don't forget that the examiner will also be looking at your use of English, including your spelling, punctuation and grammar.

# Mock controlled assessment 1

## Research task

You are to carry out an investigation of a website operated by a business in the replica sports kit industry and produce your own web page. Your investigation will have two parts:

### Part one

Using the website you have chosen, identify the features (content and layout) that make the website effective in communicating with its customers. You should pay particular attention to the website's home page. As part of your findings, you should produce a screen print of the website's home page, and write a report identifying those features of the website that are effective, and those features that could be improved.

### Part two

You need to design a web page for the following business:

*Football Greats is a new business that specialises in selling historic football kit replicas. It sells replica kits for all major British and international teams. For a fee the company will also produce hand-made replicas of any football kit.*

Once you have completed your web page, produce a screen print and a justification of why you have designed your web page in the way you have chosen.

*240*

### Good places to start

- www.football-shirts.co.uk
- www.umbrofootballkits.co.uk
- www.prostar.co.uk
- www.subsidesports.com
- www.clublinefootball.com
- www.soccerkits.com

For historic and custom-made kits:

- www.historickits.co.uk
- www.customkit.com
- www.team-colours.co.uk
- www.myfootballkit.com

# Research and planning

## Part one

Your teacher or tutor will probably recommend that you use a specific website. They will choose one that has plenty of features and aspects that you can write clearly about, focusing on the content and layout. Each website is going to be different in terms of its layout, design, navigation, purpose, length, complexity and other features. There will also 'be different ways in which customers can make contact with, and purchase from, the business.

The website's home page should feature all the key elements of a good website:

- There should be clear navigation so that customers can find what they are looking for with the minimum number of mouse-clicks.
- Navigation for different products should be featured either at the top left or the bottom and it should be clear that customers can click on these words or images to take them to the relevant pages.
- There should be an easy way for the customer to be able to contact the business, either by telephone or by email.
- There should be links to additional information, most importantly the 'about us' feature, as many of these businesses do not have a physical presence on the high street and are only virtual businesses. Customers like to be assured that the business is a solid and professional organisation.

- How are images used on the website? Are there photographs of actual products, or artists' impressions?
- How does the customer make a purchase? Is it an easy process?
- What guarantees does the business offer regarding payment security?
- Once you have entered the website, how straightforward is it to return to the home page?
- What objects and text can be clicked on?
- What is the overall look of the website? Is it consistent?
- How easy is the text to read and how large are the photographs and illustrations? Can they be clicked on to be enlarged?

## Part two

You will need to combine your research of a business that provides off-the-peg, current kits with that of a business that offers a customised kit service. Make sure that you spend a little time thinking about how the business's name is going to appear:

- Will you use a logo?
- What is your overall colour scheme?
- Remember that you will have to put in some illustrations or photographs. These need to be clear and not hidden by a dark background.
- Make sure that your text can be easily read.
- Make sure that your navigation is clear.

- Ensure that you offer easy ways for customers to contact your business.
- What will you feature on your home page? Will it be a simple design or something more complex?

Remember that you will have to produce a screen print of your home page. Most importantly you need to justify why you have designed your web page in the way you have chosen. Bear in mind the issues that you looked at in part one. These were:

- Features
- Content
- Layout
- Communication with customers.

How have you tackled each of these issues? What have you learned from existing websites to lead you to design your web page in way you have? Which of the features did you find particularly effective and have you incorporated them? If you were a customer visiting this website, what would be your overall impression?

# Mock controlled assessment 2

## Research task

You are to carry out an investigation of an emailed newsletter sent by a business operating in the travel industry, and then produce your own email newsletter. Your investigation will have two parts:

### Part one

Using the email newsletter you have chosen, identify the features (content and layout) that make the emailed newsletter effective in communicating with its customers. You should pay particular attention to the purpose of the newsletter. As part of your findings, you should produce a screen print of the emailed newsletter and write a report identifying those features you consider to be effective, and those that could be improved.

### Part two

You need to design an email newsletter for the following business:

*Find a Travel Partner is a small travel agency that specialises in finding and matching ideal travel partners for expedition-style holidays throughout the world. Many of its customers are in their early twenties and are looking for exciting and active holidays but do not wish to travel alone. Customers can book holidays through the agency and also be matched up with other travellers who are looking to share the same kind of experiences.*

Once you have completed your email newsletter, produce a screen print and write a justification of why you have designed your email newsletter in the way you have.

242

### *Good places to start*

A number of businesses routinely send out travel-related newsletters with holiday offers and travel guides to existing customers or those that have subscribed to the service. Some examples include:

- www.holidaydiscountcentre.co.uk
- www.traveldk.com
- www.easyjet.com
- www.crusadertravel.com
- www.thomson.co.uk
- www.monarch.co.uk

There are other websites that focus on finding ideal travel partners, including:

- www.mango-tree.com
- www.travelpackers.com
- www.travelbite.co.uk

# Research and planning

## *Part one*

Using their customer databases, businesses are able to create personalised email communications in the form of newsletters. A business will already have captured data relating to the preferences, age, previous bookings and other information of each individual customer. This makes it possible for them to personalise any communication that they send to a particular customer. It will primarily focus on offers and information that are directly relevant to that customer. Email newsletters will be sent out in bulk using an automated process. The business will have used search queries in their database to match particular types of information and offers, in order to make each email more focused and of interest to each customer.

The newsletter will be professionally laid out and careful consideration will have been given to its content. It will also have a number of clickable hyperlinks, which take the customer directly to the business's website or a particular part of that website. This will enable the customer to find out more information, request further information or make a booking.

What is particularly important with an email newsletter is that the customer has given permission for the business to send these communications. This is known as 'opting in'. Either the customer has requested that the business send the newsletter, or they have agreed that it is acceptable for the business to send them newsletters when they have contacted the business either to request information or to make a booking. This makes the email newsletter particularly valuable as a marketing tool as it is targeted at a group of individuals who are particularly interested in what the business has to offer. The customer should be able to recognise the newsletter, as it will have the same colours, layout, logos and other features that they have become familiar with when they have visited the business's website (a recognisable brand or house-style).

When you look at an email newsletter you need to consider not only the content and layout, but also how effective it is in achieving what you think was its purpose:

- Is it designed simply to pass on information?
- Is it to make announcements?
- Is it to encourage the customer to contact the business?
- Is it to generate sales?
- Is it to generate contributions or feedback from the customer?

You may discover that the newsletter aims to do most of these things, and you should comment on whether the content, layout and design is effective in achieving these goals.

## *Part two*

Pay particular attention to the specific needs of the type of customer who will have subscribed to this type of newsletter. They are independent travellers. They are not interested in visiting highly popular tourist resorts. They are adventurous, but are looking for others who are similar to them to travel with. This is the unique aspect of this type of travel agency. It not only performs the tasks and duties of a travel operator, but also provides this additional service.

Just as you would be considering precisely how you would decide on content and layout for a website, these aspects are equally important for a newsletter. It needs to be striking, interesting, relevant to the customer, and probably to include one or more pictures. It needs to have hyperlinks that take the subscriber to the business's website, or perhaps to other sites where they can find out more information about exciting destinations.

Look at the overall layout of the newsletter that you investigated in Part one. What are its vital features? You must incorporate as many of these as possible. Finally you will need to screen print your email newsletter, and justify why you have designed it this way. By all means refer back to the best features of the email newsletter that you looked at in Part one. Hopefully you will have identified the effective features and incorporated them into your own version.

# Picture credits

The publishers would like to thank the following for permission to reproduce images in this book.

p. 2: Tesco plc; p.4: © Kozachenko Sergey/Fotolia.com; p.7: ©KonstantinosKokkinis – Fotolia.com; p.8: ©Andrea Danti – Fotolia.com; p.9: (l) ©Paul Fleet – Fotolia.com, (r) ©Hedgehog – Fotolia.com; p.11: ©Andrew Skinner – Fotolia.com; p.12: © adistock/Fotolia.com; p.13: © Piotr Sikora/Fotolia.com; p.14: © iQoncept/Fotolia.com; p.16: © Eugeny Gripas/Fotolia.com; p.17: © brunoil/Fotolia.com; p.18: © artSILENSEcom/Fotolia.com; p.20: © artSILENSEcom/Fotolia.com; p.21: © artSILENSEcom/Fotolia.com; p.26: ©Thorsten/Fotolia.com; p.27: © victor zastol'skiy/Fotolia.com; p.29: © Living Legend/Fotolia.com; p.30: © green308/Fotolia.com; p.32: (l) Forgiss/Fotolia.com, (r) © Vasilyev Dmitry/Fotolia.com; p.33: © Roman Sakhno/Fotolia.com; p.34: © Daniel Gilbey/Fotolia.com; p.36: © Nmedia/Fotolia.com; p.38: (t) © Dan Marsh/Fotolia.com, (b) © diego cervo/Fotolia.com; p.39: © Yegor Korzh/Fotolia.com; p.41: The Fairtrade Foundation; p.45: © Soja Andrzej/Fotolia.com; p.46: © Fredy Sujono/Fotolia.com; p.47: © AKS/Fotolia.com; p.48: © Heino Pattschull/Fotolia.com; p.49: © Haris Rauf/Fotolia.com; p.50: © vladislav susoy/Fotolia.com; p.51: © Paul Fleet/Fotolia.com; p.52: © Shutterfan/Fotolia.com; p.53: © Alex Paterov/Fotolia.com; p.55: © Samu/Fotolia.com; p.56: © cornelius/Fotolia.com; p.57: © erwinova/Fotolia.com; p.58: © Jürgen Schanz/Fotolia.com; p.59: © drx/Fotolia.com; p.60: © vege/Fotolia.com; p.61: © Sergey Ilin/Fotolia.com; p.62: © V. Yakobchuk/Fotolia.com; p.63: © PictureLake/Fotolia.com; p.64: © kmit/Fotolia.com; p.67: (l) © TEA/Fotolia.com, (r) © nexusseven/Fotolia.com; p.69: ©AKS – Fotolia.com; p.71: ©nikla – Fotolia.com; p.77: © Serg Myshkovsky/Fotolia.com; p.83: © terex/Fotolia.com; p.84: © Tinka/Fotolia.com; p.87: © Pedro Diaz/Fotolia.com; p.95: (l) © TEA/Fotolia.com, (r) © nexusseven/Fotolia.com; p.97: © Emilia Stasiak/Fotolia.com; p.98: © Stephen Coburn/Fotolia.com; p.99: © ioannis kounadeas/Fotolia.com; p.102: © Tom Denham/Fotolia.com; p.108: © Brian Jackson/Fotolia.com; p.109: © illu24/Fotolia.com; p.110: Patricia Briggs; p.111: © zentilia/Fotolia.com; p.113: (t) © auris/Fotolia.com, (b) mipan/Fotolia.com; p.114: © cemil adakale/Fotolia.com; p.117: © artSILENSEcom/Fotolia.com; p.119: © Lorelyn Medina/Fotolia.com; p.120: Microsoft product box shot reprinted with permission from Microsoft Corporation; p.123: Microsoft product box shot reprinted with permission from Microsoft Corporation (×2); p.125: (t) © Feng Yu/Fotolia.com, (b) © Vlad Kochelaevskiy/Fotolia.com; p.126: © Dmitry Sunagatov/Fotolia.com; p.127: (t) © Erick Nguyen/Fotolia.com, (b) © twenty205/Fotolia.com; p.128: easyJet ; p.133: © Valery Potapova/Fotolia.com; p.134: © frenta/Fotolia.com; p.139: © Val Thoermer/Fotolia.com; p.140: (l) © KonstantinPetkov/Fotolia.com, (r) © cornelius/Fotolia.com, (b) © dja65/Fotolia.com; p.142: © Kozachenko Sergey/Fotolia.com; p.145: © pressmaster/Fotolia.com; p.148: © Thorsten/Fotolia.com; p.149: © Nmedia/Fotolia.com; p.150: © MarFot/Fotolia.com; pp.152, 153, 154, 158, 159, 160, 161, 162, 163, 165, 167, 168, 169, 172, 173, 176, 177, 180, 198, 201, 220: Microsoft product screen shots reprinted with permssion from Microsoft Corporation; p.154: © Marc Dietrich/Fotolia.com; p.155: © Fotolial/Fotolia.com; p.164: © Domen Colja/Fotolia.com; p.169: © Johnny Lye/Fotolia.com; p.170: Patricia Briggs; p.174: © KonstantinosKokkinis/Fotolia.com; p.175: © Alexander Orlov/Fotolia.com; p.176: © artida/Fotolia.com; p.177: © Yevgeniya Ponomareva/Fotolia.com; p.178: (t) © Scott Maxwell/Fotolia.com, (b) © Mellimage/Fotolia.com; p.179: © artSILENSEcom/Fotolia.com; p.181: East Anglian Daily Times/Archant Regional; p.182: (l) © Jan Spurny/Fotolia.com, (c) © Alexandr Mitiuc/Fotolia.com, (r) © jaddingt/Fotolia.com; p.185: © Miqul/Fotolia.com; p.195: © Creativeapril/Fotolia.com; p.188: © Thorsten/Fotolia.com; p.190: © Graça Victoria/Fotolia.com; p.192: (l) © chin yong teh/Fotolia.com, (r) © Nikolai Sorokin/Fotolia.com; p.193: (l) © Sean Gladwell/Fotolia.com, (r) © jenny/Fotolia.com; p.194: © rgbspace/Fotolia.com; p.196: (l) © Mark Poprocki/Fotolia.com, (c) Patricia Briggs, (r) © vectormaniac/Fotolia.com; p.204: © Adkok/Fotolia.com; p.205: © Alexander Kataytsev/Fotolia.com; p.206: © M.Tomczak/Fotolia.com; p.207: © willsphots/Fotolia.com; p.208: © Bocos Benedict/Fotolia.com; p.210: © Tomasz Rzymkiewicz/Fotolia.com; p.212: cteconsulting/Fotolia.com; p.212: © Fribourg/Fotolia.com; p.214: © endostock/Fotolia.com; p.215: © Andres Rodriguez/Fotolia.com; p.216: (l) © Konstantin Yolshin/Fotolia.com, (b) © PixAchi/Fotolia.com; p.217: © ratselmeister/Fotolia.com; p.218: (t) © David Humphrey/Fotolia.com, (l) © Dzmitry Sukhavarau/Fotolia.com, (r) © Mike301/Fotolia.com; p.219: © alphaspirit/Fotolia.com; p.220: © Marc Dietrich/Fotolia.com; p.221: © Franck Boston/Fotolia.com; p.222: (t) © Luis Leonardo/Fotolia.com, (b) © Nmedia/Fotolia.com; p.223: © Ramin Khojasteh/Fotolia.com; p.224: (t) © AAA/Fotolia.com, (b) © AAA/Fotolia.com; p.225: © photlook/Fotolia.com; p.230: © Kozachenko Sergey/Fotolia.com; p.233: © daniel sainthorant/Fotolia.com; p.234: © flucas/Fotolia.com; p.237: © Vladimir Wrangel/Fotolia.com; p.239: © Paul Malsch/Fotolia.com.

Every effort has been made to contact copyright holders, but if any have been inadvertently overlooked, the publishers will be happy to make the necessary amendments at the first opportunity.

# Index

*Bold page numbers refer to key term definitions.*

246